T0355932

Warfare parenting

A Daily Battle Plan to
Fight for Your Child

Laine Lawson Craft

BroadStreet
PUBLISHING

BroadStreet Publishing® Group, LLC
Savage, Minnesota, USA
BroadStreetPublishing.com

Warfare Parenting: A Daily Battle Plan to Fight for Your Child
Copyright © 2025 Laine Lawson Craft

9781424568802 (faux leather)
9781424568819 (ebook)

Cover and interior by Garborg Design Works | garborgdesign.com

Printed in China

25 26 27 28 29 5 4 3 2 1

Faithful warrior parents, your love fused with
Scripture and prayer cuts through the darkness
as you battle for your prodigal's return and restore
your family through God's love and grace.

Introduction

Before the first light of dawn, thoughts of your distant child burden your heart and consume your mind. Nights and days merge in a tumultuous whirl of fervent prayers and tears for your prodigal. My journey mirrors yours; my own three children once ventured far from the safety of faith. Each step away pierced my heart. Yet here I stand and declare a profound truth: hope is alive, and victory is possible.

I forged this book from my own trials and triumphs. Through my darkest hours, Scripture and prayers sustained me while I waited on God to restore my children to the light of Christ. These devotions contain God-inspired, soul-awakening truths from one warrior parent to another. They're your rallying cry against despair, your spiritual sustenance in this relentless battle.

Hold tight to every promise that touches your heart. While the world offers temporary and quick fixes, we embrace the lasting power of Scripture, a mightier force than any worldly logic, and anchor our hope in God's eternal promises. Mark the passages that challenge and then restore your faith, even as your prodigal roams. These words are your fuel, sparking fervent prayers and divinely guided dialogues and giving you strength when doubt tries to stop you. The storms may rage, but God is transforming our tearful pleas into joy. Today victory can be ours—now and forever!

Testimony in the Trials

Do you ever wonder about the point of all the pain you experience? Can good really come out of your child's rebellion? Check out Mark 5:20: "He went away and began to proclaim in Decapolis what great things Jesus had done for him; and everyone was amazed" (NASB). The man in this verse was once a total outcast plagued by demons. But when Jesus got hold of him, not only was the man transformed, but his story also became a catalyst for awe and faith in others.

What if the trials you and your wayward child are facing now are just the prelude to an amazing testimony? One that not only amazes but also draws others to hope and faith. All three of my prodigal children have testimonies of God delivering them from Satan. Now they are whole, healed, and free. Keep the faith, for today's struggle is tomorrow's testimony.

Your child's story doesn't have to end with rebellion. God is in the business of writing plot twists that blow our minds. So stand firm. You're not fighting just for your child but for the fantastic story that will come out of this. Ready for the world to be amazed? Believe in Jesus' power.

Dear Father, thank you for making a testimony out of my child's trials and tests. In Jesus' name. Amen.

A Good Father's Gift

You may be in a rut, but even though it's hard, you can find help in Luke 11:11–13.

> Which one of you fathers will his son ask for a fish, and instead of a fish, he will give him a snake? Or he will even ask for an egg, and his father will give him a scorpion? So if you, despite being evil, know how to give good gifts to your children, how much more will your heavenly Father give the Holy Spirit to those who ask Him? (NASB)

As you're praying for your wayward child, let me reassure you: God's not handing out snakes or scorpions. His gifts are good. And you're not just asking for any gift; you're asking for the Holy Spirit to intervene, to transform your child from the inside out.

Your prayers are not whispers in the wind; they're a direct line to a Father who knows how to give good gifts. So let's keep asking. Let's expect miracles because, trust me, God's in the business of exceeding expectations. When we ask for the Holy Spirit for our children, God is ready to pour it out because he is an even better parent than we are.

Dear Father, thank you for giving good gifts when I ask. In Jesus' name. Amen.

Divine Detours

Have you ever felt like you're banging your head against a wall when you're trying to reach your wayward child? Even when you follow a careful plan, your efforts fall short. Let's look at Acts 16:7 for encouragement. "When they had come up to Mysia, they attempted to go into Bithynia, but the Spirit of Jesus did not allow them" (ESV). Here we see that even Paul and his team faced divine detours. They had plans, but the Spirit of Jesus said, *Not that way*.

I know it's tough. Your plan is mapped out—interventions, tough love, ultimatums. But what if God is redirecting you for a reason? Divine detours aren't roadblocks. They're rerouting you to something better. Maybe you've been praying fervently for your child and want to charge ahead to fix things. But God might be whispering, *Take a step back and let me lead*. The Spirit knows what's up. Maybe it's not the right time for that tough conversation, or perhaps a better opportunity for reconciliation is coming.

Trust the process and the planner. You're not in this alone. God has your back. Keep praying, keep believing, and be open to God's detours. They often lead to divine destinations.

Dear Father, thank you for leading the way as I pray for my child's victory. In Jesus' name. Amen.

A Light in Dark Moments

Look, there's no sugarcoating it—parenting a wayward child is a journey marred with sleepless nights and endless worry. But Isaiah 30:18 tells us,

> The LORD longs to be gracious to you,
> and therefore He waits on high
>   to have compassion on you.
> For the LORD is a God of justice;
> how blessed are all those who long for Him.
> (NASB)

Isn't that just like God? When everything seems out of control, he's actually setting the stage for his grace and mercy. God isn't late; he's divinely timely. He waits for the perfect moment to intervene in such a way that we know it was he and he alone.

Your child might be lost in the world right now, but understand this: God is waiting for the perfect moment to show his mercy, to turn their life around in a way that only he can. If your child turns to him with longing, God's not just going to save them, but he's also going to make it a grand display of his grace. God's timing is always perfect even when our patience is running thin. His grace and compassion have the power to leave everyone in awe.

Dear Father, thank you for your grace, which can cover my child. In Jesus' name. Amen.

Divine Fire

Today let's talk fire—divine fire, to be precise. Look at 1 Kings 18:38.

> The fire of the LORD fell and consumed the burnt offering and the wood, and the stones and the dust; and it licked up the water that was in the trench. (NASB)

Picture Elijah alone against 450 prophets of Baal, outnumbered but never outpowered. Why? Because God showed up in a blaze of glory, consuming everything.

Now let's switch gears to you. As you stare down harmful influences, negative friends, or destructive habits in your child's life, you might feel outnumbered, but remember that you're never outpowered with God on your side. God's fire didn't just burn Elijah's sacrifice; it also consumed everything. Talk about thorough! God wants to do the same in your child's life by destroying what has led them astray.

Just like Elijah had to prepare the altar before the fire fell, you must keep laying down your prayers and tears. Prepare the ground for God to move. When the fire of God falls, it won't leave anything untouched. Expect a miraculous change and know that the God who answered Elijah with fire will answer you too.

Dear Father, thank you for burning off anything that hinders my child's freedom. In Jesus' name. Amen.

A New DNA

Today let's jump right into 1 John 3:9: "No one who has been born of God practices sin, because His seed remains in him; and he cannot sin continually, because he has been born of God" (NASB). This powerful verse hits where it hurts with our wayward kids. But it's not a condemnation; it's an invitation to understand God's transformational power.

As parents, we've planted seeds in our children—values, love, lessons, and prayers. But there's another seed we may have overlooked: God's seed. When we know Christ, our spiritual DNA changes. God's seed now abides in us, urging righteousness. What does this mean for prodigals? If your child once knew God but is now lost, remember that God's seed is still there, able to be revived. Even if they've never known God, transformation is one divine encounter away. This should give us parents hope.

Transformation isn't an overnight fix but a process. When God steps in, real change isn't only possible; it's also inevitable. Your child may be lost but not too far gone for a God whose seed changes essence. With God, nothing is impossible. Don't give up hope or fighting. God's seed has the power to transform lives.

Dear Father, thank you for the truth today that your people can't remain in sin if they are born of you. In Jesus' name. Amen.

Miraculous Transformation

Do you believe your prodigal is too old for God to rescue? We see in Acts 4:22 that "the man on whom this sign of healing was performed was more than forty years old" (ESV). Peter and John healed a man who was over forty years old. Imagine the years of disappointment, heartache, and perhaps even resignation he and his family must have faced.

But God stepped in and changed everything— completely and miraculously. Like that man, your wayward child is never too old for a touch from God. Sometimes the struggle continues for years. Maybe you're living with that kind of disappointment. Let's not forget that forty years was a long wait for a miracle, yet God moved powerfully. Don't lose hope. Don't stop praying.

God specializes in turning the impossible into the possible. He takes the broken, lost, and disconnected and breathes life into them. Age is just a number. Time is just a measure. God's power is limitless, and his timing is perfect. Your child might be a prayer away from their own Acts 4:22 moment. A miraculous transformation could be right around the corner. Let's remember that God's not finished yet.

Dear Father, thank you for this reassurance today that my child will never be too old for your touch. In Jesus' name. Amen.

Unfailing Love from Above

The path we walk isn't easy. Our hearts get stretched to their limits, yet somehow we still manage to find room for love. Isn't that incredible? I think of Psalm 57:10: "Your steadfast love is great to the heavens, your faithfulness to the clouds" (ESV).

God's love is as expansive as the sky. When you look up, don't just look at clouds or stars; see a tangible reminder of how big God's love is for you and your wayward child. God's love is higher than the tallest mountain you could climb in your struggle. No matter how far your child strays, they can't outdistance God's love. His faithfulness stretches way past the limits of our vision. If his love reaches the heavens, it can reach that dark pit where your child might be and pull your child into his marvelous light.

Even in the darkest moments, especially when you don't feel it, God's love remains unchanging, unfailing. It's not a fleeting emotion; it's a rock-solid promise. That love is the fuel you need to keep pressing forward. Use that unfathomable love as your touchstone in this battle. Let it fill you with hope and guide your steps. Your love for your child is powerful, but God's love is unstoppable.

Dear Father, thank you for your unchanging and eternal love.
In Jesus' name. Amen.

A Parent's Cry Heard

Do you feel like your pleas for your wayward child are just ricocheting off the heavens? Lean into Matthew 20:32–33: "Jesus stopped and called them, and said, 'What do you want Me to do for you?' They said to Him, 'Lord, we want our eyes to be opened'" (NASB).

Here's the powerful truth: Jesus stopped. Amid the crowd, the noise, and the chaos, he stopped and listened to the cries of the blind men. Why? Because he heard a sincere cry for help. Do you feel like you're amid your own turmoil, battling for your child's soul? The Savior is tuned in to your cries too. But he's not just hearing; he's also asking, *What do you want me to do for you?*

So be specific. Name what you're asking God to do for your child and trust that Jesus is stopping to listen, just like he did with the blind men. Keep the faith. He hears you and is poised to act. Get ready. You might find your child's "eyes" being opened in ways you never imagined. Remember this scene in your darkest moments, when it feels like your prayers are vanishing into thin air. Jesus isn't distant. He's attentive and caring.

Dear Father, thank you for showing me today that you hear my cries for help for my child. In Jesus' name. Amen.

A Reality Check for Parents

While you're caught between praying and relentlessly sacrificing for your child, you might find yourself wondering, *Why isn't God hearing me? I've been good.* You can feel like you're on an endless roller coaster when trying to please God by works alone. Luke 13:26–27 reminds us not to mistake familiarity with Jesus for a real, soul-deep relationship. "You will begin saying, 'We ate and drank in Your presence, and You taught in our streets!' And yet He will say, 'I do not know where you are from'" (NASB). Following Christ isn't about going through religious motions. God sees the heart! He knows when we're genuine in our faith and when we're ticking spiritual checkboxes.

So as you fight for your child, get honest with God. No shortcuts, no compromises. Your relationship with him must be the main event, not a sideshow. When you are real with God, he gets real in your situation. Authenticity breeds miracles, dear parent.

Get your knees dirty in prayer. Open that worn Bible. Start speaking life over your child and see what happens. God can show up when you least expect him but most need him. Your authenticity could be the breakthrough you've been waiting for.

Dear Father, thank you for allowing me to come to you just as I am and for always being there. In Jesus' name. Amen.

The God of Impossibilities

Do things look impossible? We see it's not true in Luke 18:27, where Jesus said, "The things that are impossible with people are possible with God" (NASB). Isn't that just a soul soother for any parent battling for their wayward child?

You've probably tried everything—conversations, interventions, and maybe even therapy. At times, it might feel like you're fighting an impossible battle. Many parents have been there. That feeling of desperation is your cue to look up.

God specializes in the impossible. He's not limited by the constraints that limit us. You might be staring at a wall so high you can't see the top, but God sees what's on the other side. Your kid might be in a pit so deep you can't reach them, but God can. So take a step back and let the God of impossibilities do his thing. Hand over the reins. You don't have to carry this burden alone. Remember, you're not the Savior; he is. Your job is to trust, believe, and hope against hope. With God, nothing is truly lost, and nothing is impossible.

Dear Father, thank you that even though my child is in the pit of sin and disobedience, nothing is impossible with you. You can turn their life around, rescue them, and heal them. In Jesus' name. Amen.

The Heart of the Gospel

Do you ever wonder if God loves us in our disobedience? We see in John 3:16–17 that

> God so loved the world, that He gave His only
> Son, so that everyone who believes in Him will
> not perish, but have eternal life. For God did not
> send the Son into the world to judge the world,
> but so that the world might be saved through Him.
> (NASB)

These verses are the cornerstone of our faith, the essence of the gospel. They're powerful, reminding us of God's unimaginable love and the lengths to which he goes to save us, including our wayward and prodigal kids, when we believe in him.

Think about it: God's love isn't a passive emotion. It's a love that sacrifices, a love that gave us Jesus. And why? So that "everyone who believes" won't just survive but will have eternal life. That's the hope we can cling to.

And let's not skip verse 17. God didn't send Jesus to condemn but to save. There's hope and redemption available, not just judgment. That should fuel our prayers for our kids who've lost their way. They're not too far gone; they're exactly who Jesus came for.

Dear Father, thank you for the saving power of Jesus and the hope for eternity with you. In Jesus' name. Amen.

Brokenness before Breakthrough

If you feel like you're at the end of your rope, then Psalm 51:17 was written just for you. "The sacrifices of God are a broken spirit; a broken and contrite heart, O God, you will not despise" (ESV). Listen up because this is pivotal. Your tears and your aching heart are not signs of weakness. They're the kinds of sacrifices God does not overlook. God doesn't despise your broken spirit; he's magnetized to it. Your openness and vulnerability before God pave the way for his divine intervention.

Sometimes when you're most broken, God does his best work. It's like you're clearing away all the barriers, all the I-can-handle-this-on-my-own attitudes, and saying, *God, I desperately need you*. That's when God steps in. That's when miracles happen.

Maybe your child is walking a path you never dreamed of by making choices that tear at your heart. Your brokenness invites God to step in and work wonders you can't even imagine. Keep laying your heart out before him. Keep being honest about your hurt, your disappointment, and your fears. Your heartache is a catalyst for God's action. Don't underestimate the power of a broken and contrite heart.

Dear Father, thank you for loving me even when I'm broken.
In Jesus' name. Amen.

Nothing's Too Big for God

Let's unpack Matthew 19:26: "Looking at them, Jesus said to them, 'With people this is impossible, but with God all things are possible'" (NASB). Parenting is tough. We encounter times when we think, *I can't do this. It's too much. My child's turnaround seems impossible!* That's when Jesus' words hit home. He told us that even when things look impossible, there's always a way with God.

Think about it. Those moments when you feel stuck or unsure how to help your child or what direction to go are exactly when God steps in. He turns our *can't* into *can* and our *impossible* into *watch this*.

This promise from Jesus is like a secret strength. You can know that no matter how big the problem, God is bigger. So when you're worried or unsure about your child's future, remember that you're not figuring it out alone. God is right beside you, and he is in it with you, making the impossible possible. Let's keep it simple: trust God. He's got this. Whatever you're facing with your prodigal, no problem is too big for God.

Dear Father, thank you for reminding me today of this powerful promise that nothing is too big for you to turn around. In Jesus' name. Amen.

Divine Intercession

I know you're fighting a spiritual battle for your child, but do you wonder if your prayers are making a dent? Let's look into a story about powerful prayer in 1 Samuel 12:17–18.

> "Is it not the wheat harvest today? I will call to the LORD, that He will send thunder and rain. Then you will know and see that your wickedness is great which you have done in the sight of the LORD, by asking for yourselves a king." So Samuel called to the LORD, and the LORD sent thunder and rain that day; and all the people greatly feared the LORD and Samuel. (NASB)

These verses show something remarkable. Samuel called on the Lord for thunder and rain as a sign, and God responded immediately. Then the people realized their sinfulness.

What if the "thunder and rain" in your situation are loud, unmistakable acts of God that capture your child's attention? Your persistent prayers could lead to divine intercession, waking your child to their need for God. Sometimes it takes a downpour before people seek shelter. It might take a divine thunderclap for your child to see the gravity of their choices. Keep praying. Samuel's prayer shook a nation. Imagine what your prayers could do.

Dear Father, thank you for showing me that you answer prayers in mighty ways. In Jesus' name. Amen.

Angelic Aid

Do you feel like you're walking through a desert, alone and worn out, while you're fighting for your child's soul? You're in good company. Let's dive into Matthew 4:11: "The devil left Him; and behold, angels came and began to serve Him" (NASB). Even Jesus, after being tempted by Satan, needed a pause, a moment of divine care. Though you've been in battle mode for what feels like an eternity, don't forget that God sends reinforcements.

There are seasons when the fight feels unbearable, when the Enemy's taunts echo loudly. But remember that divine help is on the way for you. Just as angels rushed to Jesus' side, they're also ready to rush to yours, equipped by the one who has ultimate victory in his hands.

As you pray and fight for your child, also allow God's messengers to minister to you. Your strength is being renewed, and you are not alone in this battle for your child's heart. God has your back, and victory is possible. Hold the line, parent. Heaven is on the move.

Dear Father, thank you for your heavenly angels, who are always ready to rush to my aid in seasons of war. In Jesus' name. Amen.

Armed for the Battle

How we need the armor of God! You gain many advantages by wearing God's armor, as seen in 1 Thessalonians 5:8: "Since we belong to the day, let us be sober, having put on the breastplate of faith and love, and for a helmet the hope of salvation" (ESV). When fighting for a prodigal child, this armor isn't just poetic language; it's also your daily clothing. The breastplate of faith and love protects your most vital organ—your heart. Why? Because your heart is what pumps out all your life-giving energies to the rest of your being. Don't allow despair to puncture that breastplate. Keep faith and love alive because God hasn't given up on your child, so why should you?

Now to the helmet of hope. If faith and love protect your heart, then hope safeguards your mind. It's easy to get lost in your thoughts, wondering where you went wrong or what you could've done differently. Please don't go there; it's a trap. Instead, focus on hope, the sure expectation that God is still in control and that he's working behind the scenes. This battle requires full armor, and God has fully equipped you for victory against Satan!

Dear Father, thank you for providing your armor and strength. In Jesus' name. Amen.

Awakening the Peace

Are you in a storm today with your wayward child? Let's plunge into Luke 8:24.

> They came up to Jesus and woke Him, saying, "Master, Master, we are perishing!" And He got up and rebuked the wind and the surging waves, and they stopped, and it became calm. (NASB)

Do you ever experience what the disciples were feeling? When the storm is raging, it can seem like Jesus is asleep on the job. But let's get one thing straight: Jesus is never absent, never asleep on your needs or your heartache. Sometimes he's just waiting for us to wake him up with our desperate calls for help. When the disciples cried out, Jesus immediately rose and calmed the storm. And he can do the same for you.

You're never alone in the tempest. When you're up late worrying, remember that a word from Jesus can still every storm—even the ones raging in your family. Cry out to him, wake him up with your pleas, and let him bring peace into your chaos. The master of the storm is with you. Keep calling out, for peace is just on the horizon.

Dear Father, thank you for the promise that no matter what storm I face with my child, you will give me calm and peace. In Jesus' name. Amen.

Battle of Desires

Do you ever feel like you are falling into sin yourself? Let's dig into 1 Peter 2:11, which says, "Beloved, I urge you as sojourners and exiles to abstain from the passions of the flesh, which wage war against your soul" (ESV). As parents fighting for our wayward kids, we often feel like sojourners and exiles—out of place in a world that doesn't understand our struggle. Our hearts ache, and letting emotions control us is so tempting, but this can lead us to make decisions based on fear, desperation, or even anger.

But Peter reminded us that these "passions of the flesh" wage war against our soul. They pull us away from God's best for us and our family. You might feel the desire to bend your rules, overlook unacceptable behavior, or even question your principles. But remember, this is a war against circumstances and influences that aim to derail you and your family from God's path (Ephesians 6:12).

So how do we abstain from these passions? First, we anchor ourselves in God's Word. Second, we continue in prayer, asking for wisdom and strength. Last, we surround ourselves with a community of faith, with people who remind us who we are and whose we are.

Dear Father, thank you for helping me make better life decisions today. In Jesus' name. Amen.

Becoming Imitators of God

Don't forget that we parents are God's children too. Because we are, Ephesians 5:1 tells us we can "be imitators of God, as beloved children" (ESV). What a call to action! Paul was telling us to mimic God. Why is this such a critical point for parents battling for their prodigals? Let's face it: if we want our wayward children to come back to the light, we have to shine it brightly in their lives. And nothing shines brighter than being an imitator of God. When you radiate his love, mercy, and patience, these characteristics become a beacon that can guide them home. It's like using a spiritual GPS!

Now I get it: imitating God sounds overwhelming. But remember, you're already his beloved child, and he has given you his Holy Spirit. So you're equipped for this even if you don't always feel like it.

Dear friends, your actions often speak louder than your words. The closer you draw to God, the brighter your beacon becomes, calling your lost one back home. It's like being a lighthouse in the fog of their confusion and rebellion. So let's get our shine on and be those imitators of God, attracting our kids back to the Father's heart.

Dear Father, thank you for helping me look and act more like you today. In Jesus' name. Amen.

Behind the Veil

Have you ever wondered what's happening behind the veil? Don't be deceived. A spiritual battle of good versus evil is going on every day. Job 1:7 gives us an intriguing glimpse. "The LORD said to Satan, 'From where do you come?' Satan answered the LORD and said, 'From roaming about on the earth and walking around on it'" (NASB).

You might feel overwhelmed by the dark influences looming over your wayward child. But remember, even Satan had to report back to God. This might seem like a heavyweight boxing match for your child's soul, but God has the final say.

Look, what you see isn't the whole story. There's a spiritual realm where battles are fought, and God has never lost a fight. So as you stand firm in the clash for your prodigal, know that the Enemy can only go so far. God has the reins. Nothing happens without passing through the hands of our mighty God first. Hold on to that and keep fighting the good fight. Amid the chaos and confusion, remember that God's power supersedes all. Your prayers, faith, and love are mighty weapons in this unseen warfare.

Dear Father, thank you that the devil must answer to you and that you have the final say for my child. In Jesus' name. Amen.

Belief and Healing

Do you struggle to maintain faith in your child's turnaround? Build your faith with John 4:50: "Jesus said to him, 'Go; your son will live.' The man believed the word that Jesus spoke to him and went on his way" (ESV). This verse tells of a father's belief in Jesus' words, which led to the healing of his son. It's a profound lesson in faith and the power of belief.

As parents of prodigals, we often find ourselves in a similar position, hoping for a change or healing in our children's lives. This Scripture passage reminds us that faith plays a crucial role in this process. Our belief in God's ability to transform our children is vital. Like the father in this passage, we must take Jesus at his word, trusting in his promises for our children's lives. This doesn't mean ignoring the reality of the situation. Instead, it's about seeing beyond current struggles and believing in the potential for God's work in our children.

Our faith can be a powerful force. Believe in your child's ability to change and hold on to the hope that, through faith, healing and transformation are possible.

Dear Father, thank you for increasing my belief that my troubled child can be healed. In Jesus' name. Amen.

Finding Joy amid the Struggle

Let's talk about joy. Yeah, I know. It's a strange topic when your heart is aching for your wayward child. But listen, there's a promise here for you. Psalm 5:11 says, "Rejoice, all who take refuge in You, sing for joy forever! And may You shelter them, that those who love Your name may rejoice in You" (NASB). God invites us to find refuge in him. And you know what comes with that refuge? Joy. No, this is not the fleeting happiness that changes with circumstances but a deep-seated joy rooted in knowing that God has you. He's your shelter in this storm you're going through.

So here's the challenge. Even amid the struggle, allow yourself to sing for joy. I know it sounds counterintuitive, but there's power in declaring joy over your life and your child's life. Remember, God promises to shelter you and those who love his name. Your joy doesn't deny your current hardship, but it's a powerful statement of faith that God is with you even when your prodigal strays far from home. Joy may seem distant, but it's closer than you think. Take refuge in God and watch how he shelters your heart and works miracles in your family.

Dear Father, thank you for the joy in your refuge. In Jesus' name. Amen.

Blessings in the Heavenly Places

Are you in need of a blessing today? Ephesians 1:3 says, "Blessed be the God and Father of our Lord Jesus Christ, who has blessed us in Christ with every spiritual blessing in the heavenly places" (ESV). Did you catch that? Every spiritual blessing!

Now I know what you're thinking. *My child is wayward; where's my blessing in that?* But stay with me here. The key word is *spiritual*. It's easy to forget our spiritual arsenal in the middle of the chaos. And let me tell you that it's stacked! You have power in prayer, authority in your words, and God's promises in your corner. Just because you can't see immediate change doesn't mean the spiritual realm isn't shaking. Your prayers are not in vain. They deposit those blessings from heavenly places right into your life, even if you can't see them yet.

So in those desperate moments, remember this: you're blessed to be a blessing, even for your wayward child. All those spiritual blessings? Use them as your secret weapons. Don't lose heart, warriors. Your spiritual blessings have a real-world impact.

Dear Father, thank you for all the blessings you have given me and continue to give graciously. Help me be a blessing to my family. In Jesus' name. Amen.

Bold Confidence in Crisis

Are you up late again worrying about your wayward child? Sometimes it is hard to be bold. Let's draw strength from Hebrews 13:6: "We can confidently say, 'The Lord is my helper; I will not fear; what can man do to me?'" (ESV). As parents, we often let fear and what-ifs consume us. The Enemy tries to whisper lies, saying our kids are beyond saving or that we've failed them too deeply. But hold on a minute! Our verse for today blasts those lies apart.

Confidence doesn't stem from perfect parenting or even perfect kids. It comes from knowing that the Lord is your helper. Picture it: God Almighty, the creator of heaven and earth, is your personal helper in this battle for your child's soul. So what if the world writes off your kid as a "bad influence" or "hopeless"? What can a person's opinion do when the creator of all is actively helping you? Zero. Zilch. Nada.

When you feel isolated or defeated, speak this verse aloud. Declare your trust in your heavenly helper and watch how his perfect love casts out fear. Stand firm and remember that no one gets the last word on your child except God.

Dear Father, thank you for being my helper. I am never alone in the war. In Jesus' name. Amen.

Equipped against Fear

Let's talk about fear. It's the Enemy's favorite tool to keep us paralyzed, especially regarding our wayward children. We fear for their choices, their health, their very souls. But today let's kick that fear to the curb. Second Timothy 1:7 says, "God gave us a spirit not of fear but of power and love and self-control" (ESV). So if God didn't give us a spirit of fear, where's it coming from? Not from him! Instead, he has armed us with power, love, and self-control. And that's a tool kit any parent would dream of.

Use that power to pray, fiercely breaking chains you can't see. Use that love to keep your heart soft toward your child even when your nerves are frayed. And that self-control? That's your secret weapon. It keeps you steady, guiding your words and actions and helping you pick your battles wisely.

God has already equipped you with everything you need for the warfare you're facing. Lean into his power, love, and self-control. You have more backup than you can possibly imagine. Through God's goodness, we can be brave.

Dear Father, thank you that fear must let go and leave in your presence. Thank you for equipping me with everything I need to win the war for my child. In Jesus' name. Amen.

The Final Sacrifice

Do you ever feel like you're running in circles trying to fix things? Maybe you've been hustling to correct your child's path, and let's be honest: it's draining. You're doing the work, but the peace you seek seems elusive. Hebrews 10:10 cuts right through this cycle of endless striving. "By that will we have been sanctified through the offering of the body of Jesus Christ once for all" (ESV). This verse tells us that we've been made holy—set apart, sanctified—through Jesus Christ's offering of himself, not for just a moment but "once for all."

The incredible thing is that this will cover your child, too, when your child is also saved. You don't have to make them perfect. You can't. Jesus did what we could never do. He made the final sacrifice that covers all sin, failures, and shortcomings of those who believe in him.

Embrace this truth today: there's no act, no ritual, and certainly no amount of parental worry that can make your child holy. Only Jesus can. Take that burden off your shoulders and place it at his feet, knowing that his one-time sacrifice has the power to change eternal destinies.

Dear Father, thank you that the death and resurrection of Jesus covered all the sins of your followers yesterday, today, and tomorrow. In Jesus' name. Amen.

Breaking Through the Blinding Darkness

Do you ever wonder why your kid can't see the obvious? How do they continue down this destructive path despite all the red flags? The Bible clearly shows us the answer in 2 Corinthians 4:4.

> In their case the god of this world has blinded the minds of the unbelievers, to keep them from seeing the light of the gospel of the glory of Christ, who is the image of God. (ESV)

Your child's actions aren't just the result of teen rebellion or a phase; they're also caused by spiritual blindness. The god of this world—Satan—covers your child's eyes. He's doing his best to keep them in the dark. But here's the good news: God specializes in opening eyes and turning on lights. Just as God said, "Let there be light" (Genesis 1:3), and there was light, he can light up your child's world with the truth.

Don't lose hope. Keep praying those powerhouse prayers that shatter the darkness. Your child may be blind now, but they're just one miracle away from seeing the light. Hold on to hope, reclaim what's been lost, and be confident that the gospel never stops shining its light.

Dear Father, thank you for loving me enough to show me the light of your goodness and for doing the same for my child. In Jesus' name. Amen.

Broken Hearts, Open Ears

Are you feeling crushed under the weight of your child's choices? Let's look at Psalm 34:17: "When the righteous cry for help, the LORD hears and delivers them out of all their troubles" (ESV). When it says "all," it means *all*. Not some, not most, but every last one of your troubles. This is the heart of a God who doesn't put conditions on his compassion. You cry out, and he hears. It's that simple.

Maybe you're thinking, *I've been crying out for a long time, and I'm still waiting.* I get it. But never mistake God's timing for his absence. He has heard you and is moving—even if you can't see his actions yet. God is often working behind the scenes, deep in the heart, and though we can't see anything happening, he is moving.

So keep crying out for help as you trust God. Your voice isn't lost in the ether; divine ears catch it. Stay open. You're closer to deliverance than you think. God hears broken hearts like they're the loudest thing in the room. He will answer your cries of deliverance. Don't give up and don't give in. God has you.

Dear Father, thank you for hearing all my cries for deliverance. In Jesus' name. Amen.

Eternal Gains

Have you ever asked yourself, *What's the point?* as you tirelessly battle for your child's soul? Let Matthew 16:26 sharpen your perspective. "What will it profit a man if he gains the whole world and forfeits his soul? Or what shall a man give in return for his soul?" (ESV). This verse is a reality check for any parent seduced by the idea that worldly success can replace spiritual health. I know it's easy to get sidetracked, wishing for good grades, great jobs, or social status for your kid. But none of that compares to the value of their eternal souls.

Don't get me wrong; wanting the best for your kid isn't bad. But when you're tempted to put spiritual matters on the back burner, remember that eternity outweighs any temporary gain. Your unyielding prayers and stubborn faith may not bring instant results, but they're an investment in the everlasting. Keep the faith. This is a long game, and what you're fighting for is infinitely more precious than anything this world offers. Stay focused, for the eternal stakes couldn't be higher. In this pursuit, balancing life's demands is essential while keeping spiritual growth at the forefront.

Dear Father, thank you for promising that your followers will spend eternity with you and leave this evil, dark world behind. In Jesus' name. Amen.

Build Faith through Prayer

Do you need to build your faith? We see how in verses 20–21 of Jude, which tell us,

> You, beloved, building yourselves up on your most holy faith, praying in the Holy Spirit, keep yourselves in the love of God, looking forward to the mercy of our Lord Jesus Christ to eternal life. (NASB)

Now isn't that just what we need to hear? We all can get discouraged, especially when dealing with our rebellious children. The fear, the sleepless nights, and the constant battles can wear down even the most steadfast parent. But here's the real deal: faith isn't built in the calm but in the chaos. When you're facing yet another setback with your child, when the Enemy whispers that all hope is lost, you must dig deep. Pray in the Holy Spirit. Let your prayers rise like sweet incense. Let them go where you can't, touching the heart of God and your child's soul.

You see, you're not throwing words into the void. You're connecting with the one true God, who is over the whole world and can set things right. Build up that most holy faith. Why? Because your prayers hold power. Because faith is the weapon that the Enemy can't stand. And with God, we're not just fighting; we're winning.

Dear Father, thank you for building up my faith when I pray for the deliverance of my child. In Jesus' name. Amen.

february

Call Out to God

I know the days are long, and the worries are longer. But let me drop a pearl of wisdom straight from Psalm 50:15: "Call upon me in the day of trouble; I will deliver you, and you shall glorify me" (ESV). That's right. God is giving you permission—a direct invitation—to call upon him when you think you can't make it through the day. That moment when your heart sinks as you think about your wayward child is your cue to pray like you've never prayed before.

Now I get it. It feels like you're fighting an uphill battle, doesn't it? But remember that God specializes in victories, especially in those situations that seem impossible. The promise here isn't just that he will hear you and deliver you. Through your testimony, you'll also inspire others and glorify the Lord. Your child's testimony could do the same. Imagine if the story of your prayers and prodigal child coming home brings someone else to God.

Let's double down on prayer today. Make it your first resort, not your last. Cry out to God and let him show you just how powerful he is. Watch God turn your story around for his glory.

Dear Father, thank you for displaying your glory and delivering me when I call out to you. In Jesus' name. Amen.

Casting Your Cares

Is your heart full of worry? In these turbulent moments, find a soothing balm in 1 Peter 5:6–7: "Humble yourselves… casting all your anxieties on him, because he cares for you" (ESV). Here we see an invitation to release our burdens to God, who cares for us immeasurably. This Scripture passage is not just a call to off-load our worries but also a reminder of the compassionate nature of God. It reassures us that our concerns, especially those we have for our children, are not ours to bear alone. God eagerly shoulders these burdens, enveloping us in his care and peace.

To cast "all your anxieties on him" requires a heart of trust. It means believing that God is actively involved in our lives and in our children's lives. He understands our fears and meets them with his comforting presence and guidance.

Let these verses encourage you to entrust to God all your worries about your child. In doing so, you open the door for his peace to enter your heart. This act of faith doesn't negate the challenges but instead places them in the hands of a loving God whose care is limitless and whose power can transform any situation.

Dear Father, thank you for allowing me to cast all my worries on you and find peace. In Jesus' name. Amen.

Choosing Faith over Fear

Today we find protection in Hebrews 11:28: "By faith he kept the Passover and sprinkled the blood, so that the Destroyer of the firstborn might not touch them" (ESV). Imagine the faith it took for Moses to keep the Passover. Sprinkling a lamb's blood on the doorposts of a house to spare the lives of the people inside sounds anything but logical. But Moses knew this act of faith was a protective barrier against a devastating threat.

Now let's fast-forward to us. We're not literally fighting off the destroyer of the firstborn, but we are battling dark forces aiming at our kids' hearts and minds. Are we prepared to take seemingly illogical steps of faith to safeguard them? The same God who rescued the firstborn children of Israel protects those who take bold steps of faith.

Prayer, fasting, and trust are your acts of Passover. No, they won't always make sense to the world or maybe even to you. But by faith, these acts serve as a hedge of protection around you as you pray for your wayward child. Trust God as Moses did. Do the "illogical." Wage war in the spiritual realm for your child's soul. Just like the Israelites, you'll be astounded by God's deliverance.

Dear Father, thank you for the power of Jesus' blood and the protection it provides. In Jesus' name. Amen.

Chosen and Empowered

Do you feel left behind and alone? We can find the truth in 1 Thessalonians 1:4: "We know, brothers loved by God, that he has chosen you" (ESV). Right now, you might feel isolated, overwhelmed, or downright defeated in your fight for your wayward child. The good news? You are chosen and loved by God. That's not just some feel-good phrase. It's a life-altering truth.

When God chose you, he equipped you with every spiritual weapon you need for battle. He sees your pain, sleepless nights, and shattered heart, and he is right there with you. Being chosen isn't about being perfect or having it all together. It's about being perfectly loved by a God who has a perfect plan. Your current situation doesn't define you; God's love does.

Remember, God's plans are not limited by your mistakes or your child's poor choices. He who chose you is faithful, and he has the power to turn any situation around. Hold on to this truth and let it strengthen your resolve as you continue to pray for your child.

Dear Father, thank you for choosing to love me even when I feel defeated. In Jesus' name. Amen.

Claim Your True Identity

Your identity as a parent may be under siege, but never forget that your true identity is unshakable in Christ. Galatians 3:26 says, "In Christ Jesus you are all sons of God, through faith" (ESV). When your child strays, it's like a gut punch to your soul. But don't lose sight of who you really are: a son or daughter of God. That's your birthright through faith. Earthly labels and mistakes don't change your heavenly identity.

And if your child has ever repented and believed in Jesus, their identity is also in Christ. Yes, even if they're so far away right now that they don't recognize themselves, God still sees them as his child, and you should too. So when you pray, cry, and fight for them, do it from this ground of faith.

And if your child has yet to believe in Jesus, know that the moment they do, they're defined not by their past but by their identity as God's child. Trust that no past waywardness can sever their access to salvation when they turn to faith in Christ. They might be prodigal today, but through Christ, they may become a prince or princess for the kingdom.

Dear Father, thank you that those who believe in you have assurance of their identity in you. In Jesus' name. Amen.

Never Too Far Gone

Do you ever feel like your efforts with your child are in vain? We find a powerful perspective in Matthew 21:31–32.

> "Which of the two did the will of his father?" They said, "The first." Jesus said to them, "Truly, I say to you, the tax collectors and the prostitutes go into the kingdom of God before you. For John came to you in the way of righteousness, and you did not believe him, but the tax collectors and the prostitutes believed him. And even when you saw it, you did not afterward change your minds and believe him." (ESV)

These verses challenge our assumptions about righteousness and acceptance in God's kingdom. Jesus highlights that those often deemed unworthy were the first to embrace John's message of righteousness. This can be a comforting reminder when our children seem furthest from the path of righteousness. They may be closer to understanding God's love and mercy than we realize. This Scripture encourages us not to judge by appearances or current behaviors. Instead, it invites us to see the potential for transformation in every child, no matter their current path. God's unfailing love can lead even the most wayward child to a place of repentance and change.

Dear Father, thank you for your love for my child. In Jesus' name. Amen.

Your Prodigal's Healing

Are you feeling like your child is in the pit of despair? Today's hope comes from Psalm 30:2–4.

> O Lord my God, I cried to you for help,
> and you have healed me.
> O Lord, you have brought up my soul from Sheol;
> you restored me to life from among those who go
>   down to the pit.
> Sing praises to the Lord, O you his saints,
> and give thanks to his holy name. (ESV)

Many parents have felt that their child is too far gone and that there's no way out for them. The good news? We serve a God who lifts souls from Sheol—that's the depths. He heals and keeps us alive when it feels like we're sinking.

I know you have gone to God with your broken heart many times. The Lord has not ignored your cries for help. God hears you, and healing is coming. Even when it looks like your child is sinking deeper, God has the power to pull them back. He is sure to pull out of the pit those who call out to him. Let's let out a battle cry of praise today. Why? Because when you praise in the waiting, you declare war on the Enemy.

Dear Father, thank you for pulling me out of the pits of despair and healing me. In Jesus' name. Amen.

Claiming God's Sovereignty

Are you overwhelmed by the relentless chaos of having a wayward child? If you feel out of control, then settle into the truth from 1 Corinthians 10:26: "The earth is the LORD's, and all it contains" (NASB). Pause and breathe in this life-changing reality: everything on this earth belongs to God, including your struggling child. They're his creations, fashioned by divine hands for divine purposes.

God is sovereign over this world. Proclaim it in your prayers, and let it shape your battle strategies. Next time the Enemy whispers lies of despair or defeat, you fire back with *Uh-uh, not today! God is in control.* You may never know why certain things happen, but you can trust that he rules over all.

God is in control. Align your parenting game plan with his truth and watch as the Almighty works in and through your life. Remember, no matter how far they wander, your child is under God's watchful eye, and the outcome is in his capable hands.

Dear Father, thank you that everything on earth belongs to you, including my child and family. I am so grateful that I can call you my own. In Jesus' name. Amen.

Close Calls with God

Do you need to reach out to God? Don't delay because as we see in Psalm 145:18–19,

> The LORD is near to all who call on him,
> to all who call on him in truth.
> He fulfills the desire of those who fear him;
> he also hears their cry and saves them. (ESV)

Your struggle with your wayward child can feel isolating, but know this: God is closer than you think when you are fighting to guide your child back to the right path. There's no need to shout or beg. Just call on him confidently. Open, honest prayer pulls God near like a magnet because authenticity is a language he understands perfectly.

You're a parent who fears God, who reverently seeks his will. That's your superpower in this battle for your child's soul. While your eyes see defiance or rebellion, God sees a life worth saving. When you cry out to God, he hears you and works to fulfill your deep, unspoken desires for your child's safety and redemption. So go ahead. Call on him. Pour out your worries, frustrations, and hopes. As you do, God listens, saves, and sets into motion plans you can't even begin to fathom.

Dear Father, thank you for allowing me to call on you. I trust that you save. In Jesus' name. Amen.

Commanding Authority

When forces try to pull our children away, too often we give in and feel powerless. But check out Luke 4:36.

> Amazement came upon them all, and they began talking with one another, saying, "What is this message? For with authority and power He commands the unclean spirits, and they come out!" (NASB)

Let's get one thing straight: you're not powerless. You serve a God who has authority over all things, even those seemingly insurmountable forces. Jesus didn't just talk; he commanded. And when he did, even unclean spirits had to obey. What could change in your life and in your child's life if you stepped into that kind of authority? Imagine praying with boldness that shakes the heavens and roots out the Enemy's schemes. You're not spewing words into the wind but commanding breakthroughs with divine authority.

So let's do this, parent. Stand in your spiritual authority and don't back down because with God, you're fighting with his might. Keep the faith. Your authority and the power found in Christ are more potent than any challenge you face.

Dear Father, thank you for giving me the authority to win the victory over the Enemy. In Jesus' name. Amen.

Counted and Cherished

Have you ever felt like your child is just another statistic, lost in a world that doesn't seem to care? Let's find hope in Matthew 10:29: "Are two sparrows not sold for an assarion? And yet not one of them will fall to the ground apart from your Father" (NASB). This verse isn't just about birds. It's also a revelation of God's meticulous care. If he keeps track of sparrows, how much more is he concerned about your child, whom God made in his image?

Listen, no matter how far your child has strayed, they haven't slipped through God's fingers. The Father has counted them, knows them, and cherishes them. You may be frustrated because your prayers haven't turned things around yet, but rest assured that God's eyes are on your child.

Pause a moment and breathe. We follow a God who leaves the ninety-nine to pursue the one who goes astray. God knows exactly where your child is and how to get them back. Hold on to this unshakable truth that God cares for your child more than you ever could. Your prayers are receiving divine attention. Your child is worth more than many sparrows, and they are never apart from God.

Dear Father, thank you that my child is never without your care. In Jesus' name. Amen.

Counting Tears and Fighting Fears

Do you feel like your emotions are so raw that your heart could flood the room? If you have stopped counting how many nights you've spent crying over your wayward child, let me share some comfort from Psalm 56:8: "You have kept count of my tossings; put my tears in your bottle. Are they not in your book?" (ESV).

God has a ledger, and he has accounted for every tear you've shed. Not one single tear escapes his notice, and you can believe that they are not wasted. They're all recorded and cherished as if collected in a heavenly bottle. All your hurt and pain—they matter to God. While society might dismiss your tears as a sign of weakness or instability, God considers them valuable and meaningful. He sees them as he works on your behalf and on the behalf of your child.

God is intimately in the struggle. Your tears haven't gone unnoticed, and your prayers haven't gone unheard. Take solace in the fact that the creator of the universe is collecting your tears, and you'd better believe he's planning to turn them into something beautiful.

Dear Father, thank you for not wasting a single tear of mine and for knowing every detail of my child's life. In Jesus' name. Amen.

Unshakable Love

Do you ever get stuck in the quicksand of worry, questioning if God's love is enough for your wayward child? Well, let me share some good news straight from Romans 8:38–39.

> I am convinced that neither death, nor life, nor angels, nor principalities, nor things present, nor things to come, nor powers, nor height, nor depth, nor any other created thing will be able to separate us from the love of God that is in Christ Jesus our Lord. (NASB)

That's right. Nothing can sever the love God has for your child. Not bad decisions, not rough crowds, not even the darkest nights of the soul. God's love is like spiritual superglue: it sticks and stays.

I get that you're in the middle of a fierce battle. Sometimes the struggle for your child's soul feels unbearable, but here's the deal: God loves your child even more than you do. His love is constant, it's relentless, and it's powerful. No matter how far your child strays, they're never out of God's reach. Remember these unshakable truths today whenever doubt tries to creep in. Your child is never too lost or too broken for God's redeeming love.

Dear Father, thank you for helping me hold on to hope because your love never fails. In Jesus' name. Amen.

The Power of the New Covenant

Is your heart aching as you watch your child slip further away? Let's get some heavenly perspective from Hebrews 12:24, which invites us to come "to Jesus, the mediator of a new covenant, and to the sprinkled blood that speaks a better word than the blood of Abel" (ESV). Let's be real: as parents, we want to mediate and fix everything for our kids, right? But there's a mediator who has us beat, and that's Jesus. He's the go-between who can mend what's broken in our families.

The "sprinkled blood" speaks of a covenant—God's unbreakable promise—far better than any earthly agreement. Abel's blood cried out for justice, but the blood of Jesus cries out for grace, mercy, and complete restoration. Remember who's fighting for you when you're at your wit's end. The one who entered the most holy place has your back, and his covenant promise over your family is more potent than any earthly bond or demonic influence.

Believe this: your covenant through Jesus is stronger than any chain pulling your child away. Don't lose heart. Keep praying and stand firm in this new-covenant promise. Grace is on the horizon, and it's packed with restoration power.

Dear Father, thank you for giving us Jesus to be our Mediator. Bring restoration between my rebellious child and me. In Jesus' name. Amen.

Courage to Face the Impossible

Do things look impossible with your child today? Let's examine 1 Chronicles 28:20.

> David also said to Solomon his son, "Be strong and courageous, and do the work. Do not be afraid or discouraged, for the LORD God, my God, is with you. He will not fail you or forsake you until all the work for the service of the temple of the LORD is finished." (NIV)

Imagine God speaking these words to you right now. Just like Solomon, you have a monumental task. Your "temple" is your home, your family, and that child who has you awake at night while you wrestle with worry and fear. David's advice to Solomon is life-giving for us today: be strong and courageous. Act! You're not alone in this seemingly impossible task of turning your child's heart to the light. The Lord God is with you, just as he was with Solomon.

God won't bail on you. He won't leave the job half-done. So why should you give up? Gather up that strength and courage that you have stored deep inside. Remember, God specializes in impossible missions. So get out there and act! No fear. No dismay. Just be a warfare parent empowered by an unfailing God.

Dear Father, thank you for supplying me with courage that erases my fear. In Jesus' name. Amen.

Covered by Grace

Are you feeling the weight of your child's choices? Return to Genesis 3:21: "The LORD God made garments of skin for Adam and his wife, and clothed them" (NASB). Imagine Adam's and Eve's guilt, shame, and despair after that fateful bite of fruit. They tried covering themselves with fig leaves—a feeble attempt, right? But here's where it gets good. God stepped in and covered them with garments of animal skin.

Guess what? You might feel like your efforts to save your child are as inadequate as covering with fig leaves. Maybe you're wrestling with guilt about where they are right now. But hear this: God has a better covering, one made of grace and love, stitched by his divine hands.

Your child's mistakes don't define them, nor do they define you. Like Adam and Eve, your child can be covered by God's grace. So lay down the burden, pick up your faith, and step into the realm where God's transformative power thrives. Your child's story is far from over. After all, if God can cover original sin, what can't he cover?

Dear Father, thank you for showing me how to parent disobedient children. The very first children you created disobeyed, making you the first parent of a prodigal. Thank you for offering a covering of grace for my child. In Jesus' name. Amen.

Crossing over to Life

Our focus today is John 5:24.

> Truly, truly, I say to you, the one who hears My
> word, and believes Him who sent Me, has eternal
> life, and does not come into judgment, but has
> passed out of death into life. (NASB)

This is a jaw-dropping promise from Jesus. It's not just
about believing but also about having a faith that moves you
from death to life. Parents, let's zoom in on the assurance
that a believer "has passed out of death into life." You're
not praying for temporary fixes. You're praying for eternal
transformation, engaging in spiritual warfare to lead your
child from spiritual insignificance into abundant eternal life.

First, never underestimate God's Word. Share it with
your child and pray it over them. Second, hold steadfast
in your faith. Jesus assures us that believing in him results
in eternal life, which applies to your child, too, when they
accept Jesus. Pray that your child will hear God's Word and
believe in the one whom the Father sent to give eternal
life. Trust that your prayers are pushing them closer to that
transition from death into life. God is on your side. With
him, your child can cross over from death to life.

Dear Father, thank you that the believer's death ends in
eternal life with you. In Jesus' name. Amen.

Crowned in Kindness

You may be a compassionate parent, but does your love for your wayward child feel more like a one-way street these days? Reflect on Matthew 25:34–35.

> The King will say to those on His right, "Come, you who are blessed of My Father, inherit the kingdom prepared for you from the foundation of the world. For I was hungry, and you gave Me something to eat; I was thirsty, and you gave Me something to drink; I was a stranger, and you invited Me in." (NASB)

God sees your kindness even when your child does not seem to notice or return it. Feeding them wisdom, quenching their spiritual thirst, and making your home a sanctuary—you do not do these in vain. The kingdom isn't just a future inheritance; it's also a present reality we build through acts of love and kindness. Even in the struggle, especially in the battle, you're laying the spiritual groundwork that transcends the here and now.

Keep the faith. Your acts of kindness are kingdom-building blocks. Hold fast. The reward far outweighs the cost. Your crown awaits. God sees your relentless love, unseen sacrifices, and unwavering commitment, and these will bear fruit in his perfect timing.

Dear Father, thank you for helping me navigate through the heartache. Your kindness is all I need today. In Jesus' name. Amen.

Crushing the Enemy

I have a powerful promise for you today from Romans 16:20: "The God of peace will soon crush Satan under your feet" (NASB). Doesn't that make you want to stand up and shout? The road with your wayward child has probably been full of bumps and detours. The Enemy has been working overtime, but let me tell you that his time is limited. God's promise is not just to defeat but to "crush" the Enemy under our feet. How awesome is that!

Your love for your child and God's unparalleled power are a recipe for a crushing defeat against any force that dares to come against your family. I know it's hard to wait, and it feels like you're in a constant war zone, but God's victory against Satan is on the horizon. Your persistence and prayers are paving the way for God to move mightily.

Don't lose hope. Instead, increase your anticipation. When we look back on our lives, we can often see how God transformed our lives and fortified our faith. Keep praying and fighting because the God of peace is about to do some crushing on your behalf. Get ready for it!

Dear Father, thank you today for reminding me that you will crush the Enemy. In Jesus' name. Amen.

Victory in the Battle

When worry for your wayward child weaves through your day, Psalm 60:12 is a victory shout. "Through God we will do valiantly, and it is He who will trample down our enemies" (NASB). These words are not just comfort; they're also your war strategy. Lean on God when the story of your child's rebellion seems like a narrative of defeat. Only with him can you continue to fight for your child. Only through him will your child ever come to believe in and trust God as you do.

As parents, we're not sidelined spectators. We're active participants, armed with hope and the power of prayer. Remember, your prodigal's path is not beyond God's redeeming reach. This knowledge should alleviate our worries today and spread hope.

You're battling for more than behavioral changes. You're fighting for a heart transformed by divine love. Wield your belief like a warrior and show God's true nature to your prodigal through your steadfast love and unwavering faith. Your unwavering trust is the battleground where God unveils his glory. Watch as he works wonders and continue to walk valiantly in faith.

Dear Father, thank you for trampling my enemies and the evil enticements of the world. In Jesus' name. Amen.

Defying Stereotypes

You might feel the odds are stacked against you and your child, but let's turn this around. Your child is not a lost cause. We've all heard that age is just a number, not a measurement of wisdom or mature behavior, as we see in 1 Timothy 4:12: "Let no one despise you for your youth, but set the believers an example in speech, in conduct, in love, in faith, in purity" (ESV). This verse is a shout-out to the young and a wake-up call for us as parents. It says not to let anyone look down on you for being young.

Could this also be a divine reminder that our children, no matter how young or naive, can set an example in these five areas? You have the power and mandate to guide your child in speech, conduct, love, faith, and purity. Your example may be what they need to return from the wilderness they're wandering in, to accept Jesus, and to begin modeling these characteristics in their own lives.

Don't count them out because of their youth or mistakes. Young people have a history of doing incredible things when guided by wisdom and love—your wisdom, your love, and, most importantly, God's.

Dear Father, thank you for not counting out my wayward child. In Jesus' name. Amen.

Discovering the Unseen Power

Our encouragement today is from Colossians 1:15: "He is the image of the invisible God, the firstborn of all creation" (ESV). Facing battles with wayward children, we often fight what we can see: the poor choices, the rebellion, or maybe the bad influences. But here Paul reminded us that there's more than meets the eye. This verse is a wake-up call to recognize who is behind the curtain of our reality. Jesus is the image of the invisible God.

What does that mean for us parents knee-deep in the battle for our children's souls? It means that the one who is in control of everything is on our side. We're not fighting alone, even against invisible spiritual enemies and unspoken fears. We're doing it with the One, "the firstborn of all creation." In other words, he predates and presides over anything and everything that exists. That includes the challenges and the chaos we're facing right now.

So let's focus less on the visible problems and more on the invisible power that reigns supreme. Rely on God's power, lean into his strength, and let him be the visible hope in your invisible battles.

Dear Father, thank you for being with me even though you might be invisible to me in the battle. In Jesus' name. Amen.

Divine Comfort in the Fight

You know those moments when you feel defeated, like you're battling alone? Well, I have good news for you. "God, who comforts the downcast, comforted us by the coming of Titus" (2 Corinthians 7:6 ESV). God knows exactly what you're going through. He knows your hurt, your exhaustion, your despair. And guess what? He's in the business of comfort.

Just like Paul found comfort through Titus, God often sends comfort through others—maybe a friend, a sermon, or a timely podcast. God will use many ways for you to feel his presence and comfort. Be open to how God may be trying to uplift your spirit. Don't discount any source of encouragement since God may speak through the unlikeliest people.

It's not just about God comforting you. It's also about you becoming a comfort to your struggling child. Remember, you're never alone. God has your back. So be encouraged today because the God of all comfort is actively involved in your fight. He will never leave you without the comfort and hope you need.

Dear Father, thank you for comforting me today and giving me hope that you are helping me comfort my wayward child. In Jesus' name. Amen.

A Labor Not in Vain

Today let's focus on 1 Corinthians 15:58: "My beloved brothers, be steadfast, immovable, always abounding in the work of the Lord, knowing that in the Lord your labor is not in vain" (ESV).

Life can feel overwhelming, like everything leads to more disappointment. But this verse reminds us that our efforts, bathed in God's grace and purpose, will not go to waste. You are a blessed child of the Lord. You are tirelessly working not for futility but for a legacy that echoes God's faithfulness. God's presence ensures that your labor is not in vain and won't lead to calamity. The Lord sees your steadfast dedication, which is shaping a future filled with his blessings.

As difficult as it is, your struggle is part of a bigger blessing. Don't let disappointments, worries, or regrets keep you from fulfilling the great work God has for you. Your unwavering faith and efforts are sowing seeds in your life and in your child's life. Your prayers and efforts are not going unnoticed. God sees you and is working even when you cannot see it.

Dear Father, thank you for showing me today that you bless my labors. In Jesus' name. Amen.

A Legacy of Enduring Faith

Do you wonder why your faith matters? We find the answer in Psalm 102:28: "The children of Your servants will continue, and their descendants will be established before You" (NASB). This verse profoundly impacts us. It reminds us that the struggle will affect more than now; it could build a faith legacy that will outlast us. Sometimes we're caught in our prodigal children's chaos. But God says, *Take a step back. This is a marathon, not a sprint.* Our faith today lays the groundwork for our children's future and beyond.

What we do can have great significance beyond what we realize. We're part of a God-authored narrative spanning generations. God promises that descendants "established" before him will be anchored, unshakable. When we feel mired, we should remember that faith has long dividends. We are not just striving to win our children back; we are also building a faith legacy firm before God.

Let's keep fighting. Your child may be prodigal today, but their story isn't over. Neither is yours. Keep believing, praying, and hoping. You're building eternal things. This struggle is hard, but your faithfulness matters for generations. God is weaving a legacy through you.

Dear Father, thank you for building a legacy through my family and for building my faith as you build eternal things. In Jesus' name. Amen.

Walking in the Light

I know how it feels to stand seemingly alone on the front line, desperately defending your child's soul. It's a place where isolation looms, and support feels just out of reach. Yet in that solitude, remember that you're enveloped in God's unfailing light. Look at 1 John 1:7.

> If we walk in the Light as He Himself is in the Light, we have fellowship with one another, and the blood of Jesus His Son cleanses us from all sin. (NASB)

During this relentless struggle, the light of Christ is your beacon of truth, your clarity in confusion, your connection to divine support, and, most of all, your hope. The blood of Jesus has cleansing power not just for you but also for your wayward child. The same God who transformed you can reach into the darkest corners where your child might be.

So walk in that divine light, parents. There's healing power there. Remember, darkness can't persist where there is light. Your prayers are lighting a path drenched in Jesus' cleansing blood for your child to find their way back. Don't lose heart. Stick with God and stay in the light. That's where miracles happen.

Dear Father, thank you for being our light and for your Son, who cleanses us from all sins. In Jesus' name. Amen.

Always Ready for Breakthrough

Do you feel like every moment is make-or-break with your wayward child? Let's tap into Matthew 25:13: "Be on the alert then, because you do not know the day nor the hour" (NASB). It's a wake-up call, isn't it? No one knows the precise moment when the final judgment will come, when the prodigal will return, or when God's timing will finally align with your long-held prayers. But we can be ready.

Being on the alert means you're grounded in faith, drenched in prayer, and geared for action. It means you're hopeful even when the night is darkest because you never know when the dawn will break.

So don't slack off. Stay motivated to keep believing God will move on your child's behalf. Keep the faith, for your vigilance is not in vain. Stay ready, for your breakthrough moment may be closer than you think. And most importantly, don't lose hope. God specializes in last-minute miracles. Keep your lamps filled and your wick trimmed. You never know when it will be time to shine. Every day is an opportunity for God's intervention, a chance for change. Your steadfast watchfulness and continuous prayers are the groundwork for God's miraculous works.

Dear Father, thank you for this motivation to keep believing and standing in faith for a breakthrough for my child. In Jesus' name. Amen.

Divine Intervention

Does the weight of your battles feel like it's just too much?
Find hope in 2 Kings 19:35.

> It happened that night that the angel of the LORD
> went out and struck 185,000 in the camp of the
> Assyrians; and when the rest got up early in the
> morning, behold, all of the 185,000 were dead.
> (NASB)

King Hezekiah faced a dire situation when
outnumbered by a menacing Assyrian army. But guess what?
In one night, the angel of the Lord struck down 185,000
Assyrian soldiers. When dawn broke, the threat was gone.

You might feel like the issues facing your wayward child
are an invincible army, relentless and overpowering. You've
probably had many sleepless nights praying for a miracle.
Take heart, for God specializes in midnight interventions.
When you think the Enemy is closing in, the angel of the
Lord is dispatched to deal with your situation in ways you
can't even fathom.

So don't lose hope. God sees your struggle and hears your
prayers. And just like King Hezekiah, you will see that God
is more than capable of intervening in powerful ways. Rest
tonight knowing your dawn is coming and may be bringing
victory with it. Your "Assyrians" don't stand a chance.

Dear Father, thank you for the hope in divine interventions
for my wayward child and family. In Jesus' name. Amen.

Shielded in Battle

Do you feel like you need a shield to protect you from the daily fights with your child? God is that shield, as we see in Proverbs 30:5: "Every word of God proves true; he is a shield to those who take refuge in him" (ESV). The emotional warfare for your child's soul feels ceaseless and overwhelming. Think about it. All those sleepless nights, all the tear-soaked prayers—they're not in vain. You're not throwing arrows aimlessly. With God as your shield, you are armed. His promises aren't flimsy guarantees but unbreakable spiritual laws. They're your armor in this gut-wrenching battle for your child's soul.

And what better shield could we ask for than the God of all creation? When lies, doubt, and fear assail you, remember that you can take refuge in him. When he says he will chase down the one lost sheep, believe him. Trust him when he says he can turn hearts of stone to hearts of flesh. Take up the shield of faith. God's Word never returns void, and he is fighting this battle with you. So let his truth encourage you today. Hold that shield high.

Dear Father, thank you for your Word, which is true, and for being my shield, which protects. In Jesus' name. Amen.

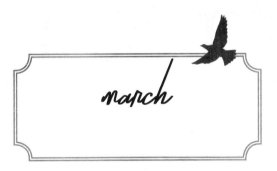

march

One God, One Path

Do you need a path to victory? Let's get into Romans 3:30: "Since indeed God who will justify the circumcised by faith and the uncircumcised through faith is one" (NASB). Let's not gloss over this. We're all under the same God—one God who justifies us by faith. When it comes to reclaiming your wayward child, it's not about religious checkboxes; it's about faith. Faith is your child's path to the victory available in Christ. Your child, wayward as they may be, is not beyond the reach of God's grace.

I know it's hard to see your child entangled in worldly traps. But remember, the same God capable of justifying you through faith can do the same for your child. Here's the real talk: God's in the business of breaking chains, and the faith that sets you free is the same faith that can set your child free. So what's our role? Keep believing. Keep praying. And remind your child that faith in God is the way home, no matter how far they've wandered. With one God and one faith, we have unity and hope.

Dear Father, thank you that faith can break my child's chains and set them free. In Jesus' name. Amen.

Don't Give Up

I know you may be worn out. Fighting for your wayward child can make even the strongest parent feel defeated. But hear this. Galatians 6:9 says, "Let us not grow weary of doing good, for in due season we will reap, if we do not give up" (ESV). Understandably, you may be on the brink of emotional and spiritual exhaustion. But giving up is not an option. Why? Because there's a "due season" coming, a harvest of good from all the love, prayer, and challenging conversations you've sown.

Think of yourself as a farmer. You plant seeds of truth, you water them with prayer, and, yes, sometimes you have to dig out the weeds of deceit or evil influences. It's grueling work, but the harvest—the rewards for the good works we do for God's glory—will be worth it.

God's economy isn't like ours. Your hard work will pay off. It may not be today, tomorrow, or even next year, but if you keep sowing goodness and love, you will reap a harvest. Trust in God's timing. Don't grow weary. Your season is coming, and it will be a bumper crop of blessings.

Dear Father, thank you for helping me not give up on doing the good that reaps a harvest for your kingdom. In Jesus' name. Amen.

Draw Near with Confidence

When the weight of your child's choices drags you down, it's easy to feel alone. But you're not. As we see in Hebrews 4:15–16,

> We do not have a high priest who is unable to sympathize with our weaknesses, but one who in every respect has been tempted as we are, yet without sin. Let us then with confidence draw near to the throne of grace, that we may receive mercy and find grace to help in time of need. (ESV)

You have the High Priest, Jesus, who's been there and gets your struggles, including the hardships you have experienced with your wayward child. The beauty of these verses is the invitation to approach God's throne— confidently—not because you're flawless but because he is. It's a grace-filled throne, not a judgmental one. At your breaking point, especially with your wayward kid, go there. Lay your burdens and despair at his feet. God is not surprised by your struggles with your child. He says, *Come*.

The big takeaway? God's grace suffices. For every sleepless night, court date, or tear shed, his grace meets us but doesn't leave us stuck. Take that divine invitation. You're not alone in the battle for your child.

Dear Father, thank you for giving grace in my greatest time of need. In Jesus' name. Amen.

Doubt to Deliverance

Are you overcome with doubt? There is no shame in it. Even those closest to Jesus sometimes felt filled with doubt. We find this in John 20:25.

> The other disciples were saying to him, "We have seen the Lord!" But he said to them, "Unless I see in His hands the imprint of the nails, and put my finger into the place of the nails, and put my hand into His side, I will not believe." (NASB)

Thomas gets a bad rap for doubting, but let's get real: Haven't we all been Thomas at some point? When we're shoulder high in the struggle, praying and fighting for our wayward children, it's easy to question if our efforts are in vain. You've heard testimonies of other parents whose prodigals have returned, yet you still doubt whether it's possible. First off, it's okay to be human. God knows our frailties. Jesus showed up for Thomas, nail scars and all. And he can show up for you and your prodigal.

The nail-scarred hands of Jesus represent his immense love for us, a love that can rescue your prodigal no matter how far they've gone. Believe it. God's love is active in the darkest situations.

Dear Father, thank you for showing up even in my doubts. In Jesus' name. Amen.

Don't Rely On Man

Today let's explore Jeremiah 17:5: "Thus says the LORD: 'Cursed is the man who trusts in man and makes flesh his strength, whose heart turns away from the LORD'" (ESV). I know that sounds heavy. Trusting in ourselves or others is a trap we all fall into, especially when we're neck-deep in the mess that comes with a wayward child. We read all the books, consult the experts, and maybe even try to control too much. We make "flesh"—ours or someone else's—our strength.

But here's the deal. The strength we need to win this battle for our children's souls isn't coming from any human source. Nope, not even from that well-meaning friend who swears by their techniques. The strength we need comes from God and God alone.

When you're entangled in the battles for your child, your heart must remain anchored in the Lord. Don't give up; just shift your trust. Take your eyes off the world's solutions and fix them on God, your true strength. Trust him to guide you and sustain you as your child wanders. God hasn't forgotten you or your child. Keep your heart turned toward him.

Dear Father, thank you that I can trust in you alone to save my child. In Jesus' name. Amen.

Embrace God's Grace

Are you feeling drained? The worry over a wayward child is intense. But listen, you're not meant to face this solo. You have a divine partner—God. According to 2 Corinthians 12:9,

> He said to me, "My grace is sufficient for you, for my power is made perfect in weakness." Therefore I will boast all the more gladly of my weaknesses, so that the power of Christ may rest upon me. (ESV)

Let's unpack this verse. *Grace* means God's unearned love. *Sufficient* means it's more than enough. And "power in weakness" is about turning our vulnerabilities, fears, and feelings of inadequacy into a stage where God's strength takes the spotlight.

Maybe you've felt weak because of your child's choices and have even doubted your parenting skills. But that weakness is God's spotlight. It's not a liability; it's a divine opportunity. Don't waste time pretending to be strong. When you're at a low point, his grace lifts you. It's sufficient, more than enough, and there for you and your child. So embrace your weakness and let God's strength flood in. Keep the faith, for his grace has enveloped you.

Dear Father, thank you that your power is brightest in my weakness. You are my strength today. In Jesus' name. Amen.

God in Your Child's Journey

Have you ever wondered how God works in your child's life, especially when they seem so far away from his path? Revelation 4:11 reminds us, "Worthy are you, our Lord and God, to receive glory and honor and power, for you created all things, and by your will they existed and were created" (ESV). This verse from Scripture beautifully echoes the truth about our children: each is a divine creation, a masterpiece made by God. In their wandering, it's this truth we must hold on to.

When our children take paths that lead them away from us or God, it's not a sign that they're lost forever. Instead, it's a part of their unique journey under God's watchful eye. He's constantly at work in their lives, shaping their story in ways only he can. We need to trust in God's plan. He's the master storyteller, and he knows the path our children are on. Our job is to pray, love, and keep faith, even when the road seems unclear. This walk with our prodigal children is a journey of faith and hope. Believe in God's unending love for them and find peace knowing he is actively involved in every moment of their lives.

Dear Father, thank you for creating everything, and may your will be done. In Jesus' name. Amen.

Overcoming Temptations

Do you feel your child constantly faces temptations and the enticements of darkness? Jesus was tempted, too, as we see in Luke 4:1–2.

> Jesus…was led by the Spirit in the wilderness for forty days, being tempted by the devil. And he ate nothing during those days. And when they were ended, he was hungry. (ESV)

These verses are a powerful reminder that strength and resilience can prevail even in moments of vulnerability. In the world of the dark web, social media, and technology at our fingertips, we see our children confronted with various temptations. Like Jesus, our children can emerge stronger and more grounded in their faith and values after facing these challenges.

Temptation is not a sign of weakness but an opportunity for growth and reliance on God. Let's encourage our children to lean into their faith during hard times. They have the strength to overcome temptations just as Jesus did if they have the power of Jesus Christ living inside them. In every challenge, there's a chance to grow closer to God. Our support and prayers for our children are crucial to helping them navigate these trials, reminding them of the strength of God's presence.

Dear Father, thank you that my family can overcome any temptation if we have the power of Jesus Christ living inside us. In Jesus' name. Amen.

The Eternal One

Do you need encouragement today? Verse 25 of Jude speaks volumes, saying, "To the only God our Savior, through Jesus Christ our Lord, be glory, majesty, dominion, and authority before all time and now and forever. Amen" (NASB). I don't know what it is if that's not a caffeine jolt for your spirit. Imagine the universe's Creator, who intricately designed galaxies and the DNA swirling inside your wayward child, being our Savior! Take a moment and let that soak in. This God—our God—is bigger than any pit your child has fallen into. Majesty, dominion, authority? He has it all, and he's in your corner.

Your child may be wandering now, but let's face it: God's majesty is unparalleled. He brings kings to their knees and rules over the chaos. He has dominion over addiction, depression, and every trap the Enemy sets for our kids.

The battles for our children's souls are not in vain when we have the one true God fighting for us. Remember, the God who was, who is, and who is to come has this, and he has you and your family too. Don't forget this truth. Keep standing, warriors, and give him the glory he's due.

Dear Father, thank you for being the Eternal One with full dominion over all, including my child. In Jesus' name. Amen.

Embracing God's Will

Understandably, you're more than ready for your child's turnaround, and you may be disappointed you haven't seen change. Ponder Luke 22:42: "Father, if You are willing, remove this cup from Me; yet not My will, but Yours be done" (NASB). Jesus was essentially at the crossroads of destiny in this moment of anguish. He was in the garden of Gethsemane, staring down the unimaginable pain of the cross. The human side of him was praying to avoid suffering, yet the divine part yielded to the Father's will.

We can relate, right? Our hearts cry, *God, if it's your will, change my child now and bring them back.* Yet in the depth of our souls, there's this whisper: *Not my will, but yours be done.*

Here's the thing. Yielding to God's will doesn't mean we're giving up on our prodigals; it means entrusting them to a higher authority. Our dreams for them may take a back seat for a while as God's perfect plan unfolds, but remember, his plans are always for the good of his people. So let's find courage in surrender, knowing that in the grand tapestry of God's will, our prodigals have a unique and divinely orchestrated part to play.

Dear Father, thank you for understanding my pain and impatience. I know you have divine plans for this world. In Jesus' name. Amen.

Healing in His Wings

Are you at your wit's end? Are you longing for a breakthrough? You can find help in Matthew 8:16–17.

> When evening came, they brought to Him many who were demon-possessed; and He cast out the spirits with a word, and healed all who were ill. This happened so that what was spoken through Isaiah the prophet would be fulfilled: "He Himself took our illnesses and carried away our diseases." (NASB)

Jesus didn't just heal some. He healed "all who were ill." The original promise from Isaiah was alive and in action. Let's bring this home: Jesus can also heal your child.

You might be dealing with a child possessed by worldly desires or addictive behaviors, but remember, Jesus still casts out spirits and heals with just a word. Your task is to bring your child to Jesus over and over through your prayers and love. He bore our infirmities and carried away our diseases. That means he's carrying your child's issues too. You're not carrying this burden alone. You have divine backup. Lean into his promises. Your child's complete healing is possible in Christ.

Dear Father, thank you for helping me see that you can set my child free no matter what battles they are fighting. In Jesus' name. Amen.

Unlocking True Life

In the chaos, it's easy to forget what we're fighting for: to take hold of that which is truly life. Your lifeline is found in 1 Timothy 6:18–19, in which Paul told Timothy to instruct the rich

> to do good, to be rich in good works, to be generous and ready to share, storing up for themselves the treasure of a good foundation for the future, so that they may take hold of that which is truly life. (NASB)

Paul spoke of rich people doing good and being generous, but it's not about just giving money or material things. This is about investing in eternal treasures that no darkness can touch. When you pray without ceasing for your child or pour love into them, even when it's hard, you store heavenly treasure. Your generosity of spirit is your spiritual investment, laying a foundation for the future.

Don't underestimate the ripple effect of your good work and generous heart. It can make a difference in the spiritual realm, weaken the Enemy's hold on your child, and allow God's light to flood in. Your sacrifices are not in vain. They pave the way for true life for you and your child.

Dear Father, thank you for helping me fight for something far more valuable than earthly wealth. In Jesus' name. Amen.

Empowered to Overcome

Do you feel powerless against the forces trapping your child? Let's gather strength from Matthew 10:1: "Jesus summoned His twelve disciples and gave them authority over unclean spirits, to cast them out, and to heal every disease and every sickness" (NASB). Did you catch that? Jesus gave authority to the disciples not just for preaching but also for casting out unclean spirits and healing. Imagine ordinary people empowered to do extraordinary things. Here's your game changer: you, too, have spiritual authority.

That's right. You're not fighting this battle unarmed. God has granted you divine authority to confront the Enemy messing with and tempting your child. Your prayers aren't just wishes but spiritual declarations that can dismantle strongholds and set your child free. Stand your ground. Use your God-given authority and call those mountains in your child's life to crumble. Declare healing, freedom, and redemption in his name. This is your weapon, and it's more potent than you think. Don't underestimate your power. The highest authority has commissioned you. Pray boldly and act decisively. Your child's breakthrough is within reach.

Dear Father, thank you for giving me the power to help heal my child. Lord, help me step into this authority. In Jesus' name. Amen.

Endurance and Faith

Being the parent of a wayward child feels like a spiritual battle because it is. There are days when you feel captive to your circumstances and other days when you're figuratively slain by heartache and disappointment. Let's learn from Revelation 13:10.

> If anyone is to be taken captive, to captivity he goes; if anyone is to be slain with the sword, with the sword must he be slain. Here is a call for the endurance and faith of the saints. (ESV)

This verse calls for two things: endurance and faith. Endurance implies that this is a marathon, not a sprint. Your child didn't go astray overnight, and the journey home may be long. As you pray, set boundaries, and exemplify Christ, you're setting the pace for a long-distance run. Then there's faith. Faith isn't wishful thinking; it's confident assurance in a God who has never failed you. It's the bedrock belief that your kid is not too far gone for God to reach. When the situation seems impossible, God does his best work.

So take a deep breath, warrior parent. This battle you're in calls for long-haul endurance and unshakable faith. And remember, you're not running this marathon alone. God is with you every step of the way.

Dear Father, thank you for building my endurance and faith.
In Jesus' name. Amen.

Unshakable Promises

Have you ever felt like the world around you is disintegrating? I mean, if it's not one thing, it's another—especially in the fight for your prodigal child, am I right? Today's life changer comes from Luke 21:33: "Heaven and earth will pass away, but My words will not pass away" (NASB). Listen, the chaos we see around us will come and go. It's just the nature of this fallen world. But God's Word? That stands forever. You can bet your life on it and the life of your prodigal.

God's promises are not only unbreakable; they're also unshakable. When the world is spinning out of control, when your child's choices make your heart ache, root yourself in the Word of God. It won't pass away, fail, or let you down. Those promises you're clinging to concerning your child are as solid as the ground under your feet.

God's Word is our firm foundation and anchor in the storm. His words will never die or come back void. Keep the faith, brave parent. No matter what changes around you, God's Word is your constant. And remember, he's still writing your family's story. Stay rooted in him and watch him work!

Dear Father, thank you for your Word, which is powerful and will never fail. In Jesus' name. Amen.

Enduring the Struggle

Do you need assurance through this tough time? Today believe 1 Peter 4:19: "Those also who suffer according to the will of God are to entrust their souls to a faithful Creator in doing what is right" (NASB). Whether it's late-night worry sessions or arguments that rip your heart apart, parenting a wayward child is a form of suffering. You're in the trenches. But here's a transformative idea: while you're in this difficult season, you're not just battling your child's choices but also learning to entrust your own soul to the faithful Creator.

God is faithful even when it seems like you're losing the battle. Your job is to continue "doing what is right" even when it seems pointless, when your child rebels more, or when the world advises you to give up. Endurance is your spiritual act of trusting God, and it's how you invite him to act powerfully in your family's life.

This verse reminds us that God is not watching from the sidelines. He's actively involved as you keep doing good, praying, loving, and entrusting your child—and yourself—to him. It's not about how strong you are. It's about how faithful God is.

Dear Father, thank you for your faithfulness and for building my trust in you even when I can't see any good. In Jesus' name. Amen.

A Turn of the Heart

Today we see how God can turn hearts! This is illustrated in Judges 10:16, which says, "They removed the foreign gods from among them and served the LORD; and He could no longer endure the misery of Israel" (NASB). This verse is powerful because it describes the Israelites making a pivotal choice: turning away from false gods and back to the one true God.

For parents of prodigals, this verse should ignite hope in our hearts. It signifies that critical moment when our prodigal children put away their "foreign gods"—be it substances, bad relationships, or harmful lifestyles—and turn back to God. Like Israel, our children, too, can reach a turning point.

Moreover, God's heart is so moved when we return to him that he can "no longer endure the misery." Imagine how our heavenly Father yearns for the return of our wayward children, much more than even we do! Remember, the same God who couldn't bear Israel's misery is fighting for your child too. So keep pressing in, warfare parents. Pray for that turn of the heart because once it happens, God will rush in like a flood.

Dear Father, thank you for being the one true God. Thank you for fighting for my prodigal to turn their heart toward you. In Jesus' name. Amen.

The Holy Spirit's Guidebook

Do you need a guidebook in the battle? We have something better to guide us: the Holy Spirit and his Word. Today's anchor is 1 John 2:27.

> As for you, the anointing which you received from Him remains in you, and you have no need for anyone to teach you; but as His anointing teaches you about all things, and is true and is not a lie, and just as it has taught you, you remain in Him. (NASB)

Can we talk about how revolutionary this is, especially when we're struggling with a wayward child? This verse tells us that the Holy Spirit within us is our ultimate guide, teaching us all we need to know. Isn't that comforting?

You're not walking blindly in this battle for your child's soul. No, you have the best possible guide: the Holy Spirit. As you pray, strategize, and reach out to your child, don't underestimate the power of divine intuition. You don't need to be a theologian or a psychologist. The Spirit has anointed you. Your child will witness a parent anchored in something so much more potent than human wisdom.

Dear Father, thank you for your anointing as I listen to that still, small voice helping me trust in your divine support in this struggle. In Jesus' name. Amen.

Eternal Perspective

Do you sometimes struggle with the worldly challenges your child faces? We can find an eternal view of these challenges in Luke 20:36: "They cannot die anymore, because they are equal to angels and are sons of God, being sons of the resurrection" (ESV). This verse invites us to see beyond immediate struggles and reminds us of our children's eternal potential. Instead of focusing solely on the earthly challenges of the here and now, let's focus on the eternal destiny that can await our children.

God hand-knit our children in their mother's womb. God so cherishes them that he has provided a way for them to spend eternity in heaven with him if they turn to him. If they don't, Matthew 25:46 says they "will go away into eternal punishment." This realization should shape how we support and pray for them, focusing on present issues and their eternal journey. Let's guide our children with this eternal perspective. Our approach then becomes infused with an urgency that transcends current problems.

We are nurturing not just for today but for the eternal future available with God. Our efforts and prayers become part of a larger, divine narrative, leading our children toward a lasting relationship with the Creator and our heavenly Father.

Dear Father, thank you for keeping my eyes focused on the eternal. In Jesus' name. Amen.

Even Demons Believe

Are you believing in God? Even demons do that. The key difference between you and them? Action. Let's get into James 2:19–20.

> You believe that God is one; you do well. Even the demons believe—and shudder! Do you want to be shown, you foolish person, that faith apart from works is useless? (ESV)

These verses challenge "comfortable Christianity," pushing us to act, especially for our wayward kids. Believing isn't enough. We have to act on that faith. Do you ever pray, *Lord, change my child*, yet stay stuck in old ways? James was clear: faith needs works. Without action, we're no different from the "foolish" people James spoke of.

You're your child's front line. Prayer is crucial, but we can't skip hands-on action. Are you battling addiction? Pray and seek help from an outside source. Are you emotionally distant? Soften your heart and be there for your child. Action coupled with faith is transformative. It's not earning God's favor but embodying a faith that doesn't back down. Show your child what living, active faith is. That's today's battle plan. Make it happen.

Dear Father, thank you for showing me today that even demons believe in you. Now I can begin acting more out of faith to help transform my child. In Jesus' name. Amen.

Not the End

Let's talk about those challenging moments when darkness seems to have an upper hand in your child's life. John 13:2 says, "During supper, the devil having already put into the heart of Judas Iscariot, the son of Simon, to betray Him" (NASB). This verse shows us that sometimes the Enemy gains temporary ground, influencing choices that have heartbreaking consequences. It feels like a "Judas moment" in your family, doesn't it? The hurt is unimaginable, but I want to pour this into your spirit today: even at the darkest moment, Jesus never lost control.

Just like Jesus knew about Judas and still carried out his plan for salvation, God also knows about your child's struggles and has an eternal plan in motion. While watching your child make harmful choices is agonizing, don't forget God's redemptive power. He's the same God who turned a betrayal into the greatest act of love the world has ever seen! So keep praying, keep believing, and keep fighting. Your child might be in a Judas moment, but Easter Sunday is coming. Your child's betrayal or rebellion is not the end of the story. God specializes in turning dark chapters into awe-inspiring victories.

Dear Father, thank you that no matter how dark in sin my child gets, your light can shine through and bring victory over the devil. In Jesus' name. Amen.

Evident Truths

Do you wonder if your child even knows the truth? Today's verse is Romans 1:20.

> Since the creation of the world His invisible attributes, that is, His eternal power and divine nature, have been clearly perceived, being understood by what has been made, so that they are without excuse. (NASB)

Even when your wayward child seems blind to the truth, remember that God's essence is woven into every aspect of life. Sometimes our children don't need to hear another sermon; they need to experience God in the real, messy, and unexpected corners of their lives.

Your prodigal child may be lost, but they're never too far gone to see the fingerprints of God all around them. Trust that at the right moment, those invisible attributes will become undeniably evident to them. Don't lose hope, for God's divine nature and eternal power are at work even if you can't see it now. What you're doing—your prayers, love, and unwavering faith—makes the invisible visible to them. Keep fighting the good fight. God's eternal power is your secret weapon and won't return void. Stand firm and remember that there are no lost causes with God.

Dear Father, thank you for the truth that what seems invisible to my child will become intimately evident in their lives with a touch from you. In Jesus' name. Amen.

Eyes Haven't Seen

Inspiration is waiting for you in 1 Corinthians 2:9.

> It is written: "Things which eye has not seen and ear has not heard, and which have not entered the human heart, all that God has prepared for those who love Him." (NASB)

Are you feeling defeated and hopeless about your wayward child? Pause. Take a deep breath. God has revealed to those who love him his breathtaking, unimaginable plan of salvation. We don't have to wonder how God will save us from our sins. We have the answer, and his name is Jesus.

You might look at your current circumstances and doubt that anything good could come from them. But God is in the business of turning messes into messages and tests into testimonies. Your view is limited, but God sees the whole timeline of human history—from heartbreak to healing, from rebellion to restoration.

Don't lose hope. The same gift of salvation that God has revealed to you is also available for your child when they come to love God. Keep loving, praying, and, most of all, believing in God's incredible gift of salvation.

Dear Father, thank you for revealing through your Spirit the good things you have prepared for me as I stand in faith. In Jesus' name. Amen.

Facing the Storm with Calm

I know you're spent, staring at a rebellious child who seems impervious to change. But let's pause momentarily and turn to Acts 6:15: "All who were sitting in the Council stared at him, and they saw his face, which was like the face of an angel" (NASB). Stephen stood before a hostile crowd, but those who looked at him saw his face shining like an angel. Why? Because he was filled with faith and the Holy Spirit.

What if, amid our battles with our wayward children, we wore the face of an angel? Not literally, of course, but what if our countenance displayed such faith, hope, and love that it could only be divinely inspired? I know it's hard. But, you see, your struggle is not just against your child. It's spiritual warfare. You need God's divine presence to sustain you. Fix your gaze on him and let him illuminate your face, demeanor, and approach. Like Stephen, when your focus is heavenward, those around you—even a rebellious child—will notice. Your kid may be challenging, but nothing is impossible with God. Let your face shine with heavenly assurance.

Dear Father, thank you for shining through me even in battles with my child. In Jesus' name. Amen.

Faith over Rules

Today we dig into Romans 4:14: "If those who are of the Law are heirs, then faith is made void and the promise is nullified" (NASB). Does your child like rules? Maybe you're anxious about your wayward child because you think they've strayed too far from the rules—be they societal norms, your family's traditions, or even your faith's doctrines. Here's the deal: if inheritance from God depended on us adhering to a bunch of rules (the law), then what would be the point of faith? And if faith doesn't matter, then the promises of God are void.

But that's not how God operates, friend. God's promise to redeem and heal is based not on rule following but on faith. As much as you may want to enforce rules to protect your child, salvation is not about the rules. Your child must have faith that God is who he says he is. So instead of leaning on a checklist of dos and don'ts, let your heart lean on faith as an example for your child. Your kid is not beyond God's reach. No one is too lost for the arms of God. The promise of reconciliation is still alive.

Dear Father, thank you that salvation depends on faith, not on rule following. In Jesus' name. Amen.

Fearless Parenting

How's your heart today? Let's look over Psalm 27:1: "The LORD is my light and my salvation; whom should I fear? The LORD is the defense of my life; whom should I dread?" (NASB). Can I get an amen? Fear loves to settle into our hearts when we think about our wayward children. The what-ifs come storming in like an uninvited guest. But let's boot them out right now. This verse is your eviction notice against fear. If God is your light, you are not walking in darkness even if it feels that way.

Your prodigal might be in a bad place right now, but remember, God is their light, too, even if they don't see it yet. While you can't control your child's choices, you can control whether you let fear rule your heart. God has your back. He's your fortress and your defense. What do you say? Let's squelch our fear and let faith rise. The God who's the defense of your life is working behind the scenes on your child's behalf. Let faith illuminate your journey, guiding you and your child to peace and security. Remember, with God as your defender, no fear is too great.

Dear Father, thank you for fighting for and defending my child. Because of you, I will not be afraid. In Jesus' name. Amen.

Feeling Faint? Find Strength

Do you feel faint from the continuous stress? Let Isaiah 40:31 uplift your spirits.

> They who wait for the LORD shall renew their strength;
> they shall mount up with wings like eagles;
> they shall run and not be weary;
> they shall walk and not faint. (ESV)

This verse speaks to the heart of every parent who has felt the weight of exhaustion and worry over a lost child. It reminds us that our strength comes from our hope in the Lord.

Our journey as parents can be draining, especially when our children are facing challenges or straying from their path. God invites us to find our renewal and sustenance in him. When we anchor our hope in him, he promises us endurance and the ability to rise above the trials—to soar like eagles. It's an encouragement to look beyond the immediate struggles and to see the bigger picture of God's plan. Our perseverance is not in vain. In God, we find the strength to continue, the grace to overcome weariness, and the faith to keep moving forward. As you place your hope in your Creator, trust that he will renew your strength and give you the power to face each day with courage and love.

Dear Father, thank you for renewing my strength when I feel like I can't go on in the battle with my prodigal. In Jesus' name. Amen.

Final Sorting

Thinking about your child's eternal destiny can either cause despair or send you to your knees in prayer. Let's lean into Matthew 13:49: "It will be at the end of the age: the angels will come forth and remove the wicked from among the righteous" (NASB). This verse cuts right to the chase, doesn't it? There's a final sorting at the end of the day—or rather, the end of the age. I know it's hard to think about, but let's face it head-on: you want your child counted among the righteous.

Guess what? Your fervent prayers and persistent faith are making an eternal difference. Even if you don't see immediate change, heaven is taking note. Your labor of love isn't in vain. It's laying the groundwork for divine intervention. Time on earth is short, but eternity is long. Very long. When you feel like giving up, keep battling, parent. When discouragement creeps in, remember that this isn't just a battle for today. It's a battle for forever. Stay strong and pray, for your child's eternal address is worth the fight.

Dear Father, thank you for fighting with me for the eternal lives of my child and my family. In Jesus' name. Amen.

When Surrounded by Trouble

Your life may feel like a minefield right now. Every step is calculated, as if you're dodging emotional explosions left and right because of your wayward child. It's a mess, and you're walking through the thick of it. Lean into Psalm 138:7: "Though I walk in the midst of trouble, you preserve my life; you stretch out your hand against the wrath of my enemies, and your right hand delivers me" (ESV). Here's the incredible promise God is making you: he's walking right alongside you. Not only that, but he's also fighting for you. Can you visualize that? God's hand is stretched out against anything and anyone coming against you and your family.

Your heart is heavy; perhaps you've wondered if God is still there. Trust me, he is. He's active in your situation, preserving you even when you're about to crumble. You're not just wandering through this trial but walking purposefully with a God who delivers. He's in the business of restoring broken lives and giving hope to those who call on him. Hold on to this verse as you navigate the complexities of parenting your challenging child. Remember, God's right hand is poised for your deliverance.

Dear Father, thank you for preserving me against the Enemy and delivering me. In Jesus' name. Amen.

Blessed in Hope

Do you sometimes feel like you are just done with your child? Find hope in Psalm 146:5: "Blessed is he whose help is the God of Jacob, whose hope is in the LORD his God" (ESV). This verse is a powerful reminder of where our steadfast support and hope lie—in God. When we feel like we can't change the course our children are on, this verse encourages us to shift our focus from our struggles to the steadfastness of God's support. It reassures us that placing our hope in God is comforting and empowering.

In times of uncertainty and stress, this verse invites us to lean into our faith. We open ourselves to his guidance, wisdom, and peace when we hope in God. This doesn't negate our efforts, but it places them in the context of a more extensive, divine support system.

Let this verse inspire you to renew your trust in God's plan for your child. It's a call to remember that we are supported by a loving God who can turn any situation and every challenge around for good.

Dear Father, thank you for being my hope and help when I want to give up on my child. In Jesus' name. Amen.

Immediate Restoration

Are you yearning for a quick turnaround for your wayward child? It can happen! We see this illustrated in Mark 10:52: "Jesus said to him, 'Go; your faith has made you well.' And immediately he regained his sight and began following Him on the road" (NASB). Notice that word *immediately*. In an instant, faith activated a miracle. God can turn your wayward child back around just as quickly. Don't let the Enemy whisper into your ear the lies that God can't turn your child around. God is the same yesterday, today, and tomorrow. He's a God who doesn't change. He is still moving in signs and wonders, even suddenly!

Here's the deal: don't underestimate the power of a moment. Your child's "immediately" could be right around the corner. Be ready; quick shifts are often the fruits of long prayers. God is still in the business of immediate turnarounds, and your family could be next in line. Ready for your "immediate" moment? Keep praying, believing, and watching for it. In this waiting period, know that every prayer you lift is a seed planted for a potential sudden breakthrough.

Dear Father, thank you for this incredible burst of hope, knowing that you can still move immediately in my life and in my troubled child's life. In Jesus' name. Amen.

april

The One True Path

I know the road is long and filled with uncertainty, especially when it comes to your wayward child. But today let's focus on an unchanging truth: Jesus. In John 14:6, Jesus said, "I am the way, and the truth, and the life; no one comes to the Father except through Me" (NASB).

Jesus doesn't mince words. He is "the way." In this chaotic world full of confusing paths and deceptive turns, his way is the one true route to restoration. Your child may be lost, veering off into dangerous detours, but remember this: Jesus is the way back. He's the GPS recalculating the route home, no matter how far gone your child seems.

And when it comes to "the truth," don't forget that Jesus can break every chain of lies entangling your child. He can set the captive free—every time. Don't let despair dictate your outlook. Stand firm in the truth that is Jesus.

Finally, let's look at how Jesus is "the life." Oh, how Jesus transforms us from the inside out, breathing life into the most broken parts. Your child's sins don't define them; Jesus does. Jesus is the way, the truth, and the life, working on your behalf and navigating your child's way back home.

Dear Father, thank you that in Jesus there is truth and life. In Jesus' name. Amen.

The Power of Trust

We're in a battle, aren't we? The fight for our wayward children is real, intense, and often heart-wrenching. But here's encouragement from 1 Chronicles 5:20, where the tribes of Israel went to war against enemy nations.

> They were helped against them, and the Hagrites and all who were with them were handed over to them; for they cried out to God in the battle, and He answered their prayers because they trusted in Him. (NASB)

God hears you when you cry out in the middle of the battle. Now your "enemy" might be different. It might be your child's addiction, depression, or lifestyle dragging your child further away from you and God. Yet the principle remains: when you cry out to God in trust, he answers. I know you're doing your best to fight for your child, but don't forget you're not alone. God is right there with you, and he's more than capable of intervening in miraculous ways when you trust in him.

Your prayers can and will move mountains. Trust in God to answer your prayers. Cry out to him in your battle, my friend. He hears you.

Dear Father, thank you that I can pray to you and trust you with my prodigal. In Jesus' name. Amen.

Following a New Path

Are you concerned your child will never be led off their dark path? We find insight in Mark 2:13: "He went out again beside the sea, and all the crowd was coming to him, and he was teaching them" (ESV). This verse captures a moment of change and new beginnings. By the lake, Jesus drew a crowd, ready to take them off their current path and guide them to a new path of understanding and life. We often see our children walking paths that concern us. They may be influenced by peers or societal pressures, much like the crowds around Jesus. Our hearts long for them to find a better way, a path that leads to fulfillment and purpose.

Jesus is always ready to teach and guide. We, too, should encourage our children to be open to his teachings and consider the wisdom and direction he offers. Our role is to pray that they may be receptive to Jesus' call, just like the crowd by the lake. Believe in the power of Jesus' teachings in your child's life. Encourage them to be open to his guidance, trusting that he can lead them onto a path of greater purpose and joy.

Dear Father, thank you for the teachings and love of Jesus that can bring my child home. In Jesus' name. Amen.

Forgiven and Forgotten

Good news today! It's found in Hebrews 8:12: "I will be merciful toward their iniquities, and I will remember their sins no more" (ESV). What relief, knowing that God's mercy isn't just for us but can also extend to our wayward kids. God promises mercy and that he will forget the sins of those who confess them. That's a fresh breeze for a weary soul, isn't it? It's not about the distance your child has strayed but the depth of God's mercy. Ever think your child's sins—or maybe your parental missteps—are unforgivable? Here's the reality: God's mercy overrules. The promise to "remember their sins no more" means past mistakes don't bind our children if they turn to God.

Transformation isn't hopeful thinking; it's a divine guarantee for those who follow him. When despair threatens to engulf you, anchor yourself in God's promise. He specializes in mercy and second chances. No one, including your child, is unreachable for him. This divine promise of mercy and forgetfulness is a lifeline. It's not just about rectifying wrongs. It's also about rewriting destinies. Trust in his unwavering love and capacity to heal.

Dear Father, thank you for forgetting all my sins and remembering them no more. Thank you for the mercy you can give to my child too. In Jesus' name. Amen.

Freed from Fear

Are you consumed with fear and anxiety over your child's future? Let Isaiah 41:10 release you from that fear.

> Fear not, for I am with you;
> be not dismayed, for I am your God;
> I will strengthen you, I will help you,
> I will uphold you with my righteous right hand.
> (ESV)

God speaks directly to our fears and anxieties, especially those we experience as parents. Watching our children navigate life, especially when they face trials or take unexpected paths, can be deeply worrying. This verse from Isaiah is a powerful reminder that God is our help even when we're concerned for our children.

This verse also encourages us to trust in God's presence and support. He promises to strengthen, help, and uphold us through every challenge. He invites us to shift our focus from our fears to his promises. When we feel overwhelmed, we can lean on his strength and guidance. This verse is not just a comfort; it's also a call to faith, faith in God's active, sustaining presence in our lives and our children's lives. Remember that God is with you and your child in moments of anxiety. He is actively working to strengthen and support you both in every circumstance.

Dear Father, thank you for understanding my fears and promising to be with me through the battle. In Jesus' name. Amen.

Silencing the Storm

Are you dealing with tumultuous situations related to your wayward child? Tap into Mark 1:34: "He healed many who were sick with various diseases, and cast out many demons. And he would not permit the demons to speak, because they knew him" (ESV). Notice something? Jesus had the authority not just to heal but also to silence the forces that were causing turmoil. Sometimes we need more than a solution; we need peace, a break from the chaos, a pause button on all the noise because the chaos keeps us in constant confusion and fear.

You have authority, too, through faith. You can't control your child's choices, but you can silence the spiritual chaos trying to bring your family down. Declare peace in your home. Tell the storm it has no voice here. Keep the faith. You're backed by the one who calms seas and silences storms. Hold the line. A moment of quiet can be just as miraculous as a cure. Believe it. Your family's peace isn't a lost cause. It's a promise waiting for you to claim. Take authority and let's silence the storm together with God's power.

Dear Father, thank you for the hope that you heal and cast out demons, silencing the chaotic storms. In Jesus' name. Amen.

Hope beyond Boundaries

Do you ever feel that your child's choices have placed them beyond hope? Let's unpack the message in Revelation 20:2–3.

> He seized the dragon…who is the devil and Satan…and threw him into the pit, and shut it and sealed it over him, so that he might not deceive the nations any longer, until the thousand years were ended. After that he must be released for a little while. (ESV)

This Scripture passage reminds us of God's supreme authority over all, even over the bottomless abyss. It's a comforting thought for us parents of prodigals, reassuring us that no distance or depth is beyond God's reach and control.

No matter how wayward, our children's paths are never out of God's sight. His ability to intervene, redirect, and protect is unmatched. In times when our children seem lost in their abysses of poor choices and bad influences, this truth brings solace. In this challenging journey, we must steadfastly trust in God's sovereignty. His power to guide and reshape lives surpasses all obstacles. Our prayers for our children should be filled with faith in God's ability to bring them back, no matter how far they have strayed. Let this be our comfort: God is actively working in their lives, and his plans are always for redemption and restoration.

Dear Father, thank you for being there no matter how dark life seems. In Jesus' name. Amen.

Wonders without Number

Today we find a hefty dose of hope in Job 5:8–9: "As for me, I would seek God…who does great and unsearchable things, wonders without number" (NASB). Whenever you feel like you're running out of answers as a parent, remember this comforting truth: God is in the business of doing things beyond your wildest dreams, wonders you can't start to count.

In the thick of parenting, especially when the going gets tough, it's easy to forget the vastness of God's capabilities. We try to fix everything on our own, but here's the thing: God is working behind the scenes, crafting solutions we couldn't imagine.

The truth in these verses isn't just a reminder; it's an invitation to lean into faith. Trust that for every challenge with your child, God has an endless supply of wonders up his sleeve. So when you're feeling overwhelmed, remember that you're partnered with the creator of "wonders without number." With him, every moment of struggle is a chance for miracles. Keep looking for those wonders. He's already at work.

Dear Father, thank you for working on solutions that provide wonders I can't imagine on behalf of my prodigal. In Jesus' name. Amen.

Generational Blessings

You're not just a parent, but you're also part of a faith lineage that goes back to Abraham. This reality is evident in Acts 3:24–25.

> All the prophets who have spoken from Samuel and his successors onward, have also announced these days. It is you who are the sons of the prophets and of the covenant which God ordained with your fathers, saying to Abraham, "And in your seed all the families of the earth shall be blessed." (NASB)

The daily struggles can blind us to this larger narrative. But God's covenant still stands even when you're fighting for your child's future. You are a steward of God's promise. So what's your role? Keep the faith, keep praying, and hold on to God's unchanging promises. The prophets spoke of "these days," and you're squarely in them, battling for your child's God-given destiny.

Embrace this: God's covenant isn't just history; it's also your family's future. Your prayers aren't futile. They're fueled by divine promise. Of course, doubt and fatigue will come, but don't let go of this covenant thread. You're part of an eternal promise that sets up your family for miraculous blessings.

Dear Father, thank you for making my family part of your lineage and legacy, which positions us for a miracle. In Jesus' name. Amen.

The Ultimate Sacrifice

You and I know the struggle is real. Our children, caught in the snares of this world, seem further away than ever. The heartache is palpable. But take heart! Let's anchor ourselves in Galatians 1:3–4, where Paul wrote,

> Grace to you and peace from God our Father and the Lord Jesus Christ, who gave himself for our sins to deliver us from the present evil age, according to the will of our God and Father. (ESV)

Jesus gave himself to free us from this evil age. He didn't just talk about it; he did it. He made the ultimate sacrifice to provide a way to deliver us—and yes, our prodigals—out of the mess we're in. This age is where all kinds of darkness entice our children. But his will is stronger than any snare the Enemy sets for our kids.

This promise is a powerful reminder that no matter how grim the situation looks, Jesus has already made the way out for your child. You might feel like you're losing your child to this "present evil age," but let's not forget who's in charge. Jesus already paid the price for their deliverance and yours.

Dear Father, thank you for delivering me from all the dark evil of the world. In Jesus' name. Amen.

From the Depths to Heights

Are you feeling low because your child's choices are breaking your heart today? Here's a lifeline from Psalm 116:6: "The LORD watches over the simple; I was brought low, and He saved me" (NASB). This verse isn't sugarcoating life. It's not saying you won't have low moments. Oh, you will. You'll feel helpless, clueless, and maybe even worthless as a parent. But God is all about the rescue. When you're at your lowest, God shines the brightest. Remember, God's in the business of saving. He's in the trenches with you and sees your broken heart and the path your prodigal has strayed from.

The word *simple* here isn't a slight. It means those of us who are helpless by ourselves. And isn't that all of us at some point? So when you're brought low, worn out from all the worrying and the sleepless nights, know that God is your coparent. He's your partner, right there, ready to save and preserve. Trust that God is with you. The Lord's preservation is not a one-time act; it's a lifetime guarantee. Your prodigal isn't beyond God's reach.

Dear Father, thank you for your rescue plan for my wayward child. I love you. In Jesus' name. Amen.

Fueling Your Prayers

You're not just any parent but a parent on a mission to win your prodigal back. The journey is rough, full of sleepless nights and relentless worry. You may wonder, *Is my prayer making any difference?* Well, let's lean into 2 Thessalonians 1:11.

> To this end we always pray for you, that our God may make you worthy of his calling and may fulfill every resolve for good and every work of faith by his power. (ESV)

This is a tailor-made prayer guide. First, it says, "We always pray for you." Continuous prayer is vital. Even when you don't see immediate results, your persistent prayers shape circumstances you can't see.

The verse then says, "God may make you worthy of his calling." This isn't about earning God's love; rather, it's about aligning your life with God's purpose. You're called to be a beacon of faith and hope for your family and others in the same boat. Lastly, the verse discusses fulfilling "every resolve for good and every work of faith by his power." This isn't your battle to win alone. God's power is at work, fulfilling your good intentions and turning them into actions that make a difference.

Dear Father, thank you for making a way for my prodigal to turn their actions around. In Jesus' name. Amen.

Keep the Faith

Isn't it amazing how a simple act can have such profound meaning? Let's dig into 1 Corinthians 11:26: "As often as you eat this bread and drink the cup, you proclaim the Lord's death until He comes" (NASB). Communion is not merely a religious routine. It's a declaration, a faith-filled proclamation that Jesus conquered death for us and our prodigals. As you take that bread and sip that wine or juice, remember that you're not just recalling history. You're also proclaiming Christ's victory over sin! When we claim the blood of Christ over our lives, the Enemy has to flee.

Why not consider communion a part of your spiritual arsenal when battling for your wayward child? Each time you partake, you are declaring the ultimate defeat of every dark force trying to claim them. It's a beautiful and powerful way to keep the faith alive and remind yourself that the Lord is not done yet, not with you or your child. In the tug-of-war for your child's soul, let communion be your tactile reminder of the Lord's eternal power to save and set you free. Let's keep proclaiming his victory until he comes. Keep pressing on, warfare parent!

Dear Father, thank you for communion, when your followers remember the blood of Christ giving us victory over evil. In Jesus' name. Amen.

Generations of Love

Do you feel like your attempts to reach your wayward child are in vain? Let's draw strength from Exodus 20:5–6: "I, the LORD your God, am a jealous God…but showing favor to thousands, to those who love Me and keep My commandments" (NASB). The struggle with your child isn't just about the here and now. It's also about planting seeds for generations to come. God promises to extend his loving-kindness far beyond your immediate circumstances, spreading it like wildfire to thousands. Imagine the impact of that love reaching your child and generations after them.

When you pour love and godly principles into a wayward child, you invest in a legacy that can transcend time. Even if you don't see immediate change, don't underestimate the ripple effect of your steadfast love and faithfulness. In your moments of doubt, cling to this promise. You are sowing seeds of faith and love that may sprout in ways you can't yet see. Stay the course. Keep loving, keep praying, and keep obeying God's commands. Your love today can echo through generations tomorrow. Believe that time and circumstance do not limit God's promise of loving-kindness.

Dear Father, thank you for your love for generations and favor over my life, my child's life, and my family. In Jesus' name. Amen.

God Goes before You

Today let's soak in Deuteronomy 20:4: "The LORD your God is the One who is going with you, to fight for you against your enemies, to save you" (NASB). This verse isn't just an Old Testament favorite; it's also your current reality. God is fighting for you and your child even when you seem to be losing ground. The battle for your child's soul might be fierce, but remember who's leading the charge.

Have you ever felt like you're fighting this alone? The good news is that you don't have to. God is not simply cheering you on from the sidelines. He's actively fighting for you and your child. Knowing that the creator of the universe is in your corner can sometimes give you that second wind you desperately need. When you're up late worried, on your knees praying, or in the counselor's office seeking guidance, God is there, fighting for you. So dig your heels in, not because you're strong but because God is beside you. You have this, valiant parent. With God leading the way, how can you not be victorious? Keep pushing. You're closer to a win than you think.

Dear Father, thank you for your fight for my child against their enemies. Thank you for being the God who saves. In Jesus' name. Amen.

God Has Equipped You

Are you feeling ill-equipped for the challenges you are facing today with your child? Today's great news is found in Psalm 18:39: "You equipped me with strength for the battle; you made those who rise against me sink under me" (ESV). This verse proves that God has already equipped you with strength and victory in your struggles. David faced many enemies throughout his life but knew God would protect and provide for him in the fight. As parents, we often face our own battles, especially as we try to guide our lost children.

This verse reminds us that God will equip us, and he will give us wisdom, strength, and patience as we navigate through the painful journey. It's an assurance that we are not alone in our struggles. God is actively arming us with the tools to face each challenge. Our enemies—whether doubts, fears, or external influences on our children—are not insurmountable with God's strength. This verse invites us to lean into God's power. Remember that God is our strength when we feel overwhelmed or underprepared. He prepares us for every battle and stands with us in every difficulty.

Dear Father, thank you for equipping me and giving me strength. In Jesus' name. Amen.

Embracing Change with Faith

It's easy to feel lost or disheartened in the wilderness of parenting challenges. Find hope and a sense of renewal in Isaiah 43:19: "Behold, I am doing a new thing; now it springs forth, do you not perceive it? I will make a way in the wilderness and rivers in the desert" (ESV). Here we see God actively working in our lives, creating new beginnings in the most unlikely places.

Watching your child struggle or stray can feel like you are wandering in a desolate wilderness. But God's promise is clear. He is bringing forth something new, something full of life and hope. Embracing this change requires faith. It means trusting in God's vision when the path isn't clear, believing that he is leading you and your child to a place of growth and restoration. Even in the driest wasteland, God promises to provide refreshing, life-giving streams of water.

This new thing might be difficult to perceive in the middle of your current struggles, but it's there. God is at work in your child's life and yours, transforming challenges into opportunities for growth and faith. As you navigate this journey, hold on to this promise.

Dear Father, thank you for being in the wilderness with my family and actively creating a way through it. In Jesus' name. Amen.

God Is with You

Facing another day of feeling defeated and desperate? Find strength in 2 Chronicles 20:17: "Do not be afraid and do not be dismayed. Tomorrow go out against them, and the LORD will be with you" (ESV). This verse was spoken to Jehoshaphat and the people of Judah, who were facing a great battle. It's a powerful reminder for us as parents that sometimes our role is not to fight but to stand firm in faith, trusting in God's deliverance.

Our instinct is to jump into action in our journey and try to rescue our children and fix their issues. However, this verse teaches us the power of standing firm, holding our ground in faith, and trusting in God's intervention. It's a call to be courageous not in battle but in belief. We're encouraged to face our challenges with the assurance that God is with us. Our steadfastness becomes a testimony of faith in God's love for us and our children.

Let this message inspire you to stand firm. In the face of difficulties, remember that the battle is the Lord's. Our faith and trust in him can bring peace and deliverance in the most challenging circumstances.

Dear Father, thank you for helping me overcome my fear and have more confidence that you are with me. In Jesus' name. Amen.

Unlocking Faith's Rewards

Do you feel like you're in a losing battle for your wayward child? Let's park here a moment and consider Hebrews 11:6: "Without faith it is impossible to please him, for whoever would draw near to God must believe that he exists and that he rewards those who seek him" (ESV). This is like a map to God's heart. Without faith, we can't please God. It sounds simple, yet it's profound, especially when your heart is breaking for your child.

Faith is that deep-rooted belief that God exists and rewards those who earnestly seek him. Let's talk about rewards. The world offers short-term fixes and momentary pleasures that can entrap a young soul. But God's rewards? They're eternal, and they begin now.

Seeking God, especially in the middle of chaos, is like a magnet for his blessings. Your faith is like a beacon, guiding your child back home even when they're far off course. Cling to your faith not just for you but for them. And trust me, God can reach your child in places you can't. Even when you can't see it, faith works behind the scenes, activating the power of God, who can do what's impossible for us.

Dear Father, thank you that as I draw close to you, my belief in you deepens, and you will reward me. In Jesus' name. Amen.

God Knows the Heart

Here is a hefty dose of comfort today. Acts 15:8 says, "God, who knows the heart, testified to them giving them the Holy Spirit, just as He also did to us" (NASB). This verse reveals a truth that's so comforting: God knows the heart. Right now, you might be seeing a version of your child far from who you raised them to be. But hang on because God's not done yet.

We often judge by what we see—actions, choices, and mistakes. God, however, looks at the heart. And that's where transformation starts. You've prayed, fought, and cried over your child's path. Maybe it feels like those prayers are hitting a brick wall. But remember, God granted the Holy Spirit to folks whom others doubted. God knows the inner transformation happening even when we can't see it.

God is working in your child's life even if the effects are not visible. The Holy Spirit can spark a change in the most unexpected ways and in the most unexpected people. You've planted seeds of faith and love, and God is nurturing those seeds in your child's heart. Your child's heart can turn toward him with one touch from God.

Dear Father, thank you for seeing into my heart and giving me the Holy Spirit. In Jesus' name. Amen.

God Has Your Prodigal Covered

Today's spiritual bread comes from Psalm 37:40: "The LORD helps them and rescues them; He rescues them from the wicked and saves them, because they take refuge in Him" (NASB). You've seen wicked influences sway your child, and it's soul crushing. But the good news is that the God we serve specializes in deliverance. When you're up at night, when your knees are sore from prayer, remember that your prodigal is not too far gone for God to reach. God can swoop in like the superhero he is and yank them out from the Enemy's clutches. Why? Because God's love is a refuge, a fortress where your child can find safety.

As you wait and pray for your child to take refuge in God, trust that God will deliver according to his promises. God has already mapped out the rescue plan and doesn't need a GPS. He knows exactly where your prodigal is and how to bring them home. So wipe those tears and lift that chin. You're not in this alone. God can deliver your prodigal. The Almighty has your back and your child's too.

Dear Father, thank you for being faithful to save and deliver my child from the wicked when they take refuge in you. In Jesus' name. Amen.

God's Perfect Timing

Are you asking, *When, God, when will you move for my child?* You can find encouragement in Genesis 21:2: "Sarah conceived and bore a son to Abraham in his old age, at the appointed time of which God had spoken to him" (NASB). Sarah and Abraham waited years for God to give them the child he'd promised them. At this time, they were old, "past childbearing" (18:11), yet God fulfilled his promise "at the appointed time."

Friends, this is a story that every parent of a wayward child should remember. I get it; you're tired. You've been praying, and maybe it feels like you've received nothing but radio silence from heaven. You're wrestling with doubt, fear, and many sleepless nights. You're wondering, *When, God, when?*

God's actions may not align with our timing, but he is never late in accomplishing his will. Let this be a divine nudge to keep praying, hoping, and crying out to him. Your child may be wayward but is never beyond God's reach. I wish I could promise you your child will return to God this year or in fifty years, but only God's promises are guaranteed. Stay the course and remember that God's delay is not his denial.

Dear Father, thank you for your perfect timing.
In Jesus' name. Amen.

Strength and Peace in the Struggle

Do you feel weak and filled with worry today? Find help in Psalm 29:11: "The LORD will give strength to His people; the LORD will bless His people with peace" (NASB). Parenting is no small feat. It stretches us, tests our limits, and sometimes leaves us weak and gasping for air. But here's a promise straight from the heart of God: he not only gives us strength but tops it off with peace.

Imagine that for a moment. Amid the chaos, the late-night worries, and the what-ifs about our kids' futures, there's a source of strength that never runs dry. And peace? It's not just any peace but the kind that settles deep in your soul, whispering, "You're not in this alone."

This verse is your reminder that, as a parent, you have backup. When you're running on empty, God steps in, filling you up with his strength and his peace.

Dear Father, thank you for understanding my struggles and providing me with strength and peace. In Jesus' name. Amen.

The Battle for Heart Change

The fight for your child feels like an ongoing war, doesn't it? Luke 11:24–26 contains a warning.

> When the unclean spirit comes out of a person, it passes through waterless places seeking rest, and not finding any, it then says, "I will return to my house from which I came." And when it comes, it finds it swept and put in order. Then it goes and brings along seven other spirits more evil than itself, and they come in and live there; and the last condition of that person becomes worse than the first. (NASB)

This is a cautionary tale not just for the individual but also for us parents. It's not enough for our children to be "cleaned up." That's an empty house waiting for more trouble. We want our children to be filled with the Holy Spirit, grounded in a life-transforming relationship with God.

Removing bad influences is a start, but what truly transforms is a heart change—a divine renewal that only God can orchestrate. God is still in the business of filling empty houses, transforming them into homes filled with his love and grace. Let's keep our house filled with God.

Dear Father, thank you for helping me keep a clean house full of love so that my child has a safe place to return to. In Jesus' name. Amen.

Turning the Tables

Our struggle with wayward kids often feels like a battle zone. The back talk, the rebellious acts, and the scorn—they can cut deep. Sometimes we might feel justified in repaying that scorn with anger or frustration. But let's turn this around. Lean into 1 Peter 3:9: "Do not repay evil for evil or reviling for reviling, but on the contrary, bless, for to this you were called, that you may obtain a blessing" (ESV).

Peter told us to bless instead of curse. Picture this: your child storms off, slamming the door. It's easy to shout back or give them the silent treatment. But what if you take a deep breath, pray, and respond in love and understanding at the right moment instead? Remember, you are at war with the devil, not with your child. It won't be easy, but remember that this is a spiritual battle.

By choosing to bless, we open the door to God's transformative power. We disarm the Enemy and set the stage for God to work miracles in our children's lives. It's not about letting them off the hook; it's about inviting God's blessing into a place where cursing used to be.

Dear Father, thank you for helping me react more calmly in the battle zone so I can give you room to transform my prodigal. In Jesus' name. Amen.

God's Rescue Mission

Jesus said, "The Son of Man has come to seek and to save that which was lost" (Luke 19:10 NASB). If you're feeling defeated, like your child is too far gone, I have a word for you: they're not too far gone. If you're losing sleep or feel anxious about what your child might be doing or where they are, shift that focus from worry to God's promise. Jesus came for this exact reason—to seek and save the lost.

Many parents know the sinking dread and the hopelessness that come when a child doesn't return home. But guess what? Your child is never out of God's reach. Like a relentless rescue team, God is tirelessly working to bring your lost one home. Your child is his creation first, and he wants them back even more than you do. Hold on to this verse when the battle gets rough. Even when your child is wandering, God is with them and longs for them to come back to his loving arms. So stay strong and keep the faith, my friend. God is in the rescue business, and he is really good at it.

Dear Father, thank you for seeking the lost, and please bring my lost child back to you. In Jesus' name. Amen.

God's Sovereignty in Chaos

Do you feel like you have lost control over your child's life? Let's breathe in some comfort from Psalm 47:3: "He subdues peoples under us and nations under our feet" (NASB). Listen up; God's in control, not just of us but also of entire nations. Are you feeling small? Remember, the same God who holds the universe also has your family in his hands. Here's the most critical point: if God can subdue nations, imagine what he can do for your child. God controls the battle and can bring your child back under his guidance. Maintain that faith, for God can bring any chaos under his divine control.

You're wrestling not just against your child's will but also against powers and principalities. The dark temptations of the world are constantly luring your child into evil. Of course, this brings chaos to your home. Thankfully, you serve a God who subdues, conquers, and reigns. Ready to relinquish control? Trust him to stop what you can't. In your most challenging moments, when it feels like every effort is slipping through your fingers, take a step back and lift it all to the one who commands the winds and waves.

Dear Father, thank you for this reminder that everything is under your control and your feet. In Jesus' name. Amen.

Taking Authority

If you're wrestling with the dark influences circling your wayward child, let's talk about the authority you have. Look at the power found in Acts 16:18.

> She continued doing this for many days. But Paul was greatly annoyed, and he turned and said to the spirit, "I command you in the name of Jesus Christ to come out of her!" And it came out at that very moment. (NASB)

Paul, annoyed by a spirit tormenting a young woman, took authority in the name of Jesus—and boom! The spirit left her.

What's bothering you today? Your child's drug habits? Their bad friends? Their apathy? The depression hovering over your child? It is time to get annoyed enough to take action, just like Paul did. You have authority, and it's time to use it.

In the name of Jesus, you can command these influences to leave your child's life. Not tomorrow, not next week, but now. This is faith in action. The same Spirit who empowered Paul is available to you. You might not see the change immediately, but don't let that discourage you. Keep commanding, believing, and, most importantly, standing in your God-given authority. God honors bold faith.

Dear Father, thank you for giving me divine authority to do miracles in your name. In Jesus' name. Amen.

When Shadows Heal

I know you're waging a war against the shadows—those unseen forces that try to pull your child away. But can we talk about a different kind of shadow today? A healing one can be found in Acts 5:15–16.

> They even carried the sick out into the streets and laid them on cots and pallets, so that when Peter came by at least his shadow might fall on any of them. The people from the cities in the vicinity of Jerusalem were coming together as well, bringing people who were sick or tormented with unclean spirits, and they were all being healed. (NASB)

Imagine being so filled with God's power that your shadow could mend a broken life. That was Peter's level of faith and divine intervention. The miracles didn't stop at Peter. They also reached the crowds and healed them, every single one.

Don't lose sight of this incredible hope. The same God who operated through Peter's shadow wants to cast his healing shadow over your family. Yes, even your wayward child is not beyond the reach of this loving, healing shadow. You're fighting with divine assistance under God's protective and powerful shadow.

Dear Father, thank you for the healing power available for my child. In Jesus' name. Amen.

God's Unfinished Business

Today we get another great dose of hope. It's found in Philippians 1:6: "I am sure of this, that he who began a good work in you will bring it to completion at the day of Jesus Christ" (ESV). If your prodigal has ever accepted Jesus, this is a megadose of hope when it seems like there's no end to the struggle with your wayward child. But let this verse sink in. On the day your child first believed, God started a "good work" in them. And God is not a quitter. That good work is not finished yet!

Now I get it; the waiting is brutal. But this isn't passive waiting. It's active trusting. And don't you dare think he's stopped working just because you can't see it. Keep praying and loving and hoping for heaven's sake. Your child might be a work in progress, but God's specialty is turning messes into messages. Warfare parents, let this promise fuel your hope today. For in his time, you'll witness the beautiful unfolding of God's perfect plan. And if your child isn't yet a follower of Jesus, keep praying for that day and the continued work of Christ in you.

Dear Father, thank you for continuing your work with those who have turned to you. In Jesus' name. Amen.

may

The Surrender Strategy

Do you feel like you have lost control of your child? Let's chat about Luke 9:23–24, where Jesus said to his disciples,

> If anyone wants to come after Me, he must deny himself, take up his cross daily, and follow Me. For whoever wants to save his life will lose it, but whoever loses his life for My sake, this is the one who will save it. (NASB)

Battles for control can consume us, especially when we are trying to guide our wayward children back home. It's natural to want to grip the steering wheel tightly, but what if the key is actually to let go?

Jesus told us that the path to real life—abundant life—is through surrender. Your battle for your child isn't lost by giving it to God; it's actually gained. When you loosen your grip and give God control, you open up a way for miracles to happen.

I know it's hard, but trust him with your child's life. Your "cross" might be your fears, sleepless nights, or ceaseless worries. Lay them down daily. Surrender, follow him, and find life in letting go. You're on the road to victory when you surrender the battle to God.

Dear Father, thank you for saving me and always being in control. In Jesus' name. Amen.

God's Wonders in the Wilderness

Do you believe in the wonders of God? Let's look at Luke's description of Moses in Acts 7:36: "This man led them out, performing wonders and signs in the land of Egypt and in the Red Sea, and in the wilderness for forty years" (NASB). Moses led the Israelites through forty years of wilderness wandering, full of uncertainty, rebellions, and setbacks. It sounds a bit like parenting a prodigal child. God used Moses to perform "wonders and signs" throughout those long years. Yes, even in the darkest times, God's power shone through. Today's verse isn't just ancient history; it's also a present promise for parents like you and me.

You might feel like you're wandering in the wilderness with your wayward child, facing endless struggles. But God's not finished. He's still in the business of performing wonders and signs. And he still has the power to pull your child out of the pit they're in right now.

Don't underestimate what God can do in wilderness seasons. Just as God led the Israelites to the promised land, he can also lead you and your child to a promised land of restored relationships and renewed faith.

Dear Father, thank you for being a God of wonders, and I believe you will perform a miracle soon. In Jesus' name. Amen.

Grace in the Chaos

Isn't it amazing how God works in mysterious ways? Second Chronicles 30:20 says, "The LORD heard Hezekiah and healed the people" (NASB). God hears and heals when we humble ourselves and pray. Many parents have been where you are, wrestling with the heartache and chaos of having a wayward child. Sometimes it feels like no matter what you do, the healing isn't happening. It's easy to blame ourselves or even feel God abandoned us.

But take heart! Just like how Hezekiah prayed for his people and God showed up in a big way, you can do the same for your child. And trust me that when God decides to move, it's life-changing. Restoration might not happen overnight or in the way we expect, but God's timing is perfect, and his healing is complete, not half-baked.

So go ahead and lay your worries at the throne of the Almighty. God is in the business of healing even when the wounds are deep and the future looks grim. God's power to heal goes beyond our understanding. Your steadfast prayers are not in vain. They're a vital connection to the God who mends broken hearts and restores lost paths. Keep your eyes on him and stay anchored in faith.

Dear Father, thank you for being a God who heals. In Jesus' name. Amen.

Great Faith, Great Results

Do you ever feel like your prayers are a constant loop of begging God for a breakthrough? Let's see an example of how God will answer in Matthew 15:28: "Jesus said to her, 'O woman, your faith is great; it shall be done for you as you desire.' And her daughter was healed at once" (NASB). Here's the key: this woman wouldn't take no for an answer. She pushed through doubt, societal norms, and even initial silence from Jesus. And because of her great faith, her child was healed on the spot. Can you imagine? Immediate transformation!

Let her tenacity light a fire under you. God sees and hears your all-persistent prayers and your unwavering faith. You're not just any parent but a parent armed with great faith. Sometimes it feels like you're shouting into a void, but let me tell you, you're not. God hears, God sees, and, most importantly, God acts. Keep pressing and keep believing. Your faith is making an eternal impact. What's stopping you? Turn up the volume on your faith and expect great things. Our God is a God of miracles. Your "as you desire" moment is coming.

Dear Father, thank you for answering my prayers that beg for my child. In Jesus' name. Amen.

Guard Your Heart

It's easy to get sidetracked when we're in the trenches, battling for our wayward kids. Don't fall into the trap Psalm 141:4 warns us about. "Do not incline my heart to any evil thing, to practice deeds of wickedness with people who do wrong; and may I not taste their delicacies" (NASB). The world offers all kinds of quick fixes and "delicacies" that promise to ease our pain or expedite a resolution. Its solutions could include the temptation to manipulate circumstances, compromise our values, or join in our children's waywardness to maintain a connection. Scripture gives us a stark reminder to guard our hearts against any evil.

Sure, the delicacies of quick-fix solutions might look appetizing, but they leave a terrible aftertaste and bring no genuine resolution. We stand on solid ground when we guard our hearts and cling to the principles of God's Word. We must align ourselves with God's will and allow the Holy Spirit to lead us. These steps are crucial because our battles require divine strategies, not human schemes. So hold tight to your integrity. Let God's wisdom guide your decisions and steps. A guarded heart is a fortress that evil cannot easily breach.

Dear Father, thank you for helping me to hear only you and to be deaf to the world's words. In Jesus' name. Amen.

Guardian Duty

Do you ever feel like you're on a solo mission, battling for your child's soul in a seemingly silent universe? Let's lean into Matthew 18:10.

> See that you do not look down on one of these little ones; for I say to you that their angels in heaven continually see the face of My Father who is in heaven. (NASB)

Talk about a revelation, right? Here's the deal: your child is never flying solo, and neither are you. God's not sitting on the sidelines. He has this whole squad of angels assigned, and guess what? They have unlimited access to the throne of Almighty God. Now, that's some heavy-hitting reinforcement!

So next time you feel isolated, remember that you're teaming up with heaven's finest. The battle for your child's heart is not yours alone. You have heavenly collaboration. Stay the course and know that with each prayer, each tear, and each hopeful step forward, a heavenly chorus echoes your love and determination. We're in this together, and with heaven on our side, the possibilities are boundless. Never forget you have the ultimate backup.

Dear Father, thank you for the heavenly collaboration so I don't feel alone in the battle. In Jesus' name. Amen.

Guidance Guaranteed

Are you overwhelmed by the twists and turns on the road to reclaiming your wayward child? Hold on to Psalm 25:8, which says, "The LORD is good and upright; therefore He instructs sinners in the way" (NASB). Who better to navigate this complex journey than the one who is both good and upright? The God who can guide sinners surely can guide us parents who are just trying to do our best.

This isn't just about getting your child back on track. It's also about your walk with God. There's comfort in knowing that he's not just the destination but also the guide. His instruction isn't reserved for the "holier-than-thou." It's also available to you and your child, sinners and seekers alike. Let God lead. He's not scratching his head, wondering what to do next in your situation. Keep the faith, for he knows the way even when you're totally lost. Lean in and remember that you will find your way with God as your compass. And you know what? That journey is a shared one, with God leading the way every step you take.

Dear Father, thank you for guiding me every step of the way.
In Jesus' name. Amen.

Your Divine Calling

Being a parent to a wayward child can sometimes make you feel like you're losing yourself. But take a moment to absorb the truth in 2 Thessalonians 2:14: "To this he called you through our gospel, so that you may obtain the glory of our Lord Jesus Christ" (ESV).

This verse reminds you that God's calling came "through our gospel." The gospel isn't just good news about salvation; it's also the life-transforming power that changes your child and you. Your struggles, dear friend, are part of a divine script, teaching you, preparing you, and, yes, also setting the stage for the glory of the Lord Jesus Christ to be revealed in you. This battle is not just about bringing your child back. It's also about obtaining "the glory of our Lord Jesus Christ." This is the ultimate endgame. The battles you're fighting, the tears you're shedding—they're shaping you for glory, both yours and Christ's.

You're not just surviving. God is shaping you for something spectacular. Lean into your divine calling because in this rough-and-tumble journey, glory is the end point. And what an end point it is! Your calling is more extraordinary than you can imagine.

Dear Father, thank you for the power of the gospel and for using my circumstances to bring you glory. In Jesus' name. Amen.

Guided Home

Is your soul tired today? You know firsthand that parenting is hard, especially when it feels like both you and your child are navigating a maze blindfolded. Does it seem like you're stumbling in the dark, desperately trying to find the way out? Here is a life-giving truth from Luke 1:78–79: "The Sunrise from on high will visit us, to shine on those who sit in darkness and the shadow of death, to guide our feet into the way of peace" (NASB).

Now let's get real for a second. As you try to navigate the unknowns, unsure of even the next step, God's not watching from the sidelines. He's actively promising to guide your steps right into the embrace of peace. And he can do the same for your prodigal.

So be intentional. Hold on to this promise with both hands. Envision God redirecting your steps, steering you away from the chaos and into a serene haven of peace that truly goes beyond your understanding. As you lean on him, watch the morning light cast away the shadows because with God, peace isn't just a distant dream. It's a divine guarantee.

Dear Father, thank you for guiding me toward your unshakable peace as my beacon in the night. In Jesus' name. Amen.

Steadfast to the End

The journey is long, but the goal is worth it all. I know how easy it is to lose confidence when we're battling for our prodigal children. But remember Hebrews 3:14, which tells us, "We have come to share in Christ, if indeed we hold our original confidence firm to the end" (ESV). The key is to hold our confidence firm to the end.

Confidence here doesn't mean arrogance or blind optimism. It means trusting that God's promises will come to pass even when we can't see any signs of it. This unwavering trust allows us to share in Christ and the victory he has won for us. When you're worried about the choices your child is making, let your confidence in Christ remind you that God is still in control.

So hold on to your confidence and don't let go no matter the situation. Even when your faith is the size of a mustard seed, it's enough for God to work miracles. You're not just fighting for today; you're also investing in eternity. Your unwavering confidence sends a powerful message to the Enemy: "My God is greater, and I will stand firm to the end."

Dear Father, thank you for the confidence you give me in the middle of the fight for my prodigal. In Jesus' name. Amen.

Embracing Imperfection

Do you sometimes wish your child could be perfect? Ecclesiastes 7:20 says, "Indeed, there is not a righteous person on earth who always does good and does not ever sin" (NASB). No one is perfect, not even the most righteous among us. If King Solomon, the wisest man, recognized human shortcomings, why do we often forget them when dealing with our prodigal kids?

Listen, it's easy to see the speck in your child's eye and ignore the log in your own. I get it! The heartache, fear, and disappointment we feel cloud our judgment. But remember, God is working in their lives just like he is in ours. We open the door to God's grace when we embrace our imperfections. We allow room for God to work miracles, and let's be real: winning back our prodigals requires nothing short of a divine intervention.

Take a moment today to be honest with yourself and with God. Confess your shortcomings but also rejoice in his grace. No prodigal is too far gone for the reach of God's arm or the touch of his grace.

Dear Father, thank you that there is no perfect person and that you don't require perfection. I am grateful that my child is never too far gone from you. In Jesus' name. Amen.

The Power of Mercy

Did your child cuss you out recently? King David had a similar experience in 1 Kings 2:8.

> Behold, you have with you Shimei the son of Gera the Benjaminite, of Bahurim; now it was he who cursed me with a painful curse on the day I went to Mahanaim. But when he came down to meet me at the Jordan, I swore to him by the LORD, saying, "I will not put you to death with the sword." (NASB)

David had every right to retaliate, but he chose mercy. Mercy isn't just overlooking an offense; it's an active, powerful choice to extend grace when it's least deserved. Mercy has transformative power.

You might be in a place where your child curses you, whether with their words, actions, or choices. Your heart aches, and you may think that the "sword"—whether that's showing tough love, severing ties, or emotionally withdrawing—is the way to go.

But what if mercy, your steadfast love, and your refusal to give up on them are the things that turn their heart back toward home? Mercy can be a heavenly strategy to win your prodigal back. Extend mercy even when it's hard. And watch how God uses it to bring your child from a place of rebellion to a place of restoration.

Dear Father, thank you for your mercy. In Jesus' name. Amen.

Healing Touch

You're in the thick of it, aren't you? You are battling for your child while clutching a shred of hope. Well, let's get some encouragement from Matthew 4:24.

> The news about Him spread throughout Syria; and they brought to Him all who were ill, those suffering with various diseases and severe pain, demon-possessed, people with epilepsy, and people who were paralyzed; and He healed them. (NASB)

This is so inspiring. Just visualize it—people from all over coming to Jesus, carrying their afflicted loved ones. They heard the buzz and then saw the evidence.

Jesus heals. He transforms. Here's your takeaway: bring your child to Jesus in prayer, just like those desperate folks did. Jesus is still moving and healing today. The world's dark lures may ensnare your child, but Jesus isn't new to this game. He's been dealing with all sorts of afflictions and chains. And guess what? He still delivers and sets people free. So go ahead and lay your child at Jesus' feet. Pray as you've never prayed before. Your faith mingled with his limitless power is an unbeatable combination. Remember, there's no affliction beyond his reach in these trying times.

Dear Father, thank you for being alive today, moving in miraculous signs and wonders. In Jesus' name. Amen.

Heard in Distress

Do you feel like your prayers bounce off the ceiling? Take heart from Psalm 18:6.

> In my distress I called upon the LORD,
> and cried to my God for help;
> He heard my voice from His temple,
> and my cry for help before Him came into His ears.
> (NASB)

Let's get this straight: when you're in distress—really in the thick of it—God is all ears. Your cries don't echo in empty spaces; they reach God's very temple. That's holy ground, my friend, and it means divine intervention is on deck.

Think about your child. They may be far from a physical temple or church, but your prayers bridge that gap. You're setting heavenly gears in motion when you cry out to God. And trust me, heaven's gears grind much mightier than earth's problems. So don't hold back. Cry out, shout, whisper, or groan. Just make sure you're directing it God's way. Your voice matters, your prayers are powerful, and God is absolutely tuned in. You're not tossing prayers into the wind but initiating a heavenly rescue mission. Your relentless spirit in prayer is a testament to your unwavering trust in God's ability to reach, restore, and redeem.

Dear Father, thank you for hearing every prayer I pray for my child and family. In Jesus' name. Amen.

Heartfelt Reflections

In the twists and turns of parenting, it's easy to get caught up in the external—how our children act, what they achieve, and what paths they choose. We can find a new perspective in Proverbs 27:19: "As in water a face reflects the face, so the heart of a person reflects the person" (NASB). This verse invites us to look deeper, reminding us that we see the essence of a person in the heart. This verse isn't about measuring success by outward appearances but about finding true value and character within. It encourages us to guide our children in nurturing a heart that reflects kindness, integrity, and compassion.

During challenging times, rather than focusing solely on external outcomes, let's foster an environment where our children can develop a strong, wise, and loving heart. Through the quiet moments, the acts of love, and the lessons learned from mistakes, their hearts grow and reflect their true selves.

Remember, your role as a parent is invaluable in shaping your child's heart. Focus on what truly matters—their inner growth and character. With patience and faith, watch as their heart reflects the beauty and complexity of who they are meant to be.

Dear Father, thank you for helping me see that I can help guide and nurture my child's heart. In Jesus' name. Amen.

Led by the Shepherd

When your child has strayed far from home, you can also feel alone in life and faith. In these times, you can find confidence in Psalm 23:1: "The Lord is my shepherd, I will not be in need" (NASB). It's a short but oh-so-powerful verse. In your toughest moments, when it feels like you have lost your way, remember that the Shepherd guides you even when you can't feel him there.

I know how deeply you ache for your wayward child. You wish you could be their ever-present guide, protecting them from harm's way. But you can't be with them twenty-four seven. However, God can, just as he's with you.

Your child may be off track right now, but they're never out of reach of the Shepherd. You must hold on to this truth and let it invigorate your prayers. Your role is to keep praying while trusting in the Shepherd's perfect ability to guide you and your child through every valley and shadow. You may not be in control, but thankfully, we know the one who is.

Dear Father, thank you for being my Shepherd. Please guide my lost child back to you. In Jesus' name. Amen.

Heaven's Blueprint

Have you ever lain in bed at night, staring at the ceiling, worried sick about where your child might end up? Second Corinthians 5:1 brings a message of hope. "We know that if the tent that is our earthly home is destroyed, we have a building from God, a house not made with hands, eternal in the heavens" (ESV). When your child is lost, it often feels like your whole world is crumbling and like everything you have built is falling down. But remember, this earthly life is just a tent—a temporary dwelling place. God has something eternal and indestructible planned.

Our children may be knocking down the tent poles right now, but that doesn't change God's heavenly blueprint. God has prepared an eternal home for all who come to him with repentant hearts. Keep fighting the good fight through prayers for your child's salvation. It's not too late for your child to find a forever home in heaven. Next time you lie awake in the middle of the night, think about God's heavenly house waiting for those who trust in him.

Dear Father, thank you for building for your people an eternal home that cannot be destroyed. In Jesus' name. Amen.

Hold On to Faith

Do you feel like even those closest to you don't get the battle you are enduring? Maybe you even feel misunderstood? Let's read Acts 14:19: "Jews came from Antioch and Iconium, and having won over the crowds, they stoned Paul and dragged him out of the city, thinking that he was dead" (NASB).
The apostle Paul was doing God's work, but folks from Antioch and Iconium turned the crowd against him. They stoned Paul and left him for dead. This hits home, doesn't it? Sometimes it feels like society—perhaps even your friends or family—has "won over" your child, leading them down a path you never wanted for them.

Remember Paul when it feels like the world has turned your child against you. Remember that people and circumstances change, and God's miracles often come when things seem most desperate. God is fighting with you in this battle for your child's soul. It might also feel like your child is "stoning" you with their choices, words, and actions, leaving you emotionally and spiritually bruised. But don't lose hope. God is with you.

Dear Father, thank you for stretching my faith and reminding me that you are with me when it seems no one understands why I am so desperate for my child to return. In Jesus' name. Amen.

Holy Spirit's Power over Waywardness

Parenting a wayward child can feel like being in a boat without oars. We exhaust ourselves by trying to throw out the perfect lifesaver, but our efforts often feel as futile as pouring a cup of water into the sea and expecting the tide to rise. Does this resonate with you? If so, let's pause and consider a profound truth in Acts 1:5: "John baptized with water, but you will be baptized with the Holy Spirit not many days from now" (NASB). This verse isn't about ancient rituals. It's about today's struggles. While our human efforts are like John's water, transformative power lies with the Holy Spirit's fire.

Jesus wasn't just prepping his disciples for the days ahead. He was speaking directly to us, worn-out parents in the battle. Our strategies, as loving and strategic as they are, can only go so far. But the Holy Spirit? He begins the real change. He's the difference between temporary fixes and lasting transformation. So let's shift our focus. Let's anchor our hopes not on our maneuverability but on the Holy Spirit's power to move mountains. Believe that your "not many days from now" moment of victory is on the horizon.

Dear Father, thank you for the life-transforming power of the Holy Spirit that can save my child. In Jesus' name. Amen.

Hope in Our Struggles

Do you need a sign from God? Perhaps you will find it today in Judges 13:6, in which the angel of the Lord visited Manoah's wife.

> The woman came and told her husband, saying, "A man of God came to me, and his appearance was like the appearance of the angel of God, very awesome. So I did not ask him where he came from, nor did he tell me his name." (NASB)

Imagine that moment: this infertile woman is about to conceive Samson, a leader with immense purpose despite his future waywardness. Isn't that just like God? He brings a message of hope when we least expect it, often in remarkable ways, reminding us that he has a plan for our children, no matter how far they've strayed.

Manoah's wife does not use the word *awesome* here casually. She was filled with awe, felt a sense of reverence, and caught a glimpse of divine intention. This story prods us to keep our eyes open for those awe-inspiring moments, those God winks that confirm our faith and keep us pushing forward. Our children, like Samson, have incredible potential. They have a divine destiny waiting to be fulfilled.

Dear Father, thank you for giving me glimpses of my child's potential. In Jesus' name. Amen.

Freedom to Love

Today's fuel for your fight comes from Romans 7:6.

> We have been released from the Law, having died to that by which we were bound, so that we serve in newness of the Spirit and not in oldness of the letter. (NASB)

Are you trapped in an unending cycle of worry, frustration, and defeat? Listen, there's a new way to fight for your prodigal child—a way directed by the Spirit of God and not just by the dos and don'ts that lead us nowhere.

Release yourself from the chains of past failures, whether your perceived shortcomings as a parent or your child's poor choices. God is offering us a new way led by his Spirit, a way that brings life, hope, and ultimate victory over sin. Serve in this "newness of the Spirit." Let go of the guilt. Let go of the fear. Embrace this new way, where the Spirit leads you in wisdom, discernment, and love. What if we fought for our kids not from a place of law but from a place of grace? Warfare parent, your love restores, your prayers empower, your hope endures, and with God, nothing is impossible.

Dear Father, thank you for providing a way for my child to be set free and start new when they turn to you. In Jesus' name. Amen.

Humble Rise

Do you feel you're low in the pecking order of successful parents? Let's soak in Matthew 23:11–12: "The greatest of you shall be your servant. Whoever exalts himself shall be humbled, and whoever humbles himself shall be exalted" (NASB). Isn't it liberating? Your value doesn't come from having the perfect family or a successful child. Thank God our children's choices don't make us who we are as parents. In God's upside-down kingdom, greatness comes through serving, loving, and, yes, even suffering.

We can get so caught up in our struggles with our wayward kids that we forget to humble ourselves before God and acknowledge that we can't do this on our own. Sometimes we even try to manipulate our children's behavior to make us seem like the greatest parents. The good news? When we lower ourselves in humility, God raises us in honor. Keep serving, keep loving, and, most importantly, keep humbling yourself before God. It's not about how great you are but how great God can be through you. Trust him. He has a passion for making the last first and the humble high.

Dear Father, thank you that I can come to you broken and low and that even though my child lives in disobedience, you can still lift us. In Jesus' name. Amen.

Ignited by the Spirit

Are you yearning for a change in your wayward child? In Luke 3:16, John the Baptist told the crowds,

> As for me, I baptize you with water; but He is coming who is mightier than I, and I am not fit to untie the straps of His sandals; He will baptize you with the Holy Spirit and fire. (NASB)

The transformation we seek doesn't come just from human efforts. It needs a divine touch. The Holy Spirit and fire—the kind that refines, purifies, and changes lives—bring real transformation. You're not in this alone. You have the most potent ally you could ever hope for.

So are you weary from fighting this battle by yourself? The Holy Spirit is willing and able to step in with transformative fire that can turn your child's life around. Let's invite him in and trust that he can ignite a fire of transformation and purity not just in our children but also in us. Nothing can be more powerful in your prodigal's life than the move of the Holy Spirit in their hearts. Hold on to hope, for the Holy Spirit has the power to transform lives.

Dear Father, thank you for the gift of the Holy Spirit, who can transform hardened hearts. In Jesus' name. Amen.

Immediate Grace

Do you need some grace to get through today? Immerse in God's grace that we find in Luke 23:43, where Jesus said to the repentant thief on the cross, "Truly I say to you, today you will be with Me in Paradise" (NASB). What's amazing here is the immediacy of grace. At the end of his sinful life, this man acknowledged Jesus, and right away, Jesus assured him of eternal life. Talk about a prodigal moment!

Sometimes we fear it's too late for our wayward kids, right? But this verse proves that as long as there's breath in someone's lungs, it's not too late for their redemption. No matter how far gone you think your child is, God's grace is instant, and his redemption is eternal. Jesus says, *I see your heart, and that's all I need to welcome you into my kingdom.* This should give us a massive boost of hope. It tells us never to give up praying and fighting for our children's futures. In one moment, in one acknowledgment of Jesus, everything can change. God's grace is instantaneous. Keep believing. After all, if a lifetime of wrongs can be made right in a moment, imagine what's possible for your child.

Dear Father, thank you for the grace that can cover all sins. In Jesus' name. Amen.

Finding Unshakable Support

Are you feeling isolated, like you're in this battle solo? You have the ultimate support—God. Psalm 54:4 says, "Behold, God is my helper; the Lord is the upholder of my life" (ESV). Even when it seems like your prayers for your wayward child echo in emptiness, God is right there supporting you. He's your unseen but ever-present backbone. Fighting for a prodigal is draining—lost sleep, heartache, endless worry. You've had setbacks, and defeat looms large. But remember, you're not alone. God is your divine partner and the sustainer of your soul. He's not a passive spectator. He's actively in the game.

Take it in. God is your helper and upholder. He's present in each whispered prayer, every shed tear, and all the tough-love decisions you make. This is a divine fact. He holds us together as we wait for the victory over evil. Let this truth empower you. You have more than just a fighting chance. You have the creator of the universe in your corner. It is time to lean on him, consult him, and let him bolster you. You don't have to do this alone because, with God, you are never alone.

Dear Father, thank you for being my divine partner in the fight for my prodigal. I am grateful that I am never alone, nor is my child. In Jesus' name. Amen.

Inner Strength to Win Your Prodigal

How's your inner tank? Are you running on empty or fueled up? Today let's refuel with Ephesians 3:16–18, where Paul explained why he prayed.

> That according to the riches of his glory he may grant you to be strengthened with power through his Spirit in your inner being, so that Christ may dwell in your hearts through faith—that you, being rooted and grounded in love, may have strength. (ESV)

Who doesn't need a dose of inner strength, especially when facing the battle of a wayward child? And this isn't any strength; it's strength with power, fueled by God's Spirit. We're talking God-level resources.

It's easy to feel helpless and weak when you see your child walking a path you never wished for them. But don't forget that you're not facing this alone. Invite Christ to dwell richly in your heart, and let your faith be your foundation. This is the starting line for any real change—inside you and, eventually, God willing, inside your wayward child. Change the angle. The struggle is real, but so is God. His strength, his power, and his Spirit are available to you. Tap into that divine source and brace yourself for the miracles to follow.

Dear Father, thank you for your strength and love for my prodigal child and family. In Jesus' name. Amen.

Instant Transformation

Do you find yourself pleading, *God, I need a miracle now*? Well, let's take a minute to reflect on Matthew 17:18: "Jesus rebuked him, and the demon came out of him, and the boy was healed at once" (NASB). "At once"—did you catch that? Not tomorrow, not eventually, but instantly. We're talking about an immediate, miraculous change that left everyone speechless. I know you've been praying, perhaps for what feels like a lifetime, for your child to be set free from whatever has a grip on them. It's easy to get discouraged, but never forget that God can quickly turn it all around.

While it's true that some battles are long, don't rule out the possibility of a sudden breakthrough. With God, a moment is all it takes to rewrite your child's story. Your quick turnaround could be just a prayer away. Your miracle could be unfolding even as you read this. God's perfect timing often comes when we least expect it. When he acts, it's powerful and profound. Don't give up on God and his miracles, for God's timing is perfect, and when he moves, you'd better believe it will be worth the wait.

Dear Father, thank you that you can cast the demons away from my child quickly. In Jesus' name. Amen.

Is Anything Too Hard for God?

Are you a stressed-out parent? Ever feel like your situation is too impossible, even for God? Numbers 11:23 has some perspective for us. "The LORD said to Moses, 'Is the LORD's hand shortened? Now you shall see whether my word will come true for you or not'" (ESV). When you are feeling limited or maybe even powerless, remember that God's not. And he's daring us to believe his Word will come true in our lives and our children's lives. God can move through your child even in the darkest hours and most turbulent times.

Your child may be straying far, but God's reach is further. Your child may be deep into sin, but our circumstances, failures, or fears don't limit God's power. We have to trust him and watch his promises unfold. So are you up for the challenge? Let's ditch our limited view and believe in a God-sized breakthrough. Ready to step into the unlimited? He's waiting to blow your mind.

This isn't about hoping for the best; it's about expecting the extraordinary. When doubts cloud your mind, remember this divine question: Is anything too hard for God? It's a call to shift your perspective, see beyond the immediate chaos, and trust in God's mighty capabilities.

Dear Father, thank you that nothing is impossible or too hard for you. In Jesus' name. Amen.

It Is Finished

Some of you may feel like the battle with your child is lost today. John 19:30 reveals where you can find victory. "When Jesus had received the sour wine, He said, 'It is finished!' And He bowed His head and gave up His spirit" (NASB). These are compelling words: "It is finished." In the heat of the battle, victory seems elusive. But hear me out; these words from Jesus are your battle cry too. Jesus spoke them as his earthly mission was coming to an end. He had faced down every temptation, pain, and loss—things we're no stranger to. When he said, "It is finished," he declared victory over sin and death, a victory which he shares with his followers. And you know what? His victory means that when your child believes in Jesus, they can escape the sin that seems to trap them.

You see, God specializes in turnarounds. When we're at the end of our rope—emotionally, mentally, or spiritually— God does his best work. He steps in to say, *I've got this.* So today let "It is finished" be your mantra. The battle over sin and death has already been won in the spiritual realm.

Dear Father, thank you for winning the battle over sin and finishing it in the Spirit. In Jesus' name. Amen.

Judgment Day

You may be battle worn, but I want us to unpack a sobering and hopeful promise: divine judgment. It sounds heavy. The good news is in Revelation 20:12.

> I saw the dead, great and small, standing before the throne, and books were opened. Then another book was opened, which is the book of life. And the dead were judged by what was written in the books, according to what they had done. (ESV)

As parents, we do everything in our power to guide our children, especially when they've gone astray. Yet despite our best efforts, they have their own free will—choices they make for better or worse.

Here's the comforting part: ultimately, God is the judge, not us. That weighty responsibility of eternal judgment? It's his to bear, not yours. God sees your child's heart, the struggles, and, yes, even the wrong decisions. He has the ultimate authority to bring them to account. Even if your child has gone far off the path, God's judgment comes with the possibility of redemption. They need only repent and believe. Breathe easier today knowing your child is never too far gone for God's mercy. Stay in the fight, but let God be God. Your child is in his hands.

Dear Father, thank you that I can put my child in your hands.
In Jesus' name. Amen.

Just a Touch

Do you feel unable to cope, like you're hanging by a thread, as you pray for a miracle for your child? Dive into Matthew 14:35–36.

> The men of that place…brought to him all who were sick and implored him that they might only touch the fringe of his garment. And as many as touched it were made well. (ESV)

Picture this: desperate people, all clamoring to touch just the edge of Jesus' cloak. And guess what? That tiny touch was enough. It was enough then, and it's enough now. A slight touch, a simple prayer, can catalyze change in your child's life. It doesn't have to be a grand gesture or a perfectly worded prayer. Just reach out in faith, believing that even a "fringe" of God's power can restore what's broken, heal what's hurting, and bring your wayward child back.

You have access to the same Jesus who performed miracles for the desperate. Extend your faith, touch the fringe, and let God do the rest. A touch of divine intervention is all your child needs. When all seems lost, know that the slightest act of faith can make a world of difference. Keep reaching. Your miracle is closer than you think.

Dear Father, thank you for your miraculous power. One touch from you can make my child well. In Jesus' name. Amen.

june

Justified by Faith

You've probably been on your knees as a parent, desperately trying to win your prodigal child back. It's exhausting. And maybe you've questioned your worthiness in the process. But read what Galatians 2:16 says.

> We know that a person is not justified by works of the law but through faith in Jesus Christ, so we also have believed in Christ Jesus, in order to be justified by faith in Christ and not by works of the law, because by works of the law no one will be justified. (ESV)

The struggle to save our children can often blur into a battle to earn God's favor through our "works." But this verse strips that notion bare and tells us that we're justified not by works but by faith in Christ.

So what does this mean for you and your prodigal child? Your faith in Jesus justifies you and demonstrates to your child the power of divine intervention. You can't earn their salvation any more than you can earn your own. It's God's battle, and he's already provided a way for your child's salvation through Christ.

Dear Father, thank you for allowing me to lay down the burden of trying to do enough or be enough. Instead, I can lean into the sufficient grace that comes through faith in Christ. In Jesus' name. Amen.

Keep Fighting for Your Prodigal

We all mess up, including some of Jesus' closest followers, as we read in John 18:27: "Peter again denied it, and at once a rooster crowed" (ESV). Peter, one of Jesus' dearest friends, messed up big time. Under pressure, he denied even knowing Jesus not once but three times. Sometimes we, too, falter in our battles for our wayward kids. Maybe we give in or lose our cool and say things we regret. But listen, that doesn't make us failures. If Peter, who walked beside Jesus, could slip up, so can we. But here's the glorious part: Peter's story didn't end there, and neither does yours. Peter was restored, and God used him mightily. His momentary failure didn't define him, and your stumbles won't define you either.

You're in this for the long haul, and there will be ups and downs. What matters is getting back up, dusting yourself off, and leaning into God's grace. His mercies are new every morning, and his strength is made perfect in your weakness. If you hear the proverbial rooster crowing over a mistake, remember Peter. Remember that God's love and grace are bigger than your shortcomings. And remember that he can use even your failures for good.

Dear Father, thank you for not tallying sins or holding them against believers. In Jesus' name. Amen.

From Far Away to Near

Are you feeling like your child is so far away? I know it can feel like your child is a million miles away—spiritually, emotionally, maybe even physically. But let's lean into the wisdom of Ephesians 2:13: "In Christ Jesus you who once were far off have been brought near by the blood of Christ" (ESV). If there's one thing this verse screams, it's hope. Your wayward child, who feels so far off from where you dreamed they'd be, can be brought near again. And don't miss how this happens: by the blood of Christ. Not by your perfect parenting, endless arguments, or the seemingly magical consequence that you hope will make them shape up. It's Jesus who can bring them back.

So let that take a weight off your shoulders. God's love and the sacrifice of Christ can reach your child no matter how distant they seem. What's your part then? Keep praying, keep loving, and keep the lines of communication open. And remember, God specializes in bringing the far-off near. He's in the business of miraculous comebacks. You keep doing your part, and trust God to do his. Hold on to hope. It's the anchor in this storm.

Dear Father, thank you for the blood of Christ, which makes it possible for my child to be close again. In Jesus' name. Amen.

Knock, Seek, Find

Nothing can stop you, warfare parent. See for yourself in Luke 11:9–10.

> I say to you, ask, and it will be given to you; seek, and you will find; knock, and it will be opened to you. For everyone who asks receives, and the one who seeks finds, and to the one who knocks, it will be opened. (NASB)

You're no stranger to persistent prayer, especially regarding your wayward child. But sometimes it feels like heaven has gone silent, and then, waiting is excruciating. Let this truth sink in: God hears you. He knows your desperation, your sleepless nights, and your heartache. He's not ignoring you. He's inviting you to keep knocking, keep seeking, keep asking.

My friend, I can tell you firsthand that your prayers aren't in vain. Remember, God specializes in the impossible, and no prodigal is too far gone. So don't give up. Keep hammering heaven with your prayers and your love because the God who promises is faithful. Even though your prayers may not be answered how or when you thought, God rewards persistence and faith. Keep knocking!

Dear Father, thank you for answering when I seek you. In Jesus' name. Amen.

Leaving Milestones to Follow

When the Israelites crossed the Jordan, God told them to set up twelve stones as a reminder of his faithfulness. Joshua 4:21–24 captures this.

> When your children ask their fathers in time to come, saying, "What are these stones?" then you shall inform your children, saying, "Israel crossed this Jordan on dry ground." For the LORD your God dried up the waters of the Jordan before you until you had crossed, just as the LORD your God had done to the Red Sea, which He dried up before us until we had crossed; so that all the peoples of the earth may know that the hand of the LORD is mighty, so that you may fear the LORD your God forever. (NASB)

This story hits home. We're crossing tumultuous rivers, wrestling with the mayhem our prodigals have caused. But here's the hope: the stones are milestones of faith and testimonies for our children to stumble upon when lost. Let's start planting these milestones by sharing testimonies even if they don't seem to listen. One day, they will remember. They'll ask, "What are these stones?" and we'll have an answer, a lifeline to throw to them.

Dear Father, thank you for creating milestones for my child. In Jesus' name. Amen.

Lessons in Obedience

Are your child's choices keeping them in trouble? Those choices may be the very things that make them change, as we see in Hebrews 5:8: "Although he was a son, he learned obedience through what he suffered" (ESV). This verse speaks volumes about the journey of growth and learning, even through suffering. It reminds us that our children can learn valuable lessons through their challenges like Jesus did. It's difficult to watch our children suffer or make mistakes. Yet this verse encourages us to see these experiences as opportunities for growth and learning. Our children's struggles can be the very thing that teaches them obedience and resilience.

We need to guide and support them with love, understanding that each challenge they face is a step toward maturity. We are called to trust in God's process, knowing he uses every experience for their good. During trials, let's encourage our children to lean into what God is teaching them. Their journey might be challenging, but it's shaping them into stronger, wiser individuals. This perspective gives us hope as we navigate the ups and downs of parenting. Each struggle allows our children to grow closer to God and learn the valuable lesson of obedience through adversity.

Dear Father, thank you that suffering can be a catalyst for my child's turnaround. In Jesus' name. Amen.

Let God's Word Dwell

I know the nights are long, and your heart is heavy, but there's hope. Let's dig into John 15:7, which says, "If you remain in Me, and My words remain in you, ask whatever you wish, and it will be done for you" (NASB). Our prayers carry power when we abide in Christ and let his words dwell richly in us. Abiding is our secret weapon in this fight for our children's souls. It isn't just a Sunday thing; it's an everyday, every moment commitment. When his words live in us, they change us. They give us hope, wisdom, and the courage to stand when everything else is falling apart. And let me tell you that when his words are in you, they'll spill out of you and touch everyone around you, especially your wayward child.

Instead of asking, *Why is this happening?* ask, *Lord, what would you have me learn?* Take those powerful words of Scripture, soak in them, and let them renew your mind and spirit. Then pray like never before for your prodigal child. With God's words as your foundation, your prayers become faith declarations that have the power to shift realities.

Dear Father, thank you for answering my prayers.
In Jesus' name. Amen.

Let Them Come

Do you feel someone is hindering your child from following God because of your child's youth? Tune in to Mark 10:14.

> When Jesus saw this, He was indignant and said to them, "Allow the children to come to Me; do not forbid them, for the kingdom of God belongs to such as these." (NASB)

Here's the great revelation of truth: God's kingdom is open for everyone to enter, especially the young. Jesus doesn't want anyone, not even your rebellious child, to be kept away when they respond to him in faith. Even if your child has made self-destructive choices, God's grace covers them the moment they start following him.

Keep the faith. Your child is never too far gone for Jesus' redemption. Sometimes it feels like your child is never going to turn around. But in the meantime, we need to maintain that spiritual welcome mat. Make your home, prayers, and heart an open pathway to God's grace. The kingdom of God is for the childlike. No matter how far off the path your child has strayed, God welcomes all who turn to him with repentant hearts. Let's welcome people into God's incredible grace with the same hospitality.

Dear Father, thank you for showing in your Word that children are precious to your heart. In Jesus' name. Amen.

God Lifts You Up

Do you feel like you and your wayward child have hit rock bottom? Find the comfort of God in Psalm 30:1: "I will exalt You, LORD, for You have lifted me up, and have not let my enemies rejoice over me" (NASB). It's one thing to be down, but it's another thing to stay down. God doesn't just provide a comforting shoulder. He also actively lifts us. The Enemy may try to bury you in despair, fear, or shame, but God's arm is never too short to snatch you back up.

I know it is so hard to praise God when you feel defeated. But even in the middle of our battle, something incredible happens when we extol—celebrate, praise, and elevate—God. Our focus shifts, our spirits lift, and suddenly, we find ourselves rising above the circumstances. Your child can experience this divine lift too. So go ahead and praise the Lord even when it hurts. God's in the business of turning pits into pedestals. You are not destined for defeat. You're destined for a divine liftoff and a complete victory over the Enemy.

Dear Father, thank you for all the ways you have lifted me up over my enemies. In Jesus' name. Amen.

Never Lose Hope

I know you're worried, worn out, and feel like giving up. But take a breath and explore John 6:40, where Jesus said,

> This is the will of My Father, that everyone who sees the Son and believes in Him will have eternal life, and I Myself will raise him up on the last day. (NASB)

Eternal life is the reward for those who come to Jesus and believe in him. Take a moment to remember that this promise holds true for you, faithful parent. In fact, this verse gives hope to *everyone* who believes, which means that no matter how far from God your child runs, they will receive eternal life if they repent and believe.

Your child may be going astray now, but that doesn't mean it's their final destination. Lean into God's promises. Let this verse today remind you that when we believe and hold on to faith, there's a promise of eternal life. That goes for you and your prodigal. Hold on to the Lord and his Word even when everything seems disastrous because when God makes a promise, he keeps it. And he's promised to raise those who believe—yes, even our formerly wayward children.

Dear Father, thank you for granting eternal life to all who believe in your Son, Jesus. In Jesus' name. Amen.

Lifting You up in Battle

It's easy to feel like you're standing alone, especially when it seems like your child is slipping further away from you and from God. Here is a lift to your soul from Psalm 109:31, which says, "He stands at the right hand of the needy, to save him from those who judge his soul" (NASB). Right now, in the middle of your struggle, God is standing at your right hand, not sitting or watching from a distance, but standing ready, like a committed copilot on a turbulent flight. God isn't an observer. He's an active defender, especially when judgment and criticism make you question your worth as a parent or your child's fate.

Imagine that! God, the creator of the universe, stands up for you and stands by you. With God at your side, no judgment can break you; no hardship can shake your faith. Remember, the world may judge your child's actions (and sometimes, unfairly, your parenting), but God's not in the condemning business. He's in the soul-saving business. Take heart. With God standing right beside you, you can stand strong when people judge you or your child.

Dear Father, thank you for being there for the needy. In Jesus' name. Amen.

Listen Up for Healing

Are you feeling swamped by advice from all directions as you seek answers about your wayward child? Zone in on Proverbs 4:20–22.

> My son, pay attention to my words;
> incline your ear to my sayings.
> They are not to escape from your sight;
> keep them in the midst of your heart.
> For they are life to those who find them,
> and healing to all their body. (NASB)

Talk about needing laser focus! The wisdom of God isn't just good advice; it's life and health. That's not just a poetic way to say it's beneficial. God's Word is the real deal, a source of divine restoration for you and your child.

So what does this mean for you? It's time to block out the noise and lean close to what God is saying. Don't let the unsolicited worldly advice bring you down. Remember, God's words aren't platitudes; they're promises. In the battles you're facing, God's Word is your weapon, strategy, and, yes, even your first-aid kit. Dig deep into the Word. Let it permeate your thoughts, prayers, and parenting approach. Keep the faith. His wisdom isn't just a road map; it's also the lifeline you've been searching for.

Dear Father, thank you for your words, which are life and healing. In Jesus' name. Amen.

The Power of Prayer

Do you need some beautiful encouragement? We get it from James 5:13: "Is anyone among you suffering? Then he must pray. Is anyone cheerful? He is to sing praises" (NASB). Isn't it comforting to know that God's Word provides answers for our highs and lows, especially as parents of wayward children? James gave us a lifeline here: pray. It sounds simple, but how often do we forget to consider prayer as our first resort?

The chaos and heartache with our wayward kids often seem too heavy to bear. Maybe your child is sick physically or emotionally or spiritually. You've tried everything— therapy, interventions, tough love—but here's a different kind of prescription: the prayer of faith. Don't underestimate the power of sincere, faith-filled prayers. God listens and acts even when it doesn't feel like he is.

Maybe you're feeling cheerful today because you see a glimmer of change in your child. Sing praises! But if today is a day of suffering, drop to your knees in prayer. Connect with God and remember that through him, you have the power to intervene in ways you never thought possible. Let your prayers be your warfare and your praise be your victory lap.

Dear Father, thank you for hearing my prayers when I'm experiencing the valley and the mountaintops with my prodigal. In Jesus' name. Amen.

The Harvest of Discipline

Do you feel guilty for punishing your prodigal? Parenting is a journey filled with moments that test our patience and resolve. The discipline we extend to our children, though challenging for both them and us, is a foundational aspect of love. Hebrews 12:11 shares, "For the moment, all discipline seems not to be pleasant, but painful; yet to those who have been trained by it, afterward it yields the peaceful fruit of righteousness" (NASB). This verse reminds us that discipline, while difficult in the moment, is a seed that grows into the peaceful fruit of righteousness.

The challenges we face when correcting our children are not in vain. They are part of a greater process of growth and learning not just for our children but for us as parents. The discomfort of discipline paves the way for a future where our children understand the value of integrity, kindness, and respect and thrive in wisdom and grace.

Let's embrace the process of discipline with faith and love, knowing that the lessons learned are building blocks for a righteous character. The path may seem tough now, but the outcome—a life marked by peace and righteousness—is worth every effort. Look forward to the beautiful harvest to come.

Dear Father, thank you for supporting my loving discipline today. In Jesus' name. Amen.

Living through Christ

Let me tell you something I've learned through all the ups and downs with my children. Our strength has limits, but God's doesn't. Look at Galatians 2:20.

> I have been crucified with Christ. It is no longer I who live, but Christ who lives in me. And the life I now live in the flesh I live by faith in the Son of God, who loved me and gave himself for me. (ESV)

This verse isn't just a nice saying; it's also a life strategy. When you're exhausted from battling for your child's soul, remember that you've been crucified with Christ, and he now lives in you. That means his strength, wisdom, and love empower you.

Your fight to win your child back isn't about your might. It's about letting Christ live through you. It's about faith—faith not in outcomes but in the one who controls the outcomes. Christ loved you so much that he gave his life for you. Don't you think that same powerful love can reach your wayward child? Instead of running on your own steam, let Christ energize you and guide you. When your child sees Jesus living in you, they know the path home. Your faith in Christ can catalyze a turnaround for your child.

Dear Father, thank you for Jesus, who lives in me. In Jesus' name. Amen.

Love's Long Game

We all know the feeling of seemingly endless battles, but we find our relief in love, as we see in 1 Corinthians 13:7: "[Love] keeps every confidence, it believes all things, hopes all things, endures all things" (NASB). That's right! Your love for your child is a force to be reckoned with, capable of enduring long sleepless nights and unimaginable fears. This love isn't a human love; it's a slice of God's eternal love. You're not sticking it out just because you have to. You're grounded in a divine love that can bear the weight of your child's choices, believe in their better selves, and hope for their ultimate return, no matter how far they've strayed.

Love endures, so you endure. Don't lose sight of this powerful truth. Even when your hope dwindles or your strength feels zapped, remember that your love—infused with the might of God—can and will endure. Keep love on your side. In your journey of endurance, let love be your compass and shield. This love is resilient, holding up under pressure, weathering storms, and never giving up. It's the kind of love that sees beyond the present struggles to the promise of what lies ahead.

Dear Father, thank you for your love, which allows me to love my child even as they rebel. In Jesus' name. Amen.

Unshakable Faith
to Stand Firm

Do you feel like your faith is tested every day as you pray for your wayward child? Have you begun to doubt your own salvation because of your struggles with your defiant child? Check out Mark 16:16, where Jesus said, "The one who has believed and has been baptized will be saved; but the one who has not believed will be condemned" (NASB).

Listen, God's promises are big. Sometimes they are too good to seem true. If we believe and live out our faith, we're not just assured salvation; we're also empowered to act. Even when it seems impossible, prayer can bring healing and transformation. By demonstrating that our faith is unshakable, we get to show our children what it looks like to have confidence in the Lord amid trials. This may be what they need to put their own trust in God and receive an unshakable salvation.

Our faith can move mountains—even mountains of rebellion, hurt, and despair. God will move on your behalf even when your faith is being tested. Ready to be unshakable? Embrace the power that comes from true belief and expect miraculous shifts. With faith, nothing's out of reach.

Dear Father, thank you for comforting me in the fight and moving supernaturally on my behalf despite my doubts. In Jesus' name. Amen.

Mending the Shattered Heart

Are you heartbroken over your child's choices? You're not the only parent who has experienced—and is experiencing—this grief, and you're not powerless. Psalm 147:3 reminds us that God "heals the brokenhearted and binds up their wounds" (NASB). Imagine God as the ultimate heart surgeon, taking each shattered piece of your heart and skillfully mending it back together. The thing is that he wants to do the same for your wayward child. Just as God binds up your wounds, he's also ready to heal the hurt, the rebellion, and the confusion in your child's life. And let me tell you something awesome: this healing goes beyond just physical well-being. It's also a soul-deep restoration.

Your child might be broken now, but God's specialty is taking broken things and making them whole. Don't lose hope. Instead, think about the mending God has done in your own life and believe he can do the same for your child. Let's trust him together to bind up the wounds in our families and bring us to a place of restoration. Believe in the transformative power of God's love. He's not patching up; he's completely renewing.

Dear Father, thank you for mending brokenness and binding up all my wounds. In Jesus' name. Amen.

Mercy Triumphs

Do you ever feel like you are being judged as a parent? Overwhelmed by the should-haves and could-haves? Let's reflect on Matthew 9:13: "Go and learn what this means: 'I desire compassion, rather than sacrifice,' for I did not come to call the righteous, but sinners" (NASB). Listen, the world wants you to believe you've failed because your child has gone astray. You may even feel another level of shame because of how your fellow believers view you. Well, the world is wrong, and not every believer can fully understand your battle. However, remember this: Jesus cares less about religious rituals and more about your compassion—your heart. And trust me, he has a massive heart for the lost, including your child.

Jesus came for the sinners, not the already saved. If your child is far from God, guess what? They're precisely who Jesus is looking for. Take the pressure off yourself. It's not about what you could've done better or differently but what God is about to do. Pour your love and compassion over your child and let God handle the rest. Your child's victory may come about when your relentless love pairs with God's transformative mercy.

Dear Father, thank you for desiring only our hearts even when they are drowning in sin. In Jesus' name. Amen.

Miraculous Breakthrough

Does it feel like you've tried everything to reach your child, but they're still lost in the dark? Acts 19:11–12 tells us,

> God was doing extraordinary miracles by the hands of Paul, so that even handkerchiefs or aprons that had touched his skin were carried away to the sick, and their diseases left them and the evil spirits came out of them. (ESV)

God performed "extraordinary miracles" through Paul. People were healed and delivered just by touching a cloth that had been in contact with him. Can you imagine?

Let's shake off any limits we've put on God. The same God who performed miracles through Paul can intervene in your child's life in unimaginable ways. It could be through an unexpected conversation with a stranger, a powerful dream, or an overwhelming sense of God's love breaking through their resistance. You may not be Paul, but your prayers have incredible power. You might not have a miraculous handkerchief, but your earnest prayers can create a spiritual environment where miracles can happen. When you're at your wit's end, remember that God's creative solutions go beyond human limitations.

Dear Father, thank you for healing the sick and setting the demon possessed free, and thank you for doing miracles today. In Jesus' name. Amen.

A New Heart

Many parents feel utterly powerless when they see their child spiraling. But let's not forget the words in 1 Samuel 10:9: "It happened, when [Saul] turned his back to leave Samuel, that God changed his heart; and all those signs came about on that day" (NASB).

If God could change Saul's heart, why not your child's? God is in the heart-changing business. The Bible contains stories of radical transformation. Paul, a former persecutor of Christians, became an influential Christian in the early church. David, a shepherd, became the king of Israel. Zacchaeus, a greedy tax collector, paid back four times over everyone he cheated. Why? Because God intervened.

Your child may be unrecognizable to you right now. If they've turned their back on everything you've taught them, don't give up because one experience with God can change a sinful lifestyle. A change of heart is entirely possible. It's God's specialty, and he's more than willing to step in. Hope is never lost because our God is a God of new beginnings and changed hearts. Watch him show up in ways that will leave you speechless. Hold on to this verse from 1 Samuel 10 as a promise of what God can do.

Dear Father, thank you for reminding me that you are in the heart-changing business. Help me believe that you can transform my child's heart. In Jesus' name. Amen.

More than Just Words

Do you feel defeated by your child? Let's unpack Deuteronomy 32:45–47.

> When Moses had finished speaking all these words to all Israel, he said to them, "Take to heart all the words by which I am warning you today, that you may command them to your children, that they may be careful to do all the words of this law. For it is no empty word for you, but your very life, and by this word you shall live long in the land that you are going over the Jordan to possess." (ESV)

Consider this: God's Word isn't merely an ancient story; it's also vibrant and life altering. Moses knew its vitality; he proclaimed God's Word as life. Let's affirm that!

When Moses declared God's words as life, he handed us a victory cry. These aren't futile words; they're seeds of hope, your arsenal against darkness targeting your child. Embed these words into your heart; they shape futures. Speak life into your child. You're not scattering words to the wind but sowing seeds of enduring life. Nourish your child with Scripture, for it is potent and never fruitless. His Word is life, never idle. It's our sustenance and strength. His Word is what fuels our hope for healing.

Dear Father, thank you for your words, which are life and strength. In Jesus' name. Amen.

Navigating a World Upside Down

Isn't it wild how today's world seems to flip-flop on what's right and wrong? Isaiah 5:20 paints a picture we know all too well. "Woe to those who call evil good and good evil, who put darkness for light and light for darkness, who put bitter for sweet and sweet for bitter!" (ESV). It's like Isaiah was talking right to us. Our kids, bless their hearts, are caught in this storm of the world's mixed-up values that are all kinds of crazy. And let's be honest: the Enemy loves to stir up this kind of chaos. But don't you dare believe he has the upper hand because he doesn't. Not when we serve a God who is the embodiment of truth itself.

You have a vital role in this whole drama. Think of yourself like a lighthouse for your child, shining God's truth and love while slicing through the fog. Your faith, your prayers, and those heart-to-hearts guided by his Spirit can lead your child back in from the sea of confusion. So even though the world seems hopelessly dark and evil, remember that your call to shine God's light is more critical than ever.

Dear Father, thank you for your light of good that can lead my child back home from the evil world. In Jesus' name. Amen.

The Power of Belief

Your wayward child's actions may break your heart right now, but let me remind you of something crucial: change starts within. We see this in Romans 10:10: "With the heart a person believes, resulting in righteousness, and with the mouth he confesses, resulting in salvation" (NASB). Believe in your heart that God is working on your child even when you don't see immediate results. Speak it out, declare their turnaround, and claim God's promises over them.

Words have creative power. When your heart's belief and your spoken confession align, heaven takes notice. Don't underestimate the power of speaking life over your child. Maybe they're not walking the straight and narrow yet, but your words can pave a path for them to return. I know this struggle feels endless, and the temptation is to give in to despair. But our God is in the business of transformation, my friend. Hold on to your faith, align your heart and mouth in believing prayer, and watch God work wonders.

Your child's current choices don't define their future. God's promises do. Remember that your faith and declarations are not wishful thinking; they are powerful acts of spiritual warfare. Believe and confess.

Dear Father, thank you for the hope in salvation. In Jesus' name. Amen.

Living a Godly Life in Battle

Believe it or not, there is a good kind of fear. Let's read 1 Peter 1:17: "If you call on him as Father who judges impartially according to each one's deeds, conduct yourselves with fear throughout the time of your exile" (ESV). What does it mean to "conduct yourselves with fear"? Before you think it's about being terrified, let me clarify. This fear is a holy reverence for God, a mindful awareness of his authority and love. It's the kind of respect that keeps you aligned with his will, especially when you are walking through challenging situations with your kid.

As parents of prodigals, we sometimes feel exiled and distanced from the life we dreamed of having. But even in this "exile," we're called to live according to God's standards. That means being consistent in love, sticking to our godly principles, and maintaining our boundaries. Why? Because our Father judges impartially, and he's watching over us. I know the strain of having a wayward child can make it easy to compromise and give in just to keep the peace. Your consistent, God-fearing actions testify to your kid. They're watching even when they are grown. One day, you may see those seeds bear fruit.

Dear Father, thank you for helping me be more like you. In Jesus' name. Amen.

Never-Ending Praise

When your wayward child has wreaked all the havoc you can take, praising God might be the last thing on your mind. Your life is filled with worry, sleepless nights, and maybe even tears. But let me share a powerful key to unlocking supernatural breakthrough: praise. We find this in Psalm 145:1, where David sang, "I will extol you, my God and King, and bless your name forever and ever" (ESV).

You see, something remarkable happens when you lift your voice in praise. The atmosphere shifts. Walls crumble. It's like a secret weapon God has given us. It's more than just singing songs or saying, "Hallelujah." It's about declaring God's goodness even when life is a mess. It's about recognizing that he is still King even when your world is falling apart.

What you focus on becomes magnified. So if you spend all your time looking at the problem—your wayward child—it's easy to lose sight of the Problem Solver. But by praising God, you're taking your eyes off the commotion and putting them on the one who can bring peace and restoration. Give it a try. In the middle of the battle, pause and give God some praise.

Dear Father, thank you that I can praise you. Help me keep my focus on you. In Jesus' name. Amen.

Never Giving Up

Do you feel like giving up when your child is walking down a path you hoped they'd never take? The verse we're digging into today is Colossians 4:2: "Continue steadfastly in prayer, being watchful in it with thanksgiving" (ESV). The urge to give up when the situation with your child seems unredeemable can be overwhelming. But what if I told you God offers a power that will sustain you? We find this power in prayer. This verse in Colossians tells us how to pray—steadfastly and watchfully.

Steadfast prayer means you're digging your heels in, not giving up until you see a breakthrough. Watchful prayer keeps you alert to God's small miracles along the way. Yes, they are happening even if they're hard to see right now. Don't miss the last part either: "with thanksgiving." It may sound crazy to give thanks when you're in the middle of a storm, but gratitude opens up space for God to move. Remember that your prayers are your most powerful tool in these difficult times. They are the lifeline to the one who can truly make a difference.

Dear Father, thank you for guiding me when I want to give up and keeping me strong while I'm waiting on you for a breakthrough. May I always praise and thank you. In Jesus' name. Amen.

Lifting the Veil

I know your heart is heavy. You're wrestling for your child's soul, but it feels like they're hidden behind a veil. Things seem very dark. But check out 2 Corinthians 3:16–17, which says, "When one turns to the Lord, the veil is removed. Now the Lord is the Spirit, and where the Spirit of the Lord is, there is freedom" (ESV). We are not talking about a metaphorical veil here, friends. We're discussing the invisible barriers between us and God. These can include fear, despair, or even spiritual oppression. But here's the best thing: the veil is lifted when you and your child turn to God. And where God's Spirit is, there's freedom! Not just a little relief—no, I mean explosive, chain-breaking freedom.

What's your next move? Turn to God not in despair but in confident hope. Let God's Spirit fill your war room as you pray for your child to also turn to the Lord. Rejoice that through Jesus, God provided a way for us to come to him and see his glory face-to-face so that we can experience his presence and become more like him.

Dear Father, thank you for lifting the veil for those who follow you so that we can see the light of hope that sets us free. In Jesus' name. Amen.

Claim Your Freedom

You are valuable to God. Take 1 Corinthians 7:23 as evidence. "You were bought for a price; do not become slaves of people" (NASB). Have you ever questioned your worth because you felt like you were bound to the situation with your wayward child? Like you were bound by worry, fear, and disappointment? I get it; I've been there. But listen up; you were bought for a price. That means you belong to God, and that's revolutionary.

You're not bound to your circumstances, but you're a child of the King. He has the ultimate authority, not the issues you're facing. If God says you're free, then you are free indeed.

So here's the strategy: stand on God's promises and claim your freedom in him. Don't give the Enemy a foothold by acting as if you're defeated. You're not! The creator of the universe is in your corner, and he has already paid the price for your victory. Walk in that freedom and watch how it shifts the atmosphere around your wayward child. Seeing your freedom in Christ may be the catalyst they need to seek the Lord as their Savior.

Dear Father, thank you for buying me with the blood of Jesus. I am so grateful I belong to you. In Jesus' name. Amen.

New Creations

Are you feeling drained and downcast? Absorb this message from 2 Corinthians 5:17: "If anyone is in Christ, he is a new creation. The old has passed away; behold, the new has come" (ESV). Isn't that refreshing? Doesn't it lift your soul? Because of your relationship with Jesus, God sees you as a new creation.

No matter how far your child has strayed, transformation through Christ is available for them too. You might see a rebellious teen or a young adult gripped by the world's lures, and it looks like things will never change, but there is still time for them to turn to God and become a new creation.

Not only can God make old things new, but he also forgets the old. The new is waiting to replace the old, and it's far more glorious than we can imagine. Keep praying, keep believing, and don't give up hope. Remember that God is in the business of making all things new, which can include your wayward child.

Dear Father, thank you for making my old things, old habits, and old wrong decisions all new and for remembering them no more. In Jesus' name. Amen.

Infinitely Precious

Do you feel like God doesn't know the intimate details of your child's life? In the midst of parenting challenges, it's easy to feel lost or forgotten by God. Yet Luke 12:7 offers us profound reassurance. "Even the hairs of your head are all counted" (NASB). This level of attention signifies God's awareness and his deep care and concern for every aspect of our lives, including our children.

This verse reminds us that we and our children are infinitely precious in God's eyes. No struggle is too small, and no worry is insignificant. When doubts arise or when the path forward seems unclear, remember that God is closely attuned to your family's needs.

Let this promise comfort and encourage you. God knows every detail. God's meticulous care and boundless love encompass you and your child, proving that you and your prodigal are precious to him.

Dear Father, thank you for the reassurance that you are in every detail of my child's life. In Jesus' name. Amen.

Now Is the Time

Are you stuck in a waiting game, praying for the perfect moment to act? Read this Scripture passage from 2 Corinthians 6:1–2.

> Working together with him, then, we appeal to you not to receive the grace of God in vain. For he says,
> "In a favorable time I listened to you,
> and in a day of salvation I have helped you."
> Behold, now is the favorable time; behold, now is the day of salvation. (ESV)

The time for salvation and change? It's now. There's a divine urgency. God's ready to move and calls you to act with him. Whether that means striking up that uncomfortable conversation with your wayward child or making a bold prayer in faith, don't delay. Time is of the essence. One second can change everything. God's grace is not a resource to be wasted. Rather, it's the essential key in your fight for your child. Seize this favorable time because God is listening and willing to help you today. Trust me, you don't want to look back and wish you'd acted sooner. Now is your moment. Act with God's favor.

Dear Father, thank you for showing me that time is urgent for my wayward child and that I need to risk acting so that they may receive the grace to change. In Jesus' name. Amen.

Obey and Display

Is there a perfect love? The answer is in 1 John 2:5: "Whoever follows His word, in him the love of God has truly been perfected. By this we know that we are in Him" (NASB). Ah, the notion of perfect love sounds like something far away, especially when we're deep in the trenches and grappling with a prodigal child. But hear me out: obedience to God's Word is the key to this perfect love. I'm not saying it's easy, but it's transformative.

By obediently standing in God's promises and principles, we activate a level of love that can heal wounds and break chains. This love isn't just for you; it's also a beacon for your lost child. Your steadfastness is a model, showing them what God's perfect love looks like even in chaotic times. God's Word isn't a list of dos and don'ts. It's a blueprint for a life soaked in divine love. As you obey his Word, you're not just doing good but also becoming a vessel of his love. And trust me, that love can draw your prodigal back into God's embrace. Obedience is your weapon, shield, and calling card for perfected love.

Dear Father, thank you for helping me know your love and for helping me be more obedient. In Jesus' name. Amen.

Trust the Author

Do you feel like the story of your wayward child is spinning out of control? Let's draw encouragement from Psalm 33:4: "The word of the LORD is upright, and all his work is done in faithfulness" (ESV). Life may feel like a shaky narrative right now, but you can find wisdom in the Bible. God's Word is upright, and there's a structural integrity to what he says and does. In its pages, we see the glory and character of a God we can trust. Even when things look like a chaotic mess, he's working faithfully to bring about his perfect will.

The Bible contains story after story of God's redemptive work in the lives of ordinary, sinful people. You can stand firm in faith, knowing your child's book isn't closed yet. Neither is yours. Your prodigal is only in a chapter of their whole life's story. When you find yourself doubting, lean into the Author. The writer of all things good has not put down his pen. Stay tuned, for the next chapter could contain a life transformation. Trust in his faithfulness because it's from that foundation that everything else makes sense. God's writing your story, and he's a master at turning plots around.

Dear Father, thank you for your Word and for writing my story. In Jesus' name. Amen.

One God, One Family

In our struggles, especially those with our wayward children, loneliness often follows us. But there's hope. Ephesians 4:4–6 says, "There is…one Lord, one faith, one baptism, one God and Father of all, who is over all and through all and in all" (ESV). When it comes to the nitty-gritty of life, especially the trials, it's easy to feel like we're on an island. The truth is that we're part of a bigger spiritual family. We all share one Lord, one faith. You are not alone, not by a long shot. God is always there with you.

This truth is super important to remember when you're fighting for your child. God is above this situation. He's in the midst of it and working through you and others. And the unity of faith means you can lean on a whole community of believers. It means you can lean on God himself. So reach out to your community. Pray hard. Get into that spiritual war room and remember that it's not just your fight. All believers are a unit under one God, equipped with the same faith. Use that unity to fuel your prayers and actions, which can help guide your kid back home. Don't lose hope. Remember, you're backed by the ultimate team.

Dear Father, thank you for being the only God. In Jesus' name.
Amen.

Divine Rescue

Have you ever felt like the world is crashing down around you, especially when you think about your wayward child? Let's journey to Genesis 19:29.

> It came about, when God destroyed the cities of the surrounding area, that God remembered Abraham, and sent Lot out of the midst of the destruction, when He overthrew the cities in which Lot had lived. (NASB)

Lot lived in a hotbed of sin, but God remembered Abraham's plea and rescued Lot. Abraham's intercession made the difference. Friend, your prayers are your child's lifeline right now. Maybe your child is in the modern-day Sodom, surrounded by choices that scare the daylights out of you. But guess what? God hears your prayers. Just as Abraham's intercession that led to Lot's rescue, your cries are before God's throne, petitioning for your child's escape from destructive paths.

God sees you. He hears your heart's cry. And he is more than capable of plucking your child from danger even when it feels like everything's going up in flames. Be encouraged that God can reach into these places of destruction and rescue you and your child. Hold tight to that unshakable faith of yours. You and God are an unstoppable force.

Dear Father, thank you for hearing my cries for my child's rescue from evil. In Jesus' name. Amen.

Reclaiming Authority

Do you feel like there is no authority in this world anymore? Let's pause and soak in the divine truth of Psalm 8:6: "You have him rule over the works of Your hands; You have put everything under his feet" (NASB). The world's darkness can easily make us feel helpless, especially when we are fighting for our wayward children. But let's not forget God has given us inherent authority over our circumstances, our lives, and, yes, even the wayward paths of our children.

When everything feels out of control, remember this verse. God put all things under our feet. This means we have the power through Christ to rule and reign. While we can't control our children's choices, we can certainly influence their paths with prayer, faith, and a heart filled with God's love. So let's step into that divine authority today. Let's bind the Enemy's plans through the power of the blood of Christ and plead God's promises over our children. And while you're at it, put yourself under God's authority because miracles happen when you're aligned with him. Remember, God doesn't make mistakes. Your child is not a lost cause, and neither are you.

Dear Father, thank you for the truth that you have full authority over everything, including my child. In Jesus' name. Amen.

Open Your Eyes

Are you facing overwhelming odds stacked against you and your wayward child? Elisha's servant felt hopeless, too, in 2 Kings 6:15–17.

> When the attendant of the man of God had risen early and gone out, behold, an army with horses and chariots was circling the city. And his servant said to him, "This is hopeless, my master! What are we to do?" And he said, "Do not be afraid, for those who are with us are greater than those who are with them." Then Elisha prayed and said, "Lord, please, open his eyes so that he may see." And the Lord opened the servant's eyes, and he saw; and behold, the mountain was full of horses and chariots of fire all around Elisha. (NASB)

When it looks like evil influences, addictions, or destructive choices surround your child, you need to tap into a greater reality. Ask God to open your spiritual eyes to see his invisible army fighting for your child. I know you're tired, but you have a God who commands legions of angels. God's army is fighting for your child's soul even if you can't see it. Let God open your eyes to his divine strategy.

Dear Father, thank you for the invisible army that fights on behalf of my child. In Jesus' name. Amen.

Overcoming Fear with Faith

Do you feel like you're walking on a tightrope between fear and faith when it comes to your wayward child? Let Mark 5:36 sink in. "Jesus, overhearing what was being spoken, said to the synagogue official, 'Do not be afraid, only believe'" (NASB). Fear can be pesky, always whispering what-ifs and worst-case scenarios and allowing our minds to go through the terrible things that might happen to our children. Fear can even paralyze us. But Jesus steps in with a counteroffer: "Only believe." It's not a suggestion. It's an alternative route, an exit ramp off the highway of fear.

When the Enemy tries to feed you lies of defeat, hold on to this: belief cancels fear. It's impossible to be genuinely afraid when fully trusting that Jesus is in control, so keep your eyes on him. When fear knocks at your door, send faith to answer it. You need to starve fearful thoughts in your mind by feeding them faith-filled thoughts. Decide to get rid of the fear. Let your faith be bigger than your fright. Jesus is right there, urging you to lean on faith, not fear. Ready to make the switch? Do it today.

Dear Father, thank you for showing me how to overcome my fear with faith. In Jesus' name. Amen.

Embracing Divine Worth

Do you sometimes question what your child's worth is in God's eyes? Find comfort and assurance in Genesis 1:27: "God created man in his own image, in the image of God he created him; male and female he created them" (ESV). This verse beautifully highlights the value God places on his children. All people—saved, unsaved, or to be saved—hold immense worth in the eyes of God because he created them in his image.

In our journey with wayward children, it's easy to feel disheartened by their choices. Yet this verse calls us to view our children through God's eyes—as precious, valued, and worthy of love and guidance. Our challenge is to mirror this divine perspective, treating our children with the love and respect they deserve, regardless of their current path. It's a reminder that their worth is inherent and unchanging, just as God's love for them is constant.

Let's draw strength from this truth. God cherishes our children. We support them with unconditional love and prayer, trusting God's plan for their lives. In embracing this divine perspective, we can guide our children with hope and faith, knowing that both we and God value and love them beyond measure.

Dear Father, thank you for loving my child. Help me see my child as you see them. In Jesus' name. Amen.

Pathway to Joy

Are you finding it hard to imagine joy while you're wading through this tough season with your child? Let's get some fresh perspective from Psalm 16:11: "You make known to me the path of life; in your presence there is fullness of joy; at your right hand are pleasures forevermore" (ESV). How beautiful is that? While you may not see it now, God has a path of life. His road map isn't a maze of dead ends; it leads to real joy.

Here's your heart lifter: the joy you're yearning for your child to experience can be found in God's presence. Yes, the same presence you invite into your prayers, home, and life is where your child's true happiness lies. No matter how far your child has fallen into the depths of sin, joy is possible when they seek the Lord.

Don't let current circumstances dictate your hope. Your troubles today are mere detours on your journey to God's best. And don't underestimate the "pleasures forevermore" part. The blessings you experience in God's presence as you follow his path last forever. Believe in God's promise of life and joy not just as a future hope but also as a present reality.

Dear Father, thank you for the true joy that is found only in your presence. In Jesus' name. Amen.

Perplexed but Prepared

Life doesn't come with a manual, especially when you're trying to guide a wayward child back to the right path. You can find some guidance in Acts 10:17.

> While Peter was inwardly perplexed as to what the vision that he had seen might mean, behold, the men who were sent by Cornelius, having made inquiry for Simon's house, stood at the gate. (ESV)

Here the Bible describes Peter, who was perplexed and trying to figure out the vision he had just received. Like Peter, you may wonder, *What does this all mean? How do I navigate this complex situation with my child?*

Even when you're perplexed, even when you don't have all the answers, God does. And he's sending "directions" your way, just like he did for Peter. In your deepest confusion, God's guidance is at work. It may not come in a dramatic vision, but trust that he's lining things up in your favor, right at your "gate"—your point of need.

Keep your ears and heart open for divine directions. It could be a sermon, a friend's timely word, or an unexpected resource that sparks a change in your child's life. The God who guided Peter is the same God who's guiding you.

Dear Father, thank you for guiding me and my prodigal. In Jesus' name. Amen.

Power over the Horde

Do you ever feel like you're up against a whole horde of issues with your wayward child? Get into Mark 5:12–13.

> They begged him, saying, "Send us to the pigs; let us enter them." So he gave them permission. And the unclean spirits came out and entered the pigs; and the herd, numbering about two thousand, rushed down the steep bank into the sea and drowned in the sea. (ESV)

First off, let's acknowledge the impossible situation Jesus was in when he faced a man possessed by not just one demon but a legion of them. The odds seemed insurmountable, but Jesus spoke, and the demons had to obey.

Does your child have their own legion of issues? It could be addiction, rebellion, or any form of darkness that has entangled your child. Here's your lifeline: Jesus could command a legion of demons, and you can access that same power through prayer. Your challenges are no match for the authority you hold in Christ. Don't be overwhelmed by the numbers or the odds. You serve a God who has dominion over legions. Step into that authority and watch those problems rush down the steep bank and out of your life.

Dear Father, thank you for your dominion over evil. Nothing is impossible for you. In Jesus' name. Amen.

Train for the Battle

Parenting a prodigal child feels like a daily battle. One minute, you're navigating emotional land mines; the next, you're dodging fiery darts of blame and guilt. You might feel like you've been drafted into a war you never signed up for. It's exhausting. Here is good news found in Psalm 144:1: "Blessed be the LORD, my rock, who trains my hands for war, and my fingers for battle" (ESV).

God is not observing from the sidelines. He's your Rock and personal trainer, training your hands for war and your fingers for battle. While you are deep in prayer, God equips you with spiritual weapons—faith, perseverance, wisdom, and unconditional love—far more powerful than any earthly arsenal. The catch is that training requires participation. If we're going to let God train our hands, we have to be willing to get them dirty. Whether diving into the Word, seeking wise counsel, or engaging in prayer warfare, your effort is pivotal.

Lean into the training. Spend time with your commander in chief, the Lord, and let him prepare you for the daily battles. As you engage more deeply with him, you'll become stronger and gain ground in the fight for your child's soul.

Dear Father, thank you for being my Rock and for being there in the battle for my child. In Jesus' name. Amen.

Pressing On

Are you finding it hard to move forward in the fight? Take a moment and reflect on Philippians 3:13–14.

> I do not consider that I have made it my own. But one thing I do: forgetting what lies behind and straining forward to what lies ahead, I press on toward the goal for the prize of the upward call of God in Christ Jesus. (ESV)

Isn't this what we do as parents, especially when we're fighting for our wayward children? We press on. Yes, missteps, mistakes, and countless what-ifs haunt our past. But focusing on yesterday's failures won't change tomorrow's possibilities.

Paul reminded us here to forget "what lies behind" not because it's easy to forget but because forgetting is essential. You can't move forward if you're always looking back. Your past doesn't define you, nor does it define your child if they turn to God. God's grace is sufficient for fresh starts and new beginnings. The prize? Complete fellowship with God in heaven. The promise of the "upward call of God in Christ Jesus" can transform your child's heart, renew your strength, and bring reconciliation and healing. The finish line is closer than you think.

Dear Father, thank you for the prize of a forever home with you as I press forward, fighting for my prodigal. In Jesus' name. Amen.

Promised-Land Moments

Have you ever had those "promised-land" moments when you see a glimpse of victory in your child's life, even amid the struggle? That's God's doing, and it's worth celebrating! Psalm 105:43–44 says,

> He brought his people out with joy,
> his chosen ones with singing.
> And he gave them the lands of the nations,
> and they took possession of the fruit
>   of the peoples' toil. (ESV)

This is a beautiful reminder that God brought his people out of hardship with joy and singing. Not only that, but he also gave them lands and possessions they didn't even work for. This shows the incredible generosity of our God. So what does this mean for you and your wayward child?

Think of it this way. God can bring your child into a promised land—a place of peace, purpose, and joy. And just as the Israelites didn't toil for the lands they received, so your child can also receive God's grace without earning it. So can you. Reclaim that joy and sing even during the battle because God can turn things around. Remember, your child is not too far gone for a promised-land moment.

Dear Father, thank you for your incredible generosity toward your people and for giving me glimpses of the promised land available for my child. In Jesus' name. Amen.

Purpose amid Pain

I've been there, crying out to God, desperate for answers. *Why, Lord? Why is my child going through this?* I'll bet that you've had your share of sleepless nights too. Here's a radical question: What if there's a purpose behind the pain? Let's see what Jesus said in John 9:3–4.

> Jesus answered, "It was neither that this man sinned, nor his parents; but it was so that the works of God might be displayed in him. We must carry out the works of Him who sent Me as long as it is day; night is coming, when no one can work." (NASB)

Your child's waywardness is heart-wrenching, no doubt about it. But what if God wants to use it not just as a lesson but as a showcase for his grace and transformation? You may see a prodigal, but God sees a platform for his glory. So here's our move: instead of asking God, *Why*, let's start asking, *What now?* What can you do today to align yourself with God's potential plan? It begins with a shift in perspective. And trust me, when God steps in, you'll be amazed by the transformation in your child and in you as well.

Dear Father, thank you for showing me that there is a purpose in my pain. In Jesus' name. Amen.

Reach Out in Faith

Have you waited years for your prodigal to return to their senses? Let's talk about Luke 8:43–44.

> A woman who had suffered a chronic flow of blood for twelve years, and could not be healed by anyone, came up behind Him and touched the fringe of His cloak, and immediately her bleeding stopped. (NASB)

Your journey with your wayward child may feel like a never-ending struggle, similar to the experience of the woman who had been bleeding for twelve long years. Like her, you may have tried everything but still feel hopeless. Guess what? She was healed by simply touching the edge of Jesus' cloak. She didn't have a grand plan; she just reached out in faith, which turned her situation around.

It might feel like you've been fighting forever, but a breakthrough could be just a touch away. Sometimes the simplest acts of faith lead to the most extraordinary miracles. Reach out to Jesus in your anguish and exhaustion, believing that even the fringe of his presence can transform your situation. Stay encouraged, steadfast parent. Your touch of faith could be the pivotal moment you've been praying for. Keep reaching. Keep believing. Your miracle is within reach.

Dear Father, thank you for the hope that my child can be healed with one touch. In Jesus' name. Amen.

One Mediator, Infinite Hope

Are you caught in the exhausting struggle of trying to steer your wayward child back on track? The stakes are high, and the spiritual warfare is intense. But our success is in our Mediator, as Paul wrote in 1 Timothy 2:5: "There is one God, and one mediator also between God and mankind, the man Christ Jesus" (NASB). This isn't just about theological doctrine. This is your lifeline. In your effort to turn things around for your child, have you been unconsciously trying to act as the mediator? It's a burdensome role that God never intended for you. Jesus Christ alone holds that title. God didn't design us to carry all the burdens alone.

Only Jesus can bridge the gap between God and humans and between you and your struggling child. He knows your heartache, and he hears your prayers. Better yet, he's interceding for your child directly to God the Father—no intermediary required. So step back and surrender control to the one who knows your child better than you ever could. In the maze of confusion, your single, unwavering point of contact is Jesus. No matter how dire the situation, rely on the ultimate Mediator.

Dear Father, thank you for Jesus, the Mediator who can guide my wayward child back. In Jesus' name. Amen.

Reclaiming Your Power

I know how easy it is to feel powerless, especially when it comes to your rebellious child. But today let's grasp the transformative power in Romans 6:11: "You too, consider yourselves to be dead to sin, but alive to God in Christ Jesus" (NASB). Get this: you are alive to God! Dead to the sins, the failures, the disappointments, you are alive to hope, redemption, and, yes, miracles. What if we apply this same principle to our parenting struggles?

You don't have to be ruled by past mistakes, yours or your child's. You don't have to be defined by the choices they're currently making. You're alive to new possibilities, fresh starts, and God's divine intervention. Start considering yourself not as a helpless, powerless parent but as a warrior parent, alive to God's transformative power. Speak life into that wayward child of yours. Believe in transformation. Pray like never before. Being "alive to God" means you have access to his strength, his wisdom, and his never-ending love. So go ahead, consider yourself empowered, full of life, and capable of winning this battle for your child's soul.

Dear Father, thank you for the fact that I am alive in you and that your transforming power can begin a fresh start for my child. In Jesus' name. Amen.

Refined by Fire

Do you feel like you are walking through fire with your defiant child? Consider Mark 9:49: "Everyone will be salted with fire" (NASB). No one gets through this life without experiencing the fiery trials of this world. The fiery trials you go through are a refining process, not a punishment. Just as we season our foods with salt, the struggles are part of the seasoning that brings out godly flavors in your life and your child's.

Stand firm and hold fast, for God is preparing you for something greater. Keep the faith. The fire you are experiencing is forging a stronger, wiser you, and it may be doing the same to your child. That heat's on, but so is God's grace. Life might feel like a furnace right now, but guess what? God is right there with you in the heat of the fire. Are you ready to embrace the refining process? Walk through this fire and come out salted, seasoned, and stronger. Although your child may be struggling, wait expectantly for the same outcome for your child.

Dear Father, thank you for the trials of life, which can make me more like you, and for the fires of life, which help me and my child become wiser. In Jesus' name. Amen.

Remember and Hold Fast

Do you struggle to keep your faith when your child seems lost? We find a faith-building reminder in verse 5 of Jude: "I want to remind you, although you once fully knew it, that Jesus, who saved a people out of the land of Egypt, afterward destroyed those who did not believe" (ESV). These verses remind us of God's power to deliver and his call for us to remain faithful. As parents of prodigals, we face the heartache of watching our children stray, yet we're called to remember God's past deliverance and to maintain our faith. When we remind ourselves of God's faithfulness, it builds our faith.

This verse teaches us that God's grace is potent and transformative. While our children might wander, God's ability to guide them back to the right path is unwavering. Let's persist in prayer and love, trusting in God's power to redeem. We must hold fast to faith, believing in his ability to turn hearts and change lives. Our faith in his power and love gives us the strength to face each day with hope and perseverance. Embrace hope, knowing God's history of deliverance reveals what he can do in our children's lives.

Dear Father, thank you for this reminder to believe and hold on to your history of miracles while building our faith. In Jesus' name. Amen.

Walking by Faith, Not by Sight

In the parenting journey, especially during times of trial, we often rely on what we see and experience in the immediate. Let's unpack a new kind of navigation in 2 Corinthians 5:7: "We walk by faith, not by sight" (ESV). We witness our children's battles and setbacks. Sometimes the visible circumstances overwhelm us. However, God invites us to see beyond the immediate. He beckons us to trust his work in our children's lives even when it's invisible.

Living by faith means believing that God is at work behind the scenes. It's trusting that he molds and shapes our children even when the evidence isn't apparent. We pray, love, and guide while leaving the results to God.

Let this verse be an anchor in turbulent times. When doubts and fears arise, remind yourself that God's plans are often unseen, unfolding in ways we cannot comprehend. As we trust that God can answer our prayers for our children, he nurtures, grows, and strengthens our own faith. Embracing this walk of faith, we find peace in knowing our trust is in a God who loves our children more than we can imagine.

Dear Father, thank you for helping me walk by faith in you, not by sight. In Jesus' name. Amen.

God Has Your Back

Are you exhausted? Listen, I understand. Battling for your wayward child can feel like an all-consuming struggle. But what if I told you that the real battle happens when you rest? We see this in Psalm 3:4–5: "I was crying out to the LORD with my voice, and He answered me from His holy mountain. I lay down and slept; I awoke, for the LORD sustains me" (NASB).

David was in a desperate situation in this psalm, yet he cried out to God and found rest. Why? Because he knew the Lord was sustaining him. You can have the same assurance. That pit in your stomach? You can trade it for peace. Those sleepless nights? You can exchange them for restful sleep, knowing God is at work. When you're tired, rest in God's embrace.

Your action plan is to cry out to the Lord in your anguish, lay down your burdens, and trust that God is fighting for you and your child. Rest in him tonight and awaken refreshed for the fight. God is sustaining you. Isn't that something? You don't have to go through this battle fatigued and frazzled. You can do it rested and reassured.

Dear Father, thank you for the rest only you can provide. In Jesus' name. Amen.

Restored Lives

Do you feel like the dreams that you had for your child are forever dead? Look at Luke 7:12–15.

> As He approached the gate of the city, a dead man was being carried out, the only son of his mother, and she was a widow; and a sizeable crowd from the city was with her. When the Lord saw her, He felt compassion for her and said to her, "Do not go on weeping." And He came up and touched the coffin; and the bearers came to a halt. And He said, "Young man, I say to you, arise!" And the dead man sat up and began to speak. And Jesus gave him back to his mother. (NASB)

These verses offer hope for the seemingly impossible. Your child may not be literally dead, but you might feel like they're spiritually or emotionally lost to you. Or maybe all the hopes and dreams you had for them seem dead. In that moment in Luke's gospel, Jesus showed us that he's in the business of bringing the dead back to life. When your heart breaks, imagine Jesus coming along and feeling compassion for you. He has the power to touch that "coffin" and say, "Arise."

Dear Father, thank you for this uplifting hope today. In Jesus' name. Amen.

Unfailing Trust

Are your nights sleepless, filled with worries about your child? Find solace in Psalm 9:10: "Those who know Your name will put their trust in You, for You, LORD, have not abandoned those who seek You" (NASB).

Here's a hard-hitting truth: trust isn't just a fair-weather friend; it's the anchor in your storm. It's what you cling to when your strength fails and fears loom large. You're not just familiar with the name of the Lord. You also know it intimately, as one knows a close friend. And it's that name—synonymous with *faithfulness*—that has never left a seeker behind, and that includes you and can include your struggling child.

The name of the Lord is a fortress, protection in battles, a beacon, and a signal of hope to the lost. When it feels like you're in a hurricane as you pray for your child, remember that your cries reach the ears of the one who calms storms with a word. You may feel you're in the depths of a nightmare, but you have access to divine intervention. Your child may seem adrift, but God holds the map and the compass to guide them back. Your love, woven with trust in God, creates a net that can catch your child.

Dear Father, thank you for never abandoning me. In Jesus' name. Amen.

Rock-Bottom Revelations

Have you ever felt like you've hit rock bottom? Struggles with your wayward child can feel like a never-ending pit. But 2 Corinthians 1:9–10 offers encouragement.

> We felt that we had received the sentence of death. But that was to make us rely not on ourselves but on God who raises the dead. He delivered us from such a deadly peril, and he will deliver us. On him we have set our hope that he will deliver us again. (ESV)

Friends, sometimes we have to hit our lowest point to discover God's power at its peak. When we're out of options, it forces us to rely solely on him. And isn't that the point? God specializes in hopeless cases and is an expert at impossible odds. God loves to beat all the odds.

If he can raise the dead, he can undoubtedly breathe life back into your situation. He can bring your prodigal out of the lure of the world and bring them back home. Sometimes it's in the darkest pits where the light of God's deliverance shines the brightest. So as you're navigating this challenging path, remember that God has already delivered you before and will do it again.

Dear Father, thank you again for this reminder that you bring dead things to life. In Jesus' name. Amen.

Rooted in Royalty

Do you ever question how God sees you? Maybe you question your worth because of your parenting mistakes or the unwise decisions your child has made. Today let's soak in John 1:12–13.

> As many as received Him, to them He gave the right to become children of God, to those who believe in His name, who were born, not of blood, nor of the will of the flesh, nor of the will of a man, but of God. (NASB)

We need this! If we believe in Jesus, we are descendants of God our King. Our identity is rooted not in the mistakes we or our children make but in the divine royalty God has granted us through his Son.

This same reality is available to our children if they receive Jesus. We should remind our prodigal kids that they could be born of God. Maybe their shame is what's keeping them from accepting the salvation Jesus offers. We need to declare with authority that they are not too far gone for God to adopt them and call them his own. Declare that they could be free from the chains binding them. God is the Father and King of all those who believe.

Dear Father, thank you for allowing me to be rooted in your royalty in heaven. In Jesus' name. Amen.

Securing Your Family's Future

Do you feel like your back is against the wall? Let's learn from 1 Chronicles 18:13: "He put garrisons in Edom, and all the Edomites became servants to David. And the LORD helped David wherever he went" (NASB). In the thick of the fight for your child's heart, remember how David partnered with God to secure his reign, turning his opponents into subjects. Like David, align your parental strategies with God's wisdom.

Don't feel trapped. Act with conviction. Set clear boundaries, offer up relentless prayers, and watch God strengthen your resolve. With him, you're not just upholding rules; you're also sculpting destinies. Parenting through rebellion is tough—no lie there. But with God as your co-commander, what seems like a siege is just a step to victory. Those wayward paths your kid is on can curve back to success stories with a little divine intervention.

Know that your back is not pressed against the wall without help coming. Keep pressing forward. Your loving discipline and hopeful perseverance are more than tactics. They are the groundwork for future victories. Nurture your hope, for with God, you're building more than a defense. You're also cultivating a legacy of faith and restoration.

Dear Father, thank you for helping me wherever I go. In Jesus' name. Amen.

Shed the Old

Do you live in a cycle of negativity, especially when it comes to your wayward child? Are you constantly reacting out of your "old self"—the worried, fearful, or angry parent? Let's focus today on Colossians 3:9–10: "You have put off the old self with its practices and have put on the new self, which is being renewed in knowledge after the image of its creator" (ESV). God is saying that it's time for a wardrobe change. Out with the old self and in with the new. The new self is continuously renewed as you become more and more like the Creator. That's God's game plan for you, and it's just as applicable to your wayward child.

Your child, wrapped up in worldly distractions, must also experience this renewal. But remember, it starts with you. By putting on your new self, you become a mirror reflecting God's image, a beacon that guides your child back to him. In this constant renewal, there's endless hope. Suit up in faith, love, and the full armor of God. Your renewed self will not only bring you closer to God, but it could also be the magnet that draws your prodigal home. As you embrace this new self, let patience, understanding, and compassion be your allies.

Dear Father, thank you for the hope in renewal. In Jesus'
name. Amen.

Shielded and Sustained

Do you feel like you're clinging to hope with everything you have? Turn to Psalm 33:18–19.

> Behold, the eye of the Lord is on those who fear Him,
> on those who wait for His faithfulness,
> to rescue their soul from death
> and to keep them alive in famine. (NASB)

Sometimes life feels like a famine—a time of barrenness when nothing seems to grow, especially when you're worried about your disobedient child. Time and time again, they defy your parenting and make poor choices. But take heart; God's eyes are on you. He's not a spectator. He's a deliverer and sustainer.

Hope in his loving-kindness isn't a wish; it's an anchor. When things are rough, this hope does more than keep you grounded. It keeps you alive. God's watching and acting in ways you can't even fathom right now. God is your shield in battle and your sustenance in famine. Divine hope anchors you, and that's where real life begins. Remember that God's vision encompasses all. He sees every challenge and hears every prayer. In this spiritual famine, his provisions are not scarce but abundant.

Dear Father, thank you for keeping your eyes on me and for rescuing those who wait on you. In Jesus' name. Amen.

Divine Reassurance

Were you up late last night? Perhaps it was another night of wrestling with hurt, worry, and what-ifs. Find relief in Acts 27:23: "This very night an angel of the God to whom I belong, whom I also serve, came to me" (NASB).

The angel reassured Paul, who was stuck in a storm, that the God he served hadn't forgotten him. Now I know you're no stranger to storms, especially the emotional and spiritual tempests that come with having a wayward child. But the God you serve and belong to is sending his messengers—maybe not visibly but through circumstances, people, or that still, small voice that says, *Keep believing*. A divine company is with you in your sleepless nights.

We serve a God who dispatches angels and orchestrates heavenly interventions even when it doesn't feel like anything has changed. So keep serving and trusting him. God has his eyes on your child just as he did on Paul in that storm. Your child's guardian angel is working overtime. Let's believe that heaven is intervening right now, giving us strength and offering our children a lifeline back to love, peace, and home.

Dear Father, thank you for creating angels who help your followers. Thank you for the angels watching over us. In Jesus' name. Amen.

Freedom from the Enemy

Do you feel like negative influences muzzle your child's life? Let's look at Matthew 9:32–33.

> As they were going away, behold, a demon-oppressed man who was mute was brought to him. And when the demon had been cast out, the mute man spoke. And the crowds marveled, saying, "Never was anything like this seen in Israel." (ESV)

Jesus didn't just restore the man's ability to speak. He also kicked out the demon that muzzled him. Now let's connect the dots. Your child might not be mute, but maybe the pressures or addictions of the world silence them. Or their struggle with self-worth and value holds them back.

There's good news. The same Jesus who cast out that demon and broke the chains of muteness is rooting for you and your child. Just one touch from Jesus and your child could be free from whatever is holding them back. One divine intervention and their true voice—aligned with God's will—will be heard loud and clear. Don't lose hope. Your prayers and God's power are a match made in heaven. Stand firm, parent, and keep praying. Miracles are happening.

Dear Father, thank you for delivering people from demons. In Jesus' name. Amen.

Slaying Giants

Are you feeling like you're facing a giant-sized disaster with your unruly child? Remember David and Goliath? Let's look at what David said to the giant he faced in 1 Samuel 17:46–47.

> This day the LORD will hand you over to me…that this entire assembly may know that the LORD does not save by sword or by spear; for the battle is the LORD's, and He will hand you over to us! (NASB)

I know your struggle with your child feels endless. It's like facing a Goliath who won't back down. But let's take a lesson from young David. He faced the giant not with the world's armor but with faith in a mighty God. And you can too.

You don't have to slay this giant by yourself. Like David, pick up your "five smooth stones" (v. 40)—prayer, faith, trust, love, and God's Word. And David didn't just pick up the stones. He also ran toward Goliath. Sometimes we must take that intimidating step forward, assured that God goes before us. So whether it's a tough conversation you need to have or boundaries you need to set, run toward that challenge. Aim your stones with precision and let God handle the rest. The battle isn't yours; it's the Lord's.

Dear Father, thank you that with you, giants do fall. In Jesus' name. Amen.

Freedom in Prayer

Do you ever feel paralyzed by the fear of what might happen to your wayward child? Immerse yourself in Psalm 34:4: "I sought the LORD and He answered me, and rescued me from all my fears" (NASB). Fear is more than an emotion. It's also a chain that binds. It can lock you up in a cell of what-ifs and worst-case scenarios. But here's your key: seeking the Lord. The act of seeking is more than just shouting into the void. It's a directed, focused call to the one who can do something about it.

There is an acronym for fear: False Evidence Appearing Real. Most things we fear will never happen. In your fears, remember that God's power is greater than the mightiest of your worries. God's response isn't a vague promise. It's a concrete deliverance from all your fears. This includes the fears you have for your child. Seek out the Lord when fear overwhelms you. Be specific. Be raw. Be real. God's in the business of liberating hearts. Stay strong. Your deliverance might be one prayer away. There's freedom waiting for you. Let's grasp it.

Dear Father, thank you for your rescue. Today I seek you more profoundly to receive deliverance from all my fears for my child. In Jesus' name. Amen.

Wiping Away Every Tear

Are you burned out from the relentless worry and stress of loving a wayward child? Picture a place where every tear is wiped away. We find this in Revelation 7:17.

> The Lamb in the midst of the throne will be their shepherd, and he will guide them to springs of living water, and God will wipe away every tear from their eyes. (ESV)

It's easy to forget, amid the chaos, the arguments, or the sleepless nights, that your child is also suffering. They might be lost now, but they're aching too. And here's the extraordinary thing: God sees both of you, and he longs for your child to trust in him as you have. The Lamb amid the throne is Jesus, and he's also the Good Shepherd, the Shepherd who relentlessly pursues every lost sheep—yours included.

When the darkness seems never-ending, when you can't see a way out for your child, remember the springs of living water, a well that never runs dry, a source of life that heals all wounds. Show your child that God desires a relationship with them so he can wipe all their tears away someday.

Dear Father, thank you for preparing a place without tears where your followers will be with you. In Jesus' name. Amen.

Snatched from Despair

Are you drowning in your troubles? It can feel like we're submerged in a sea of fear and uncertainty when we're dealing with a wayward child. But look at what happened in Acts 8:39: "When they came up out of the water, the Spirit of the Lord snatched Philip away; and the eunuch no longer saw him, but went on his way rejoicing" (NASB). What a lesson for us! Sometimes God suddenly changes our circumstances. One moment, you're drowning, and the next, you're lifted up, gasping for air but grateful. Your child may still be struggling, but let's not forget the victories, no matter how small.

Let's rejoice in the tiny improvements and the immense power of God to snatch us from despair. God can snatch your child from poor choices and life-dominating sins. And just as the eunuch continued his journey with a rejoicing spirit, you, too, can go on your way, fueled by the hope and faith that God is at work even when you don't see it. Keep praying that God will snatch you and your child from despair and let your heart find reasons to rejoice.

Dear Father, thank you that you can snatch my child from the darkness of the world and set them free, giving an excellent reason for rejoicing. In Jesus' name. Amen.

The Power of Being Known

Isn't it comforting to realize that God knows you? Find this in 1 Corinthians 8:3: "If anyone loves God, he is known by Him" (NASB). In your tireless battles for your wayward child, the creator of the universe knows you. He sees your struggles, your tears, and your prayers. Why is this a big deal? Because being known by God is a secret power the Enemy can never touch. Your relationship with God becomes your fortress, a stronghold in the fight against evil influences over your child.

You've probably had many moments when you felt alone on this battlefield. But you're not. God knows you and is right there with you, crafting a battle plan specifically tailored for your family.

So as you go about spiritual warfare, take the truth of this verse from 1 Corinthians with you today. Let it empower your prayers and fuel your hope. Lean into your relationship with God and let that connection saturate every decision, action, and prayer for your child. When you are known by God, dear warfare parent, miracles are on the horizon. This knowledge that God knows and loves you is a source of immense strength and comfort.

Dear Father, thank you for knowing me and my child, and I'm grateful that to be known by you means you love me intimately. In Jesus' name. Amen.

Speak to Your Mountain

Are you staring down a mountain-sized issue with your child, like drug or alcohol abuse, porn, rebellion, or more? Read Mark 11:22–23.

> Jesus answered and said to them, "Have faith in God. Truly I say to you, whoever says to this mountain, 'Be taken up and thrown into the sea,' and does not doubt in his heart, but believes that what he says is going to happen, it will be granted to him." (NASB)

Bold words, right? But don't just read them; speak them. Speak to that mountain you're facing—be it addiction, rebellion, or despair. A child can create many problems that can appear to be not just one mountain but a mountain range.

Today I challenge you as a warfare parent to elevate your faith and speak God's truth over the impossible. Reject doubt and believe that your words have divine authority. Take that mountain or the full mountain range through the power of Jesus in you. God gave you the authority to speak to your mountains and expect a shift. So are you ready to start moving mountains? Unleash your faith and watch those obstacles tumble like mountains that crumble.

Dear Father, thank you for moving mountains for my child through Jesus. In Jesus' name. Amen.

Spirit-Fueled Boldness

Do you feel God's Spirit? Let's look deeper in Judges 6:34: "The Spirit of the LORD covered Gideon like clothing; and he blew a trumpet, and the Abiezrites were called together to follow him" (NASB). In this verse, Gideon was stepping up to lead his people against their oppressors. And guess what? He was not going it alone. The Spirit of the Lord came upon him, energizing and equipping him for battle. It was a divine empowerment for an impossible task.

Doesn't parenting a prodigal child feel like an impossible task sometimes? But just like Gideon, we don't have to go it alone. When we invite the Spirit of the Lord into our situation, we're not relying on human wisdom or strength but tapping into divine power.

And you know what's amazing? When we step out in Spirit-fueled boldness, others rally around us—just like the Abiezrites did for Gideon. Our courage can inspire our family, friends, and even other struggling parents, creating a community of warriors fighting for their children's hearts. So next time you feel overwhelmed, remember that you have the Spirit of the Lord on your side. Blow your proverbial trumpet, gather your support group, and step boldly into the fray.

Dear Father, thank you for your Spirit, who covers me. In Jesus' name. Amen.

Spiritual Awakening

Is your child spiritually asleep? Acts 20:9 offers a relatable moment.

> There was a young man named Eutychus sitting on the window sill, sinking into a deep sleep; and as Paul kept on talking, Eutychus was overcome by sleep and fell down from the third floor, and was picked up dead. (NASB)

This story of Eutychus is about more than an accident. It's also a metaphor for awakening. The young man fell into a deep sleep, leading to a literal fall, much like our children can sometimes drift into spiritual lethargy, losing their footing in faith.

Watching our children fall away from their beliefs can be heart-wrenching. But Eutychus' story doesn't end with the fall. He was miraculously brought back to life, symbolizing hope and renewal. This account reassures us that no matter how deep our children's spiritual sleep, there is always hope for revival. Just as Paul intervened for Eutychus, God is ready to step in for our children.

Let's keep this story close to our hearts as we pray for our children. It's a powerful reminder that God can awaken them from any spiritual slumber and restore them to life. Our prayers and faith can be catalysts for their spiritual awakening.

Dear Father, thank you for miraculously bringing the dead back to life. In Jesus' name. Amen.

Joy after the Storm

Could you use a dose of comfort and joy? Look at Acts 20:12: "They took away the boy alive, and were greatly comforted" (NASB). Remember Eutychus, the boy who fell from the third-floor window? In the aftermath, Peter brought Eutychus back to life, and the people were "greatly comforted."

Our wayward kids may have us pacing floors and losing sleep, but let's not forget the powerful aftermath when God steps in. Not only was Eutychus restored, but everyone around him found great comfort. It was a community win, echoing far beyond just one parent's desperate prayer.

God can write through your child's life a testimony of hope and comfort to you, your family, and perhaps even strangers who hear the story. So while the struggle with your prodigal may feel like an isolating and never-ending ordeal, remember that the comfort God provides is often collective. Hold on for your own moment of great comfort. Believe me, the impact of God's saving grace always ripples through hearts, renewing faith and inspiring others to believe in miracles.

Dear Father, thank you for this reminder today. It helps me believe that my prodigal is never too far gone for rescue and that you will always provide comfort and joy. In Jesus' name. Amen.

Transforming Family Chaos into Peace

Are you wondering if your child is beyond transformation? Let's look at the heart of Colossians 1:21–22.

> You, who once were alienated and hostile in mind, doing evil deeds, he has now reconciled in his body of flesh by his death, in order to present you holy and blameless and above reproach before him. (ESV)

Talk about a journey—from alienation to reconciliation, from hostility to peace. Isn't that the transformation we're yearning for in our families?

If you're in the middle of a struggle with your wayward child, these verses aren't just about your transformation. They're also a powerful reminder of your child's potential transformation. The God who reconciled us—when we were broken, flawed, and rebellious—is the same God who can reconcile our children back to himself and, by extension, to us.

Think about that. He took us from being "hostile in mind" to being "above reproach before him." That same power is available for your child no matter how far they've wandered or how entrenched in the battle they seem. Trust that the God who transformed you can transform your family too. Your child's current rebellion doesn't have to be their final destination because redemption is possible with God.

Dear Father, thank you that my child is not immune to your transforming touch. In Jesus' name. Amen.

Stand Firm

I know you're in the fight of your life for your child. Every bit of wisdom counts when you're battling for a soul. That's why I want to direct your attention to John 14:30: "I will not speak much more with you, for the ruler of the world is coming, and he has nothing in regard to Me" (NASB). Jesus tells us plainly the "ruler of the world" has no power over him. But Satan sure tries to wield power over our kids, doesn't he? Sometimes the devil will trick you into thinking he has some sway. Please don't buy into it.

Here's the deal: the Enemy can only enter where he finds an open door. Keep your spiritual house clean. Pray, fast, and stand on the Word of God. Ensure your armor is on so that when the Enemy comes, he finds nothing in your family to latch on to.

The world's ruler continuously seeks weak spots, but remember, he's already defeated. He has nothing on Jesus, and if you're in Christ, he has no claim on you. Let that encourage you to fortify your spiritual boundaries. Put on that spiritual armor and rest assured that you're backed by the one whom the Enemy can never conquer.

Dear Father, thank you that nothing keeps my child from you.
In Jesus' name. Amen.

Stay Alert, Stay Ready

Are you uncertain if your prodigal will return or if things will ever change? Lean into Mark 13:32–33.

> About that day or hour no one knows, not even the angels in heaven, nor the Son, but the Father alone. Watch out, stay alert; for you do not know when the appointed time is. (NASB)

Are you feeling out of the loop about when Jesus will return? You're in good company. Even angels and Jesus don't know the "when." We don't have a timetable, but we have a promise: God is at work. In the meantime, we're called to be alert and ready. Sometimes we are so tired and want to stay in bed, or we just run out of energy. But we need to stay alert, especially as we pray for God's touch for our lost children.

Your child's turning point could happen today, tomorrow, or years from now. Only God knows when events will take place according to his perfect timing and divine will. Don't snooze on your prayers or your faith as you wait to see how God's plan unfolds.

Dear Father, thank you that you will return to take your followers to eternity with you. Please help me stay alert and believe you can turn my child's life around. In Jesus' name. Amen.

Healing at the Heart

Are you frustrated that your child seems far from where they should be? Find peace in Mark 2:17.

> Hearing this, Jesus said to them, "It is not those who are healthy who need a physician, but those who are sick; I did not come to call the righteous, but sinners." (NASB)

Let's get real. Your child might be in a bad spot, but that's exactly where Jesus loves to show up. He's not intimidated by brokenness; he's drawn to it. Remember, a hospital isn't for the healthy but for the sick. Think of your home, prayers, and love as spiritual ICUs.

So go ahead and keep praying for your wayward child. Keep the faith. Doctors don't abandon patients who need them most, and neither does God. Stand strong. Jesus didn't come for the picture-perfect lives. He came for the broken, the complex, the lost. Your child isn't too far gone. They're precisely where the Great Physician can work a miracle. Hold on to that truth and never let go. In this journey, understand that every prodigal's path is a testament to God's relentless pursuit. Jesus specializes in turning the hopeless into stories of hope.

Dear Father, thank you for coming for the sick. I believe you can make my child well. In Jesus' name. Amen.

Straight Paths

It's tough to navigate the confusing maze of emotions, decisions, and confrontations when a child has gone astray. It's like walking through a foggy forest filled with traps. Find hope in Psalm 5:8: "Lord, lead me in Your righteousness because of my enemies; make Your way straight before me" (NASB).

Take heart! This is an incredible promise here. God can make your way straight even when it seems like there's no clear path. He leads in righteousness. That's his flawless character we're talking about. And you know what that means? You can rely on him to guide you past the foes of doubt, guilt, and despair.

Here's what you need to do: ask for divine guidance. That's it. God promises to lead you, so don't shy away from asking. Surrender your own logic and emotions to his righteousness, and he'll pave a straight path for you through this tough time. God is with you. So let him take the lead, and you'll find that even in the dark and confusion, his way is straight and sure. What a loving promise from our heavenly Father.

Dear Father, thank you that you can make my child's crooked ways straight and that you can straighten my way too. In Jesus' name. Amen.

Strength in Weakness

Parenting is a journey marked by moments of both triumph and challenge. In times when you feel overwhelmed or inadequate, find God's comfort in 2 Corinthians 12:9.

> He said to me, "My grace is sufficient for you, for my power is made perfect in weakness." Therefore I will boast all the more gladly of my weaknesses, so that the power of Christ may rest upon me. (ESV)

This verse is a gentle reminder that God's strength is present and made perfect in our weaknesses. Feeling weak or incapable as a parent is not uncommon, especially when we face difficult situations with our children. Whether we're dealing with behavioral issues, emotional struggles, or life's unpredictable turns, our limitations become glaringly evident. It's in these moments, however, when God's grace shines brightest.

God's assurance, "My grace is sufficient for you," is a powerful declaration that his unending support and strength are always available to us. His grace is enough to carry us through every parenting hurdle, every moment of self-doubt, and every situation in which our strength falls short. Embrace this promise. In every challenging moment with your child, remember that God's power is at its best when you feel you're at your weakest.

Dear Father, thank you for your grace and strength. In Jesus' name. Amen.

Submitting to God

You and I know that the battle for our kids is no joke. We're wrestling with evil influences trying to claim them. And let's be honest; sometimes it feels like we're losing, right? Here is winning news from James 4:7: "Submit yourselves therefore to God. Resist the devil, and he will flee from you" (ESV). James told us to resist the devil but first to submit to God. Submission is often misunderstood. It's not about admitting defeat. It's about aligning with the ultimate power source. When we submit to God, we're plugging in to his strength, wisdom, and strategies. Then the Enemy has to flee!

Let's get practical. Are you trying to fix your child's life with your strategies? Have you been leaning on your own understanding, scouring the internet for solutions, or getting everyone's advice? Pause. First submit to God. Get into his presence. Listen for his guidance.

The devil knows he doesn't stand a chance against a God-submitted parent. When you stand firm in God, not only will the Enemy flee, but you'll also show your child what real strength looks like. Align with God. Then stand up and resist those dark forces with God-fueled might.

Dear Father, thank you for defeating the Enemy. I surrender my prodigal and my life to you. In Jesus' name. Amen.

Surrounded but Not Defeated

Do you feel like you're cornered on all sides? Let Psalm 118:11 speak life into you. "They surrounded me, yes, they surrounded me; in the name of the LORD I will certainly fend them off" (NASB). The battle for your child's soul has you surrounded by temptations, bad influences, and poor choices. I get it. It's like an army encircling your home, and you're standing there, shield up, feeling outnumbered.

However, this verse from Scripture doesn't end with us being surrounded. It ends with triumph "in the name of the LORD." When the King of kings is in your corner, the odds change drastically. It's not you against the world; it's the world against God. And friend, those aren't great odds for the world! God has already overcome the evil world.

So look those armies in the eye, the ones made up of despair, addiction, or rebellion—whatever form it's taking in your child's life right now—and let them know they picked the wrong family to mess with. Call out to God. Use his name, the name that makes demons flee and mountains move. The blood of Christ can crush the devil in his tracks.

Dear Father, thank you, for though evil influences surround my child, you can fend them off. In Jesus' name. Amen.

God's Divine Clock

Do you ever wonder what God's clock looks like? We find the answer in 2 Peter 3:8–9.

> Do not let this one fact escape your notice, beloved, that with the Lord one day is like a thousand years, and a thousand years like one day. The Lord is not slow about His promise, as some count slowness, but is patient toward you, not willing for any to perish, but for all to come to repentance. (NASB)

I know waiting is hard. Every day feels like a lifetime when you pray for your wayward child to return to the Lord. But remember, God's clock doesn't tick like ours. In his infinite wisdom, he has this timing thing down to an exact science.

He's being patient. He wants all to come to repentance—even our prodigal sons and daughters. So what feels like an agonizing delay to us is God's grace window staying open just a smidgen longer for our children to walk back through. Lean on God's unchanging nature. Your prayers are bombarding heaven, and God's timing will ensure they land when and where they should. God's patience is not absent. The promise of divine timing allows more people to experience redemption. Trust him.

Dear Father, thank you for allowing more people to come to you in your perfect timing. In Jesus' name. Amen.

A Full Heart

Are you eager to see the day your child turns around? Let Psalm 54:7 encourage you. "He has saved me from all trouble, and my eye has looked with satisfaction upon my enemies" (NASB). Our God is a deliverer, my friend. When it seems like the Enemy is winning, don't forget who has the final say. Picture that day when you'll look upon your past troubles. They are resolved and defeated.

Hold on to this promise. God can rescue your child from their wayward path, and you might see it with your own eyes. Can you imagine the satisfaction? But it's not just about seeing the problem solved. It's also about witnessing the transformation. Imagine your child, once lost, now found; once far, now close. Think of the joy, the gratitude, the peace you will feel. It will be a testimony of God's grace, a story of redemption that you can share with others, bringing them hope too.

Are you ready for that day? Lock on to hope and envision the triumph that's possible. It will be a heart-filling, joy-spilling kind of day!

Dear Father, thank you for always being ready to deliver my child from the Enemy and rescue them from trouble. In Jesus' name. Amen.

The Aha Moment

Are you holding your breath, waiting for your child's aha moment of transformation? Take in Mark 15:39: "When the centurion, who was standing right in front of Him, saw that He died in this way, he said, 'Truly this man was the Son of God!'" (NASB). Sometimes it takes a critical moment to jolt us into awareness of God. The centurion had his, and perhaps all your child needs is one of their own. What looks like an ending could be a new beginning in disguise. Many times, the end of a road is the start of God's new path for our lives.

Even in the darkest hour, a spark of realization can ignite change. Your child's story isn't over, and neither is God's work in them. They are in a chapter of the story of their life. Only God knows the ending of their story.

Let's hold on to the promise that revelation and transformation are always possible. We may have the aha moment and not even recognize it. And remember, the best aha moments often come when we least expect them.

Dear Father, thank you that you can reveal to my child who you are and deliver them through the power of your love in a heavenly aha moment. In Jesus' name. Amen.

Embracing Your Unique Calling

Are you feeling like you have failed somewhere as a parent? Let's read 1 Corinthians 7:7: "I wish that all men were even as I myself am. However, each has his own gift from God, one in this way, and another in that" (NASB). Do you feel unequipped to win your child back? Think again. God has gifted you in a unique way to reach your wayward child. Just like Paul had a special calling to spread the gospel, God has chosen you for the challenging but rewarding job of guiding your child back to wholeness.

Don't compare your journey to anyone else's. Your gifts are uniquely tailored for you alone. Maybe you have the gift of relentless love, or perhaps you're a prayer warrior unlike any other. Whatever it is, lean into it. Your unique gift could be what brings your child back to a life of purpose and joy. Remember, your gift is a weapon against the Enemy's plans for your family. Embrace it and stand confidently. God has given you everything you need to be a good parent and win this battle.

Dear Father, thank you for gifting me with the unique opportunity to reach out to my lost child. Thank you for equipping me for this battle. In Jesus' name. Amen.

The Authority of Heaven

Are you fighting feelings of helplessness? Your help is found in John 3:31.

> He who comes from above is above all; the one who is only from the earth is of the earth and speaks of the earth. He who comes from heaven is above all. (NASB)

What a potent reminder that when we're grappling with earthly struggles—yes, even the heartache over our wayward children—we can lean into the authority of the one who is above all. Jesus comes from heaven, so he has a perspective and an unmatched power. We often get bogged down in the earthly details, the day-to-day battles with our kids, feeling like that's the only reality. But this verse puts us in check: our Lord is above all this. And because he's above all, he has the ultimate say.

In the middle of our spiritual warfare for our children's souls, let's not forget the power and position of the one we're fighting alongside. We're under the authority of the one who is above all earthly matters. So go ahead and claim this divine authority in your prayers and actions. You're not fighting aimlessly. You're aligned with the power from above.

Dear Father, thank you for ruling from heaven over all the earth, including my child. In Jesus' name. Amen.

God's Promises Hold True

Have you ever felt like the promises in the Bible are too good to be true? Let's talk about Joshua 21:44–45, where it says,

> The LORD gave them rest on every side, in accordance with everything that He had sworn to their fathers, and no one of all their enemies stood before them; the LORD handed all their enemies over to them. Not one of the good promises which the LORD had made to the house of Israel failed; everything came to pass. (NASB)

Isn't that amazing? The Israelites saw every promise from God fulfilled—no exceptions. Here's the takeaway: if God could do it for them, he can do it for you and your wayward child.

I know it feels like a forever fight when you're in the battle. But God's Word doesn't return void. You and your family can depend on his promises. Believe in his power to deliver, heal, and set free. Even when life seems impossible, remember that God specializes in the impossible. God's promises are your armor in this battle for your prodigal's soul. Stand firm, knowing not one word he has spoken will fail.

Dear Father, thank you for the promises you give to your people. In Jesus' name. Amen.

The Battle Isn't Yours

The struggle with your child feels like a constant battle. But consider this from 2 Chronicles 20:15.

> Listen, all you of Judah and the inhabitants of Jerusalem, and King Jehoshaphat: This is what the LORD says to you: "Do not fear or be dismayed because of this great multitude, for the battle is not yours but God's." (NASB)

Sometimes we feel like the world's weight is on our shoulders and that we have to fix everything. We see our kids making poor choices and think we must wrestle them back on the right path. But hear this: the battle is not yours. It's God's. God is already fighting for your child even when you don't see it. Maybe the Enemy throws all sorts of temptations your child's way, and you're scared you've lost them for good. But let me reassure you that God is bigger than any problem your family faces.

All we can do is surrender the situation to the one who already has the victory. The God who crushes armies and makes ways where there were none can surely guide your child back home. Just trust him and stop carrying the burden yourself.

Dear Father, thank you for taking full control over my child and fighting the battle for them. In Jesus' name. Amen.

The Cost of Ignorance

Are you tired of watching your child make foolish choices and ignore God? Psalm 53:1 says, "The fool has said in his heart, 'There is no God.' They are corrupt, and have committed abominable injustice; there is no one who does good" (NASB).

The world's noise can drown out wisdom, making it easy for our children to play the fool. The corruption of our world is so vast and permeates every aspect of our lives. Everything around us is enticing us toward the darkness. It seems sometimes easier to join them than to fight it. But you and I know better. Denying God leads nowhere good. Even though it's gut-wrenching to watch your child flounder, remember that God is still in control. The arrests, the lies, the manipulating, the anger, and more all may be consequences of your child's foolishness. But God has a way of turning things around, even for the fools among us.

Pray like never before. God specializes in heart transformations. No fool is too far away for a divine turnaround. Ready for a miracle? Invite God into the foolishness and expect a big change for your prodigal.

Dear Father, thank you for being in control. Only you can bring my foolish child back into your ways. In Jesus' name. Amen.

Trust and Pour

Does it feel like you're carrying the weight of your wayward child's choices? Find relief in Psalm 62:8: "Trust in Him at all times, you people; pour out your hearts before Him; God is a refuge for us" (NASB). Isn't that a relief? We can trust God with the mess, the confusion, and, yes, even the waywardness. We don't just trust him sometimes. We trust him "at all times." Even when things look bleak, God's got this. He's our refuge, our safe space to let it all out. Our challenge is to trust God when we are in the heat of the battle with our rebellious children.

Now are you ready to pour out your heart to God? The weight gets lighter when you do. Release your worries, your disappointments, and your fears to him. He can handle it. God's not just listening; he's also leaning in to bring restoration and healing.

It's okay to feel drained. Trust me, I've been there. But don't lose hope. Lean on God and let him be your eternal strength. After all, isn't it time we let the creator of the universe step in and turn things around?

Dear Father, thank you that I can trust you at all times. You are my refuge. In Jesus' name. Amen.

The Divine Mystery

Maybe you need a divine reality check today. Let's look at Proverbs 30:4, which poses critical questions.

> Who has ascended to heaven and come down?
> Who has gathered the wind in his fists?
> Who has wrapped up the waters in a garment?
> Who has established all the ends of the earth?
> What is his name, and what is his son's name?
> Surely you know! (ESV)

This passage serves as a divine reality check. As you find yourself waist-deep in the struggles, the failures, and the endless questions concerning your wayward child, this is God gently tugging at your spirit, asking, *Do you know who I am?*

Let's get real: parenting a prodigal can make us think we must be all-knowing, all-powerful, or ever present. But this verse reminds us that only God is all these things, and he has our back.

If you've been burdened trying to find all the answers, let yourself off the hook. You need to entrust your child to the one who knows all the answers. In the grand scope of life, your trials are but a mist, a fleeting moment. The one who holds the wind, the waters, and the entire earth also has your child in his hand.

Dear Father, thank you for this assurance that you have established the world, including my child. In Jesus' name. Amen.

The Door to Transformation

The relentless struggles with your child can leave you searching for answers. But listen, you're not powerless. Consider John 10:9: "I am the door; if anyone enters through Me, he will be saved, and will go in and out and find pasture" (NASB). Jesus refers to himself as "the door," the way to true life and safety. As a struggling parent grasping for answers, consider Jesus as the entrance to a transformed family life. Your prodigal may be out there lost, but Christ is the door through which they can find their way back home—back to peace, joy, and righteousness.

Today let's lean into this promise. Start with prayer. Have that difficult conversation. Extend grace when it's the last thing you want to do. Through Jesus, we're not aiming just for behavioral changes; we're also talking about soul transformation.

You may have banged on many doors for help— therapists, self-help books, even desperate Google searches late into the night. While those have their place, don't forget the Door who swings wide open with love, acceptance, and transformation for your lost child. God's door is always available and ready to walk through.

Dear Father, thank you for Jesus, the door of transformation for those who believe. In Jesus' name. Amen.

The Enduring Love That Waits

Do you believe in God's enduring love that waits forever and is everlasting? Psalm 100:5 tells us, "The Lord is good; his steadfast love endures forever, and his faithfulness to all generations" (ESV). If you ever need a boost of hope, keep this verse close to your heart. Why? Because God's love isn't a one-time event; it's everlasting. Imagine that—his love never ends, not even when our kids stray. When doubt tries to creep in, remember his faithfulness reaches all generations. Yes, including our prodigals.

His love isn't waiting for our children to clean up their act. It's already there, steadfast and unchanging. He's not waiting for them to become sober or go to church so he can love them. What a comfort to know that his love and faithfulness are there as a safety net, present even before our children return.

And in those moments when you feel like giving up, lean on this truth: God's love is a constant in this ever-changing world. Your unwavering belief in his love is a powerful force capable of bridging the widest gaps and healing the deepest wounds. Keep loving your child because God's love endures.

Dear Father, thank you for your goodness and for your love, which are everlasting and faithful to all generations. In Jesus' name. Amen.

september

Embracing God's Righteousness

Does it seem as if your child is too far away from God's touch? We find encouragement in Romans 3:22–23.

> It is the righteousness of God through faith in Jesus Christ for all those who believe; for there is no distinction, for all have sinned and fall short of the glory of God. (NASB)

You know what's liberating? Realizing you're not alone in this. We all fall short, not just your child. The real battle here isn't against flesh and blood; it's spiritual warfare.

That righteousness you're after? You can't achieve it alone and certainly can't force it on your child. It's a God-given gift, made possible through faith in Jesus. That good news is life-transforming, right? Let's look at it differently. Pray for a faith-fueled turnaround for your child instead of agonizing over their missteps. Pray for your child to receive a deep understanding of God's righteousness that can dispel the darkness looming over your family.

God is in your corner, and his righteousness is primed to transform your life, your struggles, and your child. It's time to trade human effort for divine righteousness through faith. The fight is far from over. But with God's righteousness, you have more than just a fighting chance.

Dear Father, thank you for not leaving me alone. I'm grateful that my child is not so deep into sin that your righteousness can't cover it. In Jesus' name. Amen.

The Eternal Spring of Life

Are you thirsty for God today? Get quenched by John 4:14.

> Whoever drinks of the water that I will give him shall never be thirsty; but the water that I will give him will become in him a fountain of water springing up to eternal life. (NASB)

This verse should help fill your thirst for God's touch. When you're thirsting for solutions, particularly for your wayward kid, entrust your child to the one who knows all the answers. Solutions that come from your own finite knowledge are like "waters" that will leave you thirsty again.

However, the water Jesus offers is a different story. This water doesn't just quench your thirst for a moment; it eradicates it and transforms into a wellspring within you that leads to eternal life. Just imagine what that could mean for your struggles. In Jesus, there are no quick fixes or half measures but a wellspring of wisdom, love, and resilience flowing out of you, covering your kid, your family, and your life circumstances.

When you're standing in the battle, feeling parched, desperate, and defeated, remember you have a wellspring inside you. God is the eternal spring of life. In him you will thirst no more.

Dear Father, thank you for filling me when I get thirsty for you. In Jesus' name. Amen.

The Fear of the Lord

Do you need refuge for your family? We find it in Proverbs 14:26–27.

> In the fear of the LORD there is strong confidence,
> and his children will have refuge.
> The fear of the LORD is a fountain of life,
> by which one may avoid the snares of death. (NASB)

Isn't this powerful? Especially for parents like you who are wrestling with the issues concerning their prodigal kid. These verses are brimming with hope and strategy.

"In the fear of the LORD there is strong confidence." This is where your warfare begins. Placing awe and reverence in God arms you with unshakable confidence. And guess what? It extends to all God's children. They "will have refuge." As you pray for your child to fear the Lord, you're fighting for them to receive a sanctuary of faith.

"The fear of the LORD is a fountain of life." Imagine your home as a fountain of life, where everyone is refreshed, renewed, and restored. When you cultivate an atmosphere of godly fear, it's like setting traps for the Enemy so your kid "may avoid the snares of death." The fear of the Lord isn't just religious jargon. It's your battle stance, refuge, and legacy.

Dear Father, thank you for allowing me to plant my feet firmly in your refuge. In Jesus' name. Amen.

The Final Judgment

Do you find it hard to see your prodigal like God sees them? Here is a good word in 1 Corinthians 4:5.

> Do not go on passing judgment before the time, but wait until the Lord comes, who will both bring to light the things hidden in the darkness and disclose the motives of human hearts; and then praise will come to each person from God. (NASB)

When our children are off course, it's tough not to pass judgment or jump to conclusions about what they're up to. But guess what? God sees what we can't, including the hidden motives of our wayward children's hearts.

God has the final say, not the world and not even our children themselves. The Lord is at work even when your child is blinded by their decisions. God's timing is perfect, and the hidden things will come to light. What's in the dark corners of your child's life won't stay hidden forever. When God shines his light on it, transformation happens. So let's let God be the judge. Our role is to keep praying, keep loving, and remember that no one is beyond God's reach. He's the one who brings the final praise. Trust him.

Dear Father, thank you for seeing the truth in my child when I can't. In Jesus' name. Amen.

Breaking the Curse

Do you feel like you're under a dark cloud? It's like no matter what you do, bad luck or worse decisions follow your family. Pause and consider Proverbs 3:33: "The LORD's curse is on the house of the wicked, but he blesses the dwelling of the righteous" (ESV).

Let's debunk the myth that you're cursed just because your child is struggling. You're not. If you're pursuing righteousness and seeking God, he promises to bless your dwelling. Your home, family, and struggling child are all included in this promise. You might be staring at the four walls of your home thinking they've seen too many fights and tears. But here's the crucial point: those walls can also be witnesses to God's blessing, to turnaround and transformation.

Keep pushing forward in righteousness even when it seems impossible or when you don't see immediate change. Your righteousness isn't just for you. It's also a legacy you build for your family. And remember, blessings follow righteousness. Hold on tight to this promise. Invite God's blessing into your home every single day. Even as your child strays, stand firm in truth and follow the Lord's ways. Keep the faith. You may be closer to a breakthrough than you think.

Dear Father, thank you for blessing my home for generations.
In Jesus' name. Amen.

The Final Warning

Here is a sober wake-up call today. It's found in 1 John 5:21: "Little children, keep yourselves from idols" (ESV). Short but massively powerful, isn't it? We live in a world jam-packed with distractions and temptations vying for our children's attention. Whether it's social media, peer pressure, substance abuse, or even relationships that lead them away from the Lord, let's call them what they are: idols.

This verse isn't meant to be a gentle nudge; it's an urgent, loving plea. And it's not just for our children; it's for us too. We might not bow down to golden statues, but do we bow our time, energy, and focus to other things besides God? In the battle for our wayward kids, we can also become consumed by our efforts, making idols out of our worries and strategies. The bottom line is that we must safeguard our hearts and theirs from anything that steals our focus from God.

Here's your challenge: make a list of things that could potentially be idols in your life or your child's life. Pray over that list and ask God to reveal the changes that you need to make. In doing so, embrace the clarity and strength that come from putting God first.

Dear Father, thank you for helping me keep my heart and home clean of idols. In Jesus' name. Amen.

The Glory in the Struggle

Do you ever find yourself crying out, *Enough, God! When will this change?* You're not alone. Even Jesus had a moment when he asked if there were another way. In John 12:28, Jesus said, "'Father, glorify Your name.' Then a voice came out of heaven: 'I have both glorified it, and will glorify it again'" (NASB).

I know your child's wayward journey makes you feel helpless. But remember this: even in the darkest corners of your child's life, God's glory can shine through. It's hard to see the silver lining in your child's rebellion. But God is saying he's already been glorified in the past, and he's going to do it again. His name will be glorified through your family's story in all the turmoil and sleepless nights.

Just like Jesus entrusted his circumstances to glorify God's name, you can do the same. Yes, the path is hard, and the fight feels endless, but you're a key part of a higher plan. God's going to use even this for his glory. That prodigal child? God may be at work right now to bring them back for his glory and your joy.

Dear Father, thank you for glorifying your name, even in my struggle. In Jesus' name. Amen.

A Symphony of Miracles

Are you craving a breakthrough? Let's read Luke 7:21: "At that very time He cured many people of diseases and afflictions and evil spirits; and He gave sight to many who were blind" (NASB). Many miracles happened in a single moment when Jesus walked on the earth. As we see in today's verse, not just one or two diseases were cured, but *many* were healed, evil spirits were cast out, and blind eyes were opened.

Do you feel like you need a miracle for your child right now? You're in good company. Just as Jesus performed multiple miracles in a single moment, he can do more than we ask or imagine, even today. Your child's situation isn't too complex or too far gone for a God who can do many miracles.

You're not asking God to work on one aspect of your child's life. You're asking him to transform their heart, mind, soul, and spirit. And God can do it—all of it—because multiple miracles are his specialty. Stay steadfast in faith. You're backed by a God who performs not just a single miracle but whole symphonies of them. Keep believing!

Dear Father, thank you for the sudden miracles you perform. Please help me wait in faith for the miracles to come soon. In Jesus' name. Amen.

A Teachable Heart

Let's plunge into Proverbs 12:1: "One who loves discipline loves knowledge, but one who hates rebuke is stupid" (NASB). Ouch, right? But let's get real; we all know that teens and young adults think they know everything. Yet God's wisdom tells us something different: loving discipline is the key to knowledge.

It can be disheartening if your child is rebelling, dismissing your guidance, or refusing to listen. But remember, a teachable spirit isn't cultivated overnight. And sometimes life needs to be the teacher. You've sown seeds of wisdom and discipline even if it doesn't feel like it right now. There may be a season of "stupid," as Proverbs puts it, but it's often a precursor to wisdom. Hold on to the promise that God can change hearts, making your child receptive to discipline and, ultimately, wiser.

Don't lose heart. Your prayers and efforts are setting the stage for God's intervention. Your child can go from rejecting reproof to embracing wisdom. During these trying times, it's important to remember that your role as a parent includes being a guide, not just a disciplinarian. It's about striking a balance between correction and understanding, guiding your child with love and patience.

Dear Father, thank you for changing hearts and being the God of intervention and healing. In Jesus' name. Amen.

The Heavenly Choir

Do you believe in heavenly hosts? Let's sink into Revelation 5:11: "I looked, and I heard around the throne and the living creatures and the elders the voice of many angels, numbering myriads of myriads and thousands of thousands" (ESV). Picture a heavenly host, a choir of angels so vast that you can't even count them. They're all around God's throne, praising him.

Why is this image essential for you, a parent battling for a wayward child? How does this change the battle? This verse is a reminder that the heavenly choir is with you. You're part of something much larger than your family's struggles. You are part of God's kingdom, and you have divine, angelic support.

It's a battle, I know. Some days, you probably feel like you're barely holding on. But on those days, remember Revelation 5:11. Visualize that choir of countless angels. Think of them as your backup, belting out anthems of hope and victory even as you feel downcast and desperate. God's heavenly hosts are a testament to his greatness and ultimate victory. And since you're a part of his kingdom, that victory over evil extends to you.

Dear Father, thank you for the peace my family can experience with a chorus of angels on our side. In Jesus' name. Amen.

The High Priest

Do you sometimes feel like you're on the front lines, battling for your child's soul? Let's cut through the noise for a moment. Hebrews 10:21 offers a fantastic reality. "We have a great priest over the house of God" (ESV). Think about it. In Jewish tradition, the high priest made atonement for the people's sins. We have Jesus, the ultimate High Priest, who has done that once and for all.

That means he's got you, and he's got your child. Jesus is not a spectator; he's active in this spiritual war you're fighting. He's advocating, intervening, and making things right in a realm we can't fully see. When the nights are long and the struggle seems too great, remember who's really in charge. You're not alone in this. We have a priest active in the fighting. We don't have to be perfect parents because we're under the leadership of the one who is perfect.

Let it build you up in the battle. Jesus is our High Priest. As you face each day, know that Jesus is interceding for you and your child. Your efforts are complemented and completed by his grace and power.

Dear Father, thank you that Jesus is not a spectator but a very present defender in the war over my child. In Jesus' name. Amen.

Eternal Hope

Sometimes as parents, we get tired. Let's examine
1 Corinthians 15:22: "As in Adam all die, so also in Christ all
will be made alive" (NASB). Is your soul heavy with worry
for your prodigal? It seems like it's the most brutal battle of
your life. But lean in and let me share a revelation. The same
Jesus who conquered death is alive and working in your
child's life.

Here's the hope: Every wrong turn, every moment
your child feels spiritually "dead," can be turned around in
Christ. As in Adam, we die—in our trespasses, mistakes,
and regrets—but Christ breathes life back into us. And yes,
he can do the same for your wayward child. Your love is
powerful, but God's love is transformative. He can awaken
what's dormant in your child and bring them to a new life of
purpose, meaning, and freedom.

Hold on to hope and let faith rise in your heart. You're
not fighting just for today. You're fighting for eternal victory.
And in Christ, victory over sin and death is already ours.
Keep the faith.

Dear Father, thank you for this uplifting truth today that
through your Son, Jesus, we are made alive in you. In Jesus'
name. Amen.

The "If You Can" Breakthrough

Does the world and everyone in your life tell you that your child's situation is impossible? Your answer is in Mark 9:22–23: "'If You can do anything, take pity on us and help us!' But Jesus said to him, '"If You can?" All things are possible for the one who believes'" (NASB). Notice Jesus' response: "If You can?" He turned the tables, shifting the focus from God's ability to our belief. And that's the key.

I know it is so hard to believe in restoration when it seems like our prodigals are way past a return. For years, they may have been making self-destructive and poor choices for their lives. But don't listen to naysayers or the world; God can make the impossible possible.

Let's get straight to the point: it's not about whether God can; it's about whether you believe he will. Doesn't this build up your faith? Activate that faith. You're not just hoping for a miracle but expecting it. Nothing's too hard for God, so don't put limits on what he wants to do. Ask God to help you to trust him to do the impossible. Ready to make room for the impossible? Believe.

Dear Father, thank you for making the impossible possible for my child and my family. In Jesus' name. Amen.

The Invitation's Open

Do you feel like your child's RSVP to a godly life got lost in the mail? Take a moment with Matthew 22:14: "Many are called, but few are chosen" (NASB). Here's the lowdown: God's unique and intimate invitation is out there, extended to many. But getting a seat isn't about earning or deserving. It's about responding. God is a patient host, and he has the table prepared and ready, waiting for your child to show up.

I know you have sent countless invitations of love, prayer, and wisdom to your child, hoping they'll come home, spiritually or literally. It's frustrating and agonizing when they don't RSVP. But remember, God is also calling them, and his invitation has eternal implications.

So don't lose hope. Continue to be a messenger for God's invitation to a whole, healed, restored, and free life. Just because they haven't responded yet doesn't mean they won't. The event isn't over, and their seat is still open. Keep praying; God's invitation has no expiration date.

Dear Father, thank you for preparing a table for believers to be with you. Thank you for waiting patiently for my child. In Jesus' name. Amen.

Spiritual Fitness

Between sleepless nights and endless worries, you might be entertaining all kinds of thoughts—maybe even falsehoods. *Did I fail as a parent? Is it too late for my child? Maybe things would be different if I had done X or Y.* Stop right there. First Timothy 4:7 says, "Have nothing to do with irreverent, silly myths. Rather train yourself for godliness" (ESV). Paul cut through the fog and advised us to train ourselves for godliness. Your focus should be on godliness, not on the what-ifs or the doomsday scenarios. When you're spiritually fit, you're better equipped to face the challenges coming your way, including the struggle for your child's soul.

Godliness brings wisdom, patience, and a strong foundation that no whirlwind of problems can shake. And remember, you're not doing this on your own. God is with you. Shift your focus from the myths and fears to something rock-solid: godly training.

Replace that time spent worrying with time in prayer and the Word. Switch out the anxiety for trust in the one who made your child and loves them even more than you do. Let godliness be your guide and strength. Your spiritual fitness is key when navigating these turbulent times.

Dear Father, thank you for helping me overcome worst-case thoughts about my child. In Jesus' name. Amen.

Even in Darkness, Light Shines

In the intricate parenting journey, we often encounter periods shrouded in darkness. Find hope in John 1:5: "The light shines in the darkness, and the darkness has not overcome it" (ESV). This verse is a profound reminder that no matter how deep the darkness seems, God's light is brighter still. His presence and guidance are constant, shining through the gloom and offering clarity, hope, and direction. When the way forward is obscured, when our efforts seem to be lost in the night, this light is our assurance that all is not lost.

As parents, we can take heart in this promise. The challenges we face, the worries that keep us awake at night are not beyond the reach of God's illuminating grace. His light can penetrate the darkest situations, bringing wisdom, comfort, and, most importantly, a path forward.

Let this verse encourage you. In times of uncertainty or despair, remember that the light of God is unyielding. It shines in and through you, offering guidance and hope. It ensures that even in the darkest moments, you are never alone, and the darkness will never prevail.

Dear Father, thank you for this powerful message of hope: no darkness will keep you from your people. In Jesus' name. Amen.

The Lord Fights for You

Do you ever feel helpless when fighting with your child? You can find your help and rescue in Exodus 14:14: "The LORD will fight for you, and you have only to be silent" (ESV). Moses spoke these powerful words to the Israelites during a moment of great fear and uncertainty. Today they remind us that even when we feel helpless, we are not alone in our battles.

As parents, we often feel we need to fix everything for our children, especially when they stray. However, this verse invites us to step back and trust God's intervention. It's a call to recognize that some battles are beyond our control and are instead in the hands of the Lord. Our role, then, becomes one of faith and stillness. Being still doesn't mean inaction; it means actively trusting God, praying, and waiting for his guidance and intervention.

In moments of worry or frustration, remember that God is with your child, fighting battles you may not even see. He is working in their life, often in ways beyond your understanding. Your stillness and trust in God can open the way for his mighty work in your child's life.

Dear Father, thank you for fighting on my behalf when I feel helpless. In Jesus' name. Amen.

The Next Generation

Are you uncertain about your child's future? Psalm 48:12–13 offers a moment of reflection. "Walk about Zion, go around her, number her towers, consider well her ramparts, go through her citadels, that you may tell the next generation" (ESV). These verses invite us to take a symbolic walk around Zion, God's city of refuge, observing its strength and beauty. God calls us to appreciate the enduring foundations and pass on this knowledge to future generations.

In the context of parenting, this Scripture passage is an encouragement to reflect on the strong foundations we've laid for our children. Despite the current paths our children have chosen, the values and teachings we've instilled in them are like Zion's towers and ramparts—strong, enduring, and significant.

Our children's journeys might be unpredictable, but their foundations are solid. We need to remember this, especially in moments of doubt or worry. This passage also reminds us of our role in passing on these values. Our experiences, faith, and wisdom are a legacy we offer our children, guiding them even when they are not with us. Trust in these teachings and values to guide them back to the right path in their own time.

Dear Father, thank you for the legacy of your love that I can pass on for generations. In Jesus' name. Amen.

One Sacrifice
Changed Everything

Sometimes it can feel like you're just putting out fires all day.
Well, guess what? Jesus felt that pressure, too, but in a divine
way, and he changed the game for all of us. Hebrews 9:26
shares,

> He would have needed to suffer often since the
> foundation of the world; but now once at the
> consummation of the ages He has been revealed to
> put away sin by the sacrifice of Himself. (NASB)

Christ's sacrifice was a one-time event with eternal
significance. No redo, no repeat—just one act that "put away
sin" forever. Imagine that power. That's the same power
available to you and your wayward child.

Here's the thing: your tireless sacrifices for your child—
while noble and meaningful—can never save them. Only Jesus'
sacrifice can. The power of what Jesus did on that cross is
enough to cover your child's past, present, and future mistakes.

So if you're feeling like you have to keep moving while
trying to make everything right, stop and remember this:
Jesus has already won the battle. All the sacrifices you feel
might never be enough have been completed in the one
ultimate sacrifice by Jesus.

*Dear Father, thank you for the truth that empowers me as I
stand in the gap for my child. In Jesus' name. Amen.*

Finding Your Child's Path

Do you feel weak? Let's draw strength from Acts 9:34: "Peter said to him, 'Aeneas, Jesus Christ heals you; get up and make your own bed.' Immediately he got up" (NASB). In this verse, Peter, filled with the Holy Spirit, healed Aeneas, who had been bedridden for eight years. Now imagine this: your struggling child, stuck in a destructive cycle, meets Jesus and immediately gets up—a changed person. That's the power of God!

I know you're tired, probably running on spiritual fumes, praying for that miracle. Let this verse remind you that Christ has the authority to heal, restore, and redeem. No matter how long-standing, your child's situation can be changed "immediately." Your fervent prayers, your sleepless nights— they're not in vain. You might be waiting for your child to "get up and make [their] own bed" to step into healing and responsibility. Hang in there. God's timing is perfect. Jesus Christ heals, and he can lift your child out of any pit they're in. Keep your faith rooted in this truth. A miracle is possible, and it can happen quicker than you think.

Dear Father, thank you for this truth: with one touch from you, everything can change suddenly. In Jesus' name. Amen.

You're Seen and Known

Parenting a wayward child can make you feel isolated, misunderstood, and even invisible. It's like no one truly understands the depth of your struggle or the magnitude of your love for that child. You might even feel like God is distant, watching from the sidelines.

Let's pause and consider what Psalm 139:1 says. "O LORD, you have searched me and known me!" (ESV). God has searched you and knows you. Picture that. The creator of the universe, who holds all things in his hands, has taken the time to search you out and get to know you intimately. You are on his radar not as a blip but as a priority. You see, no matter how lonely it feels, you're not alone in your parenting journey. God is with you, grasping every detail, every hidden tear, every desperate prayer. And let's be honest: if anyone can get to the heart of what's going on with your child, it's God.

So when the weight of your situation is about to tip you over, remember this comforting truth. You are known by a God who cares and is intricately involved in your life and, by extension, in your child's life. That's your divine advantage, warfare parent.

Dear Father, thank you for knowing me intimately. In Jesus'
name. Amen.

The Path to True Righteousness

Seeing our kids trying to fill a God-shaped void with worldly pursuits is heartbreaking. Paul said in Romans 10:3, "Not knowing about God's righteousness and seeking to establish their own, they did not subject themselves to the righteousness of God" (NASB). Maybe your child is striving for validation in all the wrong places—popularity, achievements, or rebellious adventures. But listen, nothing but God's righteousness can bring the peace and purpose they crave.

I know it's gut-wrenching to watch them chase after fleeting highs. You want to yell, "Hey, the answer isn't out there; it's right here with God!" But sometimes they must learn the hard way. And let's be real. Haven't we all had to learn some difficult lessons?

Don't lose heart. Remember, no one is too far gone for his saving grace. Your child might think they figured it all out, but God's love has a way of breaking through even the thickest walls. Lean into your faith and let God's righteousness do its work. His grace is sufficient and can transform even the most wayward hearts. Take comfort in the fact that God's arms are always open.

Dear Father, thank you for the hope that my child may one day realize that all they need is you. In Jesus' name. Amen.

Soul-Deep Suffering

Do your child's choices crush you? See how Jesus can empathize with you in Mark 14:34: "He said to them, 'My soul is deeply grieved, to the point of death; remain here and keep watch'" (NASB). Jesus gets it. He knows soul-deep suffering, the kind that pushes you to your limits. Jesus needed his friends to help him endure the grief. Remember, you're not alone when it feels like you're bearing the unbearable.

This season might have you down, but it's not your end. You may feel crushed under the weight of burdens, but you're called to keep watch, to stay hopeful. Why? Because Jesus, who suffered deeply, also conquered sin and brought redemption. The death and resurrection of Jesus is your only hope for victory.

Hold on a little longer. I know your suffering seems too great. Your situation may appear as dark as Gethsemane—the place where Jesus prayed before his crucifixion—but remember, resurrection morning follows. Ready to persevere? Keep watch for the miracles only God can bring. He's not a distant savior but a present help in times of trouble.

Dear Father, thank you for your Son, who knows the excruciating pain of the burdens I feel I can't bear. Thank you for being with me through it all. In Jesus' name. Amen.

Navigating Temptation

Are you tired of feeling desperate? Let's examine 1 Corinthians 10:13.

> No temptation has overtaken you except something common to mankind; and God is faithful, so He will not allow you to be tempted beyond what you are able, but with the temptation will provide the way of escape also, so that you will be able to endure it. (NASB)

Do you feel stuck in a loop of anguish over your wayward child? This struggle is common, but it's also one that God has prepared you to handle. He will never allow the weight of this battle to crush you.

Even when you're staring temptation in the face—tempted to give up, to doubt God, or to be consumed by fear—there's always a way out. God has already mapped the escape route for you. You've got this because he's your divine GPS. He shows you the way and gives you the strength to get there. In this challenging journey, remember that God has your back. He's empowering you to endure every trial and equip your child to find their way of escape from the Enemy's traps. His unending support fortifies your resilience and faith.

Dear Father, thank you for providing a way for me to escape despair. In Jesus' name. Amen.

Hope in Trials

Facing the heartache of a child entangled in legal troubles can leave parents feeling lost and disheartened. First Peter 2:13–14, though challenging, invites us to view these earthly systems and their consequences through the lens of faith.

> Submit yourselves for the Lord's sake to every human institution, whether to a king as the one in authority, or to governors as sent by him for the punishment of evildoers and the praise of those who do right. (NASB)

Authorities and the law are instituted by God and serve purposes beyond our understanding, including the correction and growth of those we love most. The moment your child faces earthly consequences, as difficult as they are, can be a turning point. Encourage your child to face this challenge with humility and responsibility, seeing it not as an end but as a step toward redemption and growth.

Meanwhile, God calls you to trust in his sovereignty, knowing he works through all situations for good. Let this trial strengthen your faith and hope in God's plan. He is with your family, guiding, refining, and redeeming. In his hands, even the most daunting situations are transformed into pathways of grace.

Dear Father, thank you for offering mercy and forgiveness to repentant hearts, even if my child breaks the law and faces the resulting consequences. In Jesus' name. Amen.

Healing in the Crowd

Perhaps you are still standing in the fight for your child's soul. Your child's cure may be near, as we see in Luke 6:17–18: "A great multitude…had come to hear Him and to be healed of their diseases; and those who were troubled by unclean spirits were being cured" (NASB). First, let's soak in the fact that people came to Jesus for two things: to hear him and to be healed. They didn't just stand around hoping things would change. They took action. They sought Jesus because they believed he could cure what ailed them—and their loved ones.

Are you desperate for a miracle? Have you been praying relentlessly for your child, fighting off discouragement? Listen, you're already in the crowd gathered around the Master. You're in the right place, doing the right thing. In our verses today, people were cured, and your situation could be too. Hold on tight, parent. You're where you need to be, and the healing power of Jesus is as available to you today as it was then. Don't let go because your miracle could be in the making. Keep that faith strong. You're closer to God's transformative power than you think.

Dear Father, thank you that you can cure my child and heal my family. In Jesus' name. Amen.

Listening to God First in Battle

Do you make decisions without going to God first? We all do. In Joshua 9, a group of neighboring men told Joshua they were from a distant country, deceiving him into making a peace covenant with them.

> "These wineskins which we filled were new, and behold, they are split open; and these clothes of ours and our sandals are worn out from the very long journey." So the men of Israel took some of their provisions, and did not ask for the counsel of the LORD. (vv. 13–14 NASB)

Joshua and the Israelites didn't consult God before making a covenant. Mistake, right?

We often make quick decisions out of fear or impatience, especially when our children are astray. Trying everything before laying it down at God's feet is tempting. But we need to consult God first in our battles for our wayward children. He shouldn't be our last resort. Take your concerns to him in prayer before making any moves. Your strategy led by God will be infinitely better than one born from desperation. Let's learn from Joshua and always ask for God's counsel first. Get his battle plan. Then watch as God's miraculous power turns your child's life around.

Dear Father, thank you for this reminder to go to you first before making quick decisions. In Jesus' name. Amen.

When God Weeps over Prodigals

Do you ever wonder how God feels about your wayward child? Look no further than Luke 19:41, which says, "When He approached Jerusalem, He saw the city and wept over it" (NASB). In this verse, Jesus wept over a city lost in its own sin, missing the opportunity for peace and salvation. He feels the same about your prodigal child—compassionate, concerned, and full of love. If you think nobody understands your pain, Jesus does, and he's right there weeping with you.

This Scripture passage doesn't just show God's emotion. It's also a call to action for us. Just as Jesus felt deeply for Jerusalem, we need to have that same spirit of compassion by not giving up on those who have strayed.

Accept this word of comfort today: God feels your pain and sees your tears. I know it's tough. It's draining. But don't lose hope. God hasn't. His heart aches for every lost soul, and that includes your child. So when you're feeling defeated and in despair, remember that you have a Savior who weeps, cares, and is tirelessly working to turn things around.

Dear Father, thank you for weeping with me and feeling the pain of my broken heart for my lost child. In Jesus' name. Amen.

The Power of *Speak, Lord*

Do you wish that God would speak directly to you? Today's verse comes from 1 Samuel 3:10: "The LORD came and stood, and called as at the other times: 'Samuel! Samuel!' And Samuel said, 'Speak, for Your servant is listening'" (NASB). This is an incredible moment in Samuel's life, but let's not miss the lesson here for us, especially for parents in the trenches with a wayward kid. Samuel's response to God is a template for us: "Speak, for Your servant is listening."

In our warfare for our families, one of the most potent stances we can take is that of a listener to God's voice. We often want to do the talking, laying out our plans, our worries, and our strategies to God. But Samuel taught us first to listen.

How does this translate into strategy? When you listen to God, you align your plans with his, and that's where the real power is. Do you want to get your prodigal back? In a loud world, where everyone is shouting to be heard, you must turn down the noise and clatter and get in a quiet place in the presence of God so that you can hear him clearly when he speaks.

Dear Father, thank you for still speaking today. In Jesus' name.
Amen.

Courage for the Fight

I want you to know that many understand your pain, your sleepless nights, and your battle-worn soul. It's tough. But today let's ground ourselves in John 16:33: "These things I have spoken to you so that in Me you may have peace. In the world you have tribulation, but take courage; I have overcome the world" (NASB). In this mess, we can quickly lose our peace. But Jesus is saying, "Take courage." Why? Because he has already defeated the Enemy who is trying to steal your child. Your situation is *not* too big for a God who has overcome the world.

We're guaranteed challenges; that's the "tribulation" part. But, oh friend, that's not the end of the sentence! Jesus has already overcome those battles for us. He's our peace in the chaos, our strategy in the confusion, and our courage in the fight.

So before you battle for your prodigal, remember that you're walking not in your own strength but in his victory. That's where your peace comes from. You don't have to muster it up; you only have to step into it. Don't let your heart be troubled. Anchor yourself in his peace and let that courage rise within you.

Dear Father, thank you for the peace of knowing you have overcome the world. In Jesus' name. Amen.

october

Finding Your Life

Do you feel like you are losing part of yourself as you try to parent your child? Let's examine Luke 17:33: "Whoever seeks to preserve his life will lose it, but whoever loses his life will keep it" (ESV). Talk about a gut punch, right? You're fighting for your wayward child, and it feels like your life is slipping away from you. You want to hold tight, control the situation, and save them. But here's the paradoxical gospel truth: you must let go to gain. Lose your life in Christ, and you'll find it anew.

In the journey for your prodigal child, it might feel counterproductive to "lose yourself" in prayer, faith, or surrender. But God's economy works differently. When you give it all to God, he takes over. And when God takes over, miracles happen. It's a tough pill to swallow, but it's liberating. In loosening your grip, you invite God to move powerfully. So go ahead and lose your life in him. Let go of it and give God control over everything. It's the best way to find your life and help lead your wayward child back home. Keep the faith.

Dear Father, thank you for allowing me to hand over my life and my child's life to you. Please help us let go of our lives so that you can take over. In Jesus' name. Amen.

Power of Unconventional Wisdom

I have something to fuel your fire today. Let's look at 1 Corinthians 1:18, where Paul wrote, "The word of the cross is foolishness to those who are perishing, but to us who are being saved it is the power of God" (NASB). How many times have you been told that your faith-based approach to parenting your wayward child is foolish or outdated? Too many to count, right? But the world doesn't get it because it can't get it. To them, it's nonsense. But to you, faith is where the real power is.

The wisdom of God often appears foolish to the world. But who cares? We're not looking for the world's approval. We're claiming God's power! Your relentless prayers, unwavering love, and belief that God's saving grace is available for your prodigal child are where life-saving change happens. Don't let anyone convince you otherwise.

Dare to continue to be "foolish," my friend. Keep believing, praying, and trusting in the cross's transformative power. Your prodigal child may not understand it now, but one day they might, and then you'll witness the power of the cross firsthand. Never stop standing strong in the power of God's wisdom.

Dear Father, thank you for keeping me strong so I can fight against the world's lies. In Jesus' name. Amen.

The Promise of Divine Protection

Do you ever feel like you need an extra level of protection as you pray for your rebellious child? Heavenly protection is certain for those who obey God, as we see in Revelation 3:10.

> Because you have kept my word about patient endurance, I will keep you from the hour of trial that is coming on the whole world, to try those who dwell on the earth. (ESV)

Let that sink in. God is saying, *Hey, I have your back because you trust me.*

We all know parenting a wayward child is like being on a battlefield. The Enemy wants to shake our faith, but God promises protection during times of trial, specifically during the end times. I know what you're thinking: *I'm living the trial. Where's the protection, God?* But remember that God's protection doesn't always mean that our immediate circumstances are changing. Sometimes it's the strength he gives us to endure, the peace amid chaos, or that unexpected phone call from your wayward child just when you feel like giving up.

Don't let your heart waver. God sees when you're enduring patiently even when the nights are long and your heart is heavy, and he's committed to standing by you. God will protect you.

Dear Father, thank you for your divine protection over me. In Jesus' name. Amen.

The Quiet Fight

Does your household need some quiet? Let's focus on
1 Thessalonians 4:11–12.

> Aspire to live quietly, and to mind your own affairs,
> and to work with your hands, as we instructed you,
> so that you may walk properly before outsiders and
> be dependent on no one. (ESV)

The journey with a wayward child can feel like a loud,
disruptive whirlwind. Sometimes it's easy to forget the
simple things. These verses gently remind us to settle down
and get back to basics. Live quietly. Mind our own business.
Work diligently. And why? So we can "walk properly before
outsiders and be dependent on no one."

Your struggle might be public, but the battle is intimate
and personal. You're showing an example to your child and
others by keeping a composed demeanor. Your behavior can
either escalate situations or inject them with God's peace.
Remember, our children are watching us even when they
seem lost. Let's show them what a life dependent on God—
not on the dark world—looks like. Try to dial down the noise,
focus on what's yours to handle, and let God do the rest.

*Dear Father, thank you that my quiet strength in you can be a
weapon to win back my child. Help me keep my eyes fixed on
you. In Jesus' name. Amen.*

The Resurrection Power in You

Are you drained, feeling like each day is a battle you're losing? Hold tight because Romans 8:11 has something for you.

> If the Spirit of Him who raised Jesus from the dead dwells in you, He who raised Christ Jesus from the dead will also give life to your mortal bodies through His Spirit who dwells in you. (NASB)

Listen up because this is your power boost. The same Spirit who raised Jesus from the dead lives in you. That means resurrection power flows through your veins. This isn't just "make it through the day" strength; this is a "raise the dead, part the seas, and bring the prodigal home" kind of power.

You might think, *But my child is so far gone.* Remember that there's no place too far for God's Spirit to reach. His love can break the hardest hearts, and his Spirit can breathe life into the driest bones, including your wayward child's. No prayer you pray, no tear you shed is in vain. That resurrection power is at work not only to sustain you but also to pursue and transform your child. Embrace the Holy Spirit, for you are armed with divine, life-giving power.

Dear Father, thank you that your Spirit and power are alive in me. In Jesus' name. Amen.

The Sacrificial Road

I know you are committed, but are you struggling with the ongoing sacrifice it takes to reach your defiant child? Lean into Mark 8:34: "[Jesus] summoned the crowd together with His disciples, and said to them, 'If anyone wants to come after Me, he must deny himself, take up his cross, and follow Me'" (NASB).

This journey with your child isn't a sprint; it's a marathon. And sometimes that cross feels heavy. Remember that the path to transformation often involves sacrifice. Your selfless love isn't going unnoticed—by your child or God. Sometimes, when your child is the hardest to love and living in utter disobedience, that is the exact time when they need love to open the doors to transformation. When they are the most unlovable is when they need love the most. Your willingness to carry this cross lays the groundwork for a miracle. Love never fails.

Taking up your cross isn't easy, but it's where you'll find Jesus walking with you most closely. The only way you can walk out of this kind of selfless love is through the power of Jesus. Ready to keep pressing on? Take up that cross and keep following him.

Dear Father, thank you for showing me the power of sacrificial love that is found only in you. In Jesus' name. Amen.

The Solution to Parenting Struggles

Are you feeling weighed down by the law of perfect parenting, which seems impossible to fulfill? Romans 8:3 is your lifeline today.

> What the Law could not do, weak as it was through the flesh, God did: sending His own Son in the likeness of sinful flesh and as an offering for sin, He condemned sin in the flesh. (NASB)

You're not alone in feeling weak or insufficient in parenting, especially when your child is lost and far from home. It's impossible to be perfect, but what you can't do, God already did. Jesus came to tackle the problem head-on, the root issue of sin that entangles both you and your prodigal.

God's Spirit offers you strength in your weakness. You're no longer fighting this battle in your power. Jesus took care of the sin issue. Our part is to lean into his Spirit for wisdom, patience, and love that we couldn't muster on our own.

You can face today's challenges with supernatural peace and resilience. With God leading the charge, you're not scraping by. You're more than a conqueror. Hold on to this promise and watch how it transforms your perspective and fuels your fight.

Dear Father, thank you for sending your Son as an offering for my sin. In Jesus' name. Amen.

God Walks before You

Do you wonder what to do next with your child? Find direction in Deuteronomy 1:30: "The LORD your God who goes before you will himself fight for you, just as he did for you in Egypt before your eyes" (ESV). This verse reassures us that just as God was with the Israelites, he is also with us in our parenting journey. What a great reminder that we are not alone in our struggles and challenges. It's easy to feel lost as parents, especially when our children are in the dark and being lured by the Enemy. When we feel this way, we can remember that God is going ahead of us, preparing the way and fighting our battles.

God's relationship with the Israelites encourages us to trust God's guidance and strength. To trust God during difficult parenting times, pray for wisdom and strength, read the Bible regularly for insight and encouragement, seek counsel from mature Christian parents and leaders, and remember God's past faithfulness shown in the Bible and your own life. Reflecting on his provision and deliverance can bolster your faith during current challenges. He is handling the situations you cannot and equipping you for the challenges you face.

Dear Father, thank you for going before me and reminding me of your faithfulness. In Jesus' name. Amen.

The Thundering Rescue

Do you need God to intervene right now? Today's insight from 1 Samuel 7:10 is an example of how God can intervene in a big way.

> Samuel was offering up the burnt offering, and the Philistines advanced to battle Israel. But the LORD thundered with a great thunder on that day against the Philistines and confused them, so that they were struck down before Israel. (NASB)

This verse paints a vivid picture of God's intervention at a critical moment. When Israel's enemy thought they were about to overrun God's people, the Lord intervened with a thunderous noise that threw the enemy into confusion and defeat.

Isn't it just like God to show up when the odds are against us? When it seems like the Enemy is gaining ground, God can intervene in powerful and unexpected ways. Don't underestimate the power of prayer and obedience. When God intervened, Samuel was presenting a burnt offering to the Lord, an act of obedience and worship. Likewise, your prayers and faithfulness are not in vain.

In your moments of desperation, remember this: God can still thunder from heaven to scatter the Enemy's plans. He is mighty to save, and he can route the enemies in your child's life just as decisively as he did for Israel.

Dear Father, thank you for when you claim a thunderous victory! In Jesus' name. Amen.

The Time of God's Favor

Ever feel like you are running out of time to reach your child? Find encouragement in 2 Corinthians 6:1–2.

> Working together with [God], then, we appeal to you not to receive the grace of God in vain. For he says,
> "In a favorable time I listened to you,
> and in a day of salvation I have helped you."
> Behold, now is the favorable time; behold, now is the day of salvation. (ESV)

This passage reminds us of the immediacy and potency of God's grace. It's a call to recognize that in every moment, God is ready to work in our lives and our children's lives. For parents of prodigals, this Scripture passage should bring our hearts an overflow of hope. It reassures us that it's never too late for God to intervene. His timing is always perfect, and his favor is always available.

Let these verses inspire you to renew your efforts in reaching out to your child. God's favor is upon us, offering hope and salvation even in the most challenging times. In embracing the immediacy of God's grace, we find the strength to continue guiding our children, trusting that God is working in their hearts right now, in his perfect timing.

Dear Father, thank you for your grace, which covers your followers for the day of salvation. In Jesus' name. Amen.

From Persecutor to Protector

Are you sick of your child's rebellious actions? Then these verses from Acts 9:3–5 are for you.

> As he went on his way, he approached Damascus, and suddenly a light from heaven shone around him. And falling to the ground, he heard a voice saying to him, "Saul, Saul, why are you persecuting me?" And he said, "Who are you, Lord?" And he said, "I am Jesus, whom you are persecuting." (ESV)

Saul was on the road to Damascus, his heart set on persecuting Christians. But God had a different plan. In a flash, Jesus confronted Saul and threw him off his course.

Just like Saul, your child isn't beyond redemption. God can and does use dramatic turnarounds to showcase his glory. After one encounter with Jesus, Saul—a major enemy of Christians—became Paul, one of the greatest missionaries. Talk about an about-face! Even if your child is rebelling against God and his ways, they can still repent and serve him. You might be staring at a Saul right now, but don't lose sight of the potential Paul. With God, the turnaround can be dramatic, earthshaking, and life-transforming. Your child's road-to-Damascus moment could be just around the corner.

Dear Father, thank you. You can immediately take my child's course and turn them around. In Jesus' name. Amen.

The Ultimate Security

Anxiety on overdrive? Can't stop imagining worst-case scenarios for your child? Let's cling to Proverbs 3:26: "The Lord will be your confidence, and will keep your foot from being caught" (NASB). Get this: your confidence doesn't come from your ability to control your child's choices or circumstances. Your confidence comes from the Lord. When you're walking through a minefield of fears and what-ifs, God has your foot, ensuring you won't trip.

And let's apply this assurance to your child too. If God is safeguarding you, imagine what he's willing and able to do for your child. The Lord can intervene even when they're making risky choices or running toward danger. I know you're wearing battle scars from your struggles, but hold your head high. Your confidence comes from a higher source—one that never fails. God's watching your step and steering your path.

Dig your heels into this promise. Let it anchor you when you start to drift into the sea of worry. In this relentless journey, lean on God's unyielding support. His strength is your fortress against every worry and fear. God is your unshakable confidence. Keep holding on to him.

Dear Father, thank you for boosting my confidence today. In Jesus' name. Amen.

The Unbreakable Bond

When your child seems more distant daily, it's easy to drown in despair, right? Well, pause for a moment and soak in comfort from John 10:28: "I give them eternal life, and they will never perish; and no one will snatch them out of My hand" (NASB). The devil is trying to snatch your child away, tempting them and luring them into the dark. But here's the good news: if your child has even a mustard seed of faith in Jesus, they are in God's hand, and no one or nothing can snatch them away. You read that right. No one.

We have to cling to this hope like a lifeline. Your prodigal may be messing up big time, but God's grip is bigger. It's a grip of eternal security, love, and redemption. Even if your child has yet to believe in God, remember that God is in the redemption business, my friend, and his currency is grace, unlimited and unearned, to anyone who follows him.

It's not about your ability to hold on to your child but God's ability to hold on to them for you. Keep praying, believing, and loving, even when it's hard. Your child isn't too far gone.

Dear Father, thank you for giving eternal life to those in your hands. In Jesus' name. Amen.

Unleashing the Power

Are you weary from the constant tug-of-war with your child's choices? Let's get a revelation from Deuteronomy 33:17, where Moses proclaimed his final blessing over the tribe of Joseph.

> As the firstborn of his ox, majesty is his, and his horns are the horns of the wild ox; with them he will gore the peoples all at once, to the ends of the earth. And those are the ten thousands of Ephraim, and those are the thousands of Manasseh. (NASB)

These words are a weapon. God describes your influence like the horns of a wild ox—strong enough to move nations. Those "horns" are your prayers, words of wisdom, love, and faith. Think about the unstoppable power they have in your child's life.

You may be going through the toughest season, where it feels like evil has the upper hand. Don't let that shake you! Use your horns—the power God has given you—to push against those forces. His divine backing can reclaim your child. No demonic influence stands a chance when you bring God into the equation. Keep pushing through, armed with God's promises. The battle is his.

Dear Father, thank you for your words written in the Bible, which I can stand on today. In Jesus' name. Amen.

The Unseen Battle

Do you ever feel like you're doing everything right but still not seeing a change in your wayward child? Let's take a look at Matthew 25:44, where Jesus described the final judgment.

> They themselves also will answer, "Lord, when did we see You hungry, or thirsty, or as a stranger, or naked, or sick, or in prison, and did not take care of You?" (NASB)

These folks missed it. They were so focused on their own understanding that they failed to recognize Jesus in the needy around them. And sometimes we can be so focused on the struggle that we miss what God is doing. The fight for your child's soul isn't just about your child; it's also a spiritual development course for you. It's easy to get so wrapped up in their issues that you overlook the Jesus moments— opportunities for grace, forgiveness, and transformative love—in your own life.

While you're fervently praying for your child, don't forget to keep your spiritual eyes open for what God wants to do in you. This battle is refining you, shaping you, and bringing you closer to God. Stay the course. Trust the process. Your child's story isn't over, and neither is yours.

Dear Father, thank you for helping me keep fighting even when I can't see the progress. In Jesus' name. Amen.

God Is Greater

When your child is lost, it feels like you're battling an army to rescue them. But today I want you to draw strength from 2 Chronicles 32:7.

> Be strong and courageous, do not fear or be dismayed because of the king of Assyria nor because of all the horde that is with him; for the One with us is greater than the one with him. (NASB)

Just pause and soak that in. Your battle may seem insurmountable, but the one who is with you is greater than any force you face. I know it's tough. You're probably emotionally drained, spiritually worn out, and mentally exhausted. But don't let the Enemy rob you of this truth: God is greater.

What do we do? We cling to God and embrace courage as our new normal. We can pray for victory for our wayward children not by our might but by God's incredible power. When we lock arms with the Lord, the odds tip in our favor no matter how hopeless the situation may look because God is greater than anything. When despair tries to take hold, replace it with determination. The outcome isn't in your hands, but the courage to face it is.

Dear Father, thank you for helping me be more courageous in the battle. In Jesus' name. Amen.

The Urgency of Transformation

Are you an exhausted parent? It's understandable. Watching your child wander is heart-wrenching. But what if I told you there's an opportunity for a new start? It is found in Acts 22:16: "Why do you delay? Get up and be baptized, and wash away your sins by calling on His name" (NASB). Paul, a man responsible for murdering countless believers, got a fresh start. He didn't delay. He got up, got baptized, and called on the name of Jesus.

It's easy to feel that your child is too far gone in the sins they've committed or that their path is irreversible. Let me remind you: if Paul, a persecutor of the church and a murderer, could start anew, so can your child.

The story isn't over. God's grace is just as available to your child as it was to Paul. What are you waiting for? The time to pray with urgency is now. Pray for your child's clean slate in the name of Jesus. Imagine their road-to-Damascus experience—their sins washed away, and their lives transformed. Your child's fresh start begins with urgent, believing prayer.

Dear Father, thank you for forgiving all our sins when we repent and for allowing us to get baptized in the name of the Father, Son, and the Holy Spirit. In Jesus' name. Amen.

The Waiting Game

I can't stand the waiting game. How many of us are experts at this, right? Let's learn from David in Psalm 40:1: "I waited patiently for the LORD; and He reached down to me and heard my cry" (NASB). If you're anything like me, you know that the struggle with a wayward child can feel like an endless season of waiting. Waiting for them to come home. Waiting for them to make the right choice. Just…waiting. But God hears our cries even when it seems we've been put on hold. Your prayers are not falling on deaf ears. God heard David's cry, and he hears yours too.

Let's redefine waiting, shall we? Waiting doesn't mean doing nothing. It means preparing, praying, and posturing your heart for the incredible works God will do. It's not a passive resignation but an active form of hope. It's a fertile ground where faith grows, and it's when you lean into God more than ever, yes, even in the chaos, even when your heart breaks over your child's choices. It's an invitation to see God show up big in a way that only he can. When you wait with expectancy, knowing God will show up, you change the waiting game.

Dear Father, thank you for increasing my patience. In Jesus' name. Amen.

White Garments of Victory

Sometimes we're tired and emotionally drained, and sometimes we feel utterly defeated. And yes, it feels like the world's influences are soiling the future we envisioned for our kids. But listen up; God sees your white garments in this spiritual battle. We see this in Revelation 3:4: "You have still a few names in Sardis, people who have not soiled their garments, and they will walk with me in white, for they are worthy" (ESV). This is awesome news for us today! Think of these white garments as your unwavering faith, consistent prayers, and unconditional love for your wayward child. You may not see it, but these make you worthy to walk with God.

Let's not let the grime of the world stain us. The Almighty reminds us that despite the mess, some of us hold strong, and our kids can too. These white garments? They're not made of linen; they're spiritual armor—light yet impenetrable.

Stand firm, warfare parent! Keep that armor bright and continue walking in faith. God is still in the game, which means we're far from losing. Keep fighting and remember that you're worthy of victory.

Dear Father, thank you for washing me white as snow and loving me unconditionally. In Jesus' name. Amen.

The Wisdom in Listening

If you're feeling so tired by the seemingly never-ending struggle with your wayward child, you're not alone. The Bible talks straight to us even when it's difficult to hear. Proverbs 15:5 tells us, "A fool rejects his father's discipline, but he who complies with rebuke is sensible" (NASB).

I know how it stings when your child dismisses your guidance or even mocks your faith. I've been there too. But the silver lining here is the word *sensible*. It hints at the power of listening and the ability to change course. Think about it: if your child isn't listening now, it doesn't mean they never will. God can stir their hearts to become receptive to discipline again, to heed your words, and to find their way back to him. Your job is to keep loving, guiding, and turning to the unchanging wisdom of God's Word for your strength and strategy.

Don't discount the power of your own willingness to listen—both to God and to your child. Sometimes we gain new avenues for connection when we're just willing to hear our children out, even if we don't agree. Intentional listening may be the catalyst for life-changing behaviors in your child.

Dear Father, thank you that I can hear you and that you make me a better listener. In Jesus' name. Amen.

Third Time's a Charm

Three is a powerful number. Let's talk about John 21:14: "This was now the third time that Jesus revealed Himself to the disciples, after He was raised from the dead" (NASB). On this third time Jesus appeared to His disciples post-resurrection, he had a point to prove. He was really alive, and his grace was in endless supply.

Let's apply this to our lives, especially when it comes to our wayward children. You may feel like you're on attempt three hundred, not just the third try, to get through to your child. But here's the beauty: Jesus doesn't give up on us, and we shouldn't give up on our children.

Grace didn't end at the cross; it began there. Each appearance of Jesus served as a fresh start, a new extension of grace, a do-over for the disciples. Imagine that kind of repeated grace being available for your prodigal child. It is! Grace is not a one-time offer. Like Jesus' repeated appearances, grace is an ongoing promise. Embrace it and know that every new day could be the day of your child's "third time"—their day of unmistakable, life-changing grace.

Dear Father, thank you for Jesus, who rose from the grave and is moving today. Thank you for the grace he offers my prodigal. In Jesus' name. Amen.

Time Is Ticking

We all know that time never stops ticking. We learn more about time in 1 Corinthians 7:29: "Brothers, the time has been shortened, so that from now on those who have wives should be as though they had none" (NASB). Paul reminded us that we're living on borrowed time. While he was talking about relationships, the lesson is clear: we must live with a sense of urgency.

Now why am I bringing this up? Because I know the days are long but the years are short when dealing with a wayward child. Sometimes we get so caught up in the day-to-day battles that we forget the larger war we're fighting—a spiritual one that's time sensitive.

God has given you this moment to act, pray, and fight for your child's soul. So don't wait. Don't say, "Maybe tomorrow things will be different." Do whatever you've been putting off now: having that difficult conversation, setting those boundaries, or ramping up your prayer life. The time has been shortened, but the power of God to bring your child back hasn't diminished. Let's use the time we have and use it well.

Dear Father, thank you for this urgent reminder to use my time wisely to bring my prodigal back home. In Jesus' name. Amen.

Touch and Transform

Are you feeling like you've done everything you can to help your wayward child? Look at this powerful and encouraging message in Mark 6:56.

> Wherever He entered villages, or cities, or a countryside, they were laying the sick in the marketplaces and imploring Him that they might just touch the fringe of His cloak; and all who touched it were being healed. (NASB)

People were desperate, feeling they had done all they could do, just like you. Maybe your child has been arrested or entered rehab once again or hasn't been home in a very long time, and you feel like you can't do any more to change their situation. Yet a simple touch of Jesus' cloak can transform their situations. What if your prayer, faith, and sheer will not to give up is that "touch" your child needs?

Keep the faith; one touch from Jesus can change everything instantly. Reach out, for God is not far. He's as close as the mention of his name. Your unwavering faith could be the conduit for your child's turnaround. Ready to stretch out in faith? Reach for him.

Dear Father, thank you that one touch from you can heal my child. In Jesus' name. Amen.

Trading Anxiety for Peace

I'll bet you could use some peace today. We discover how to find it in Philippians 4:6–7.

> Do not be anxious about anything, but in everything by prayer and supplication with thanksgiving let your requests be made known to God. And the peace of God, which surpasses all understanding, will guard your hearts and your minds in Christ Jesus. (ESV)

Okay, let's be real. Not being anxious about "anything" sounds like a tall order, especially when your child is going astray. But the apostle Paul isn't just throwing out a command; he's giving us the secret sauce—prayer and supplication with thanksgiving.

Do you have worries? Pray. Do you have urgent needs? Pray. When we pour out our hearts to God, we should also include thanksgiving. Why? Because gratitude redirects our focus from the problem to the Problem Solver. Even in the middle of chaos, find something to be thankful for.

And here comes the promise: "The peace of God, which surpasses all understanding, will guard your hearts and your minds in Christ Jesus." This peace is not worldly; it's heavenly. It doesn't mean the problems will vanish instantly, but you'll have a peace that doesn't make sense to the world.

Dear Father, thank you for replacing my anxiety with your peace. In Jesus' name. Amen.

Prayer Warriors Unite

You and I both know the fight for our prodigals is a real spiritual battle. Today's life changer comes from Psalm 35:1: "Contend, LORD, with those who contend with me; fight against those who fight against me" (NASB). The power of this verse lies in its raw simplicity. You're asking God to roll up his sleeves and get down in the trenches with you. And guess what? He's more than willing! If it feels like you're fighting alone, understand that God is not sitting on the sidelines. He's eager to step in and throw divine punches on your behalf. Remember, he's even more invested in your child's future than you are.

It's time to start praying this verse over your and your child's lives. Every time you feel overwhelmed, pause and speak this verse out loud. Let it be your battle cry. God has your back. So lace up those warrior boots and get to work. With God fighting for you, no struggle is too great, and no child is too far gone. Ask other warrior parents to join you in prayer. In your moments of desperation, when the odds seem stacked against you, let this verse be your rallying call.

Dear Father, thank you for fighting against evil for my child. In Jesus' name. Amen.

Train Them Up

Are you feeling defeated? Proverbs 22:6 says, "Train up a child in the way he should go; even when he is old he will not depart from it" (ESV). This verse isn't a guarantee but a guiding principle. It's the light on the path when everything else goes dark. If your child has strayed, it doesn't mean you've failed. Remember, free will is a powerful thing. Even God's first children—Adam and Eve—chose their own way.

Imagine your efforts as seeds planted deep within your child's soul. You've watered them with love, nurtured them with discipline, and shone upon them with your faith. It's hard when winter-like seasons seem to silence growth. But take heart, dear friend. Spring is God's promise, and it can come to every heart you've tended.

If your child seems miles away from the path you've set for them, don't lose hope. You've done the training and laid the foundation of faith and values. Trust the God of restoration to do the rest. Realize that the path you've laid isn't forgotten. It's imprinted in your child's heart. Life may lead them in circles, but circles can lead back to where they started—back to the values you've instilled.

Dear Father, thank you for giving me wisdom to instruct my child so they may remember your ways. In Jesus' name. Amen.

Transformed by Faith

Have you ever wondered if your child can truly change? Here is a powerful example filled with hope in Acts 8:9: "There was a man named Simon, who had previously practiced magic in the city and amazed the people of Samaria, saying that he himself was somebody great" (ESV). Simon's story in Acts is a testament to transformation. He was known for sorcery, misleading many, yet his life took a remarkable turn toward faith, and he was baptized.

No matter how deep in sin our prodigals appear, change can come. This narrative speaks to us as parents of prodigals. It reminds us that transformation is always possible, no matter how far our children may seem to have strayed. Their current path does not define their future.

We need to believe in their potential for change. Like Simon, our children can move from a life of confusion and misdirection to one of purpose and faith. This change often begins with our prayers, hope, and unwavering belief in their ability to transform. Let Simon's story be a source of encouragement. It illustrates that through faith and the work of the Holy Spirit, even those who seem lost in their ways can find a new path in Christ.

Dear Father, thank you for being a God of transformation. In Jesus' name. Amen.

Spiritual Warfare 101

Warfare parent, if you've ever felt ill-equipped or overwhelmed in your fight for your child's soul, you'll find 2 Corinthians 10:3–4 liberating.

> Though we walk in the flesh, we are not waging war according to the flesh. For the weapons of our warfare are not of the flesh but have divine power to destroy strongholds. (ESV)

Here's the big revelation: you're not fighting this battle alone, and you certainly can't fight with worldly weapons. This struggle for your child's future, this constant tugging at your heart, is spiritual warfare.

So quit relying solely on human wisdom and methods. I'm talking about worrying late into the night or endlessly searching the internet for solutions. Your God-given weapons have divine power. They can actually demolish strongholds—the ones trapping your child.

Imagine you're armed with weapons forged by God himself: prayers that pierce through the darkness, faith that shatters doubt, and a love that even your wayward child can't shake off. When we bring God into the equation, things start to shift. Strongholds crumble. This is not a fair fight, and that's a good thing. You're empowered by a heavenly Father who wants your child back as much as you do.

Dear Father, thank you for your divine power that destroys strongholds. In Jesus' name. Amen.

Faith beyond Outcomes

Do you struggle today to trust God's outcome? In the fiery trials of parenting a prodigal child, Daniel's words in Daniel 3:17–18 offer profound courage and demonstrate authentic trust in God.

> If it be so, our God whom we serve is able to rescue us from the furnace of blazing fire; and He will rescue us from your hand, O king. But even if He does not, let it be known to you, O king, that we are not going to serve your gods nor worship the golden statue that you have set up. (NASB)

Like Shadrach, Meshach, and Abednego, we stand at the edge of the furnace, trusting in God's power to bring our children back. Yet our faith is also grounded in a sobering "even if He does not."

This passage isn't about giving up hope but deepening our trust in God's sovereignty. We must understand that our ultimate trust in God transcends the outcomes we desire. While we continue to pray, hope, and believe for our children's return, we rest in the peace that, regardless of the path they choose, our faith and devotion to God remain unwavering. Trust deeply in God's presence through every challenge that honors him, regardless of the outcome.

Dear Father, thank you for helping me trust you deeply. In Jesus' name. Amen.

True Religion

You're still waging war for your wayward child, and it feels like you're in the battle all alone. Let me remind you that the battle isn't just about what you're fighting against but also what you're fighting for. James 1:27 is our wake-up call today. "Religion that is pure and undefiled before God the Father is this: to visit orphans and widows in their affliction, and to keep oneself unstained from the world" (ESV).

God is not as interested in our religious activities as he is in how we demonstrate his love. And let's be honest: we're called to love our households first. Our struggling kids, who might as well be spiritual orphans lost in the world, desperately need to see God's love in action.

The call to "visit orphans and widows" also means being there for your child in their emotional and spiritual affliction. Show up for them even when it's hard, especially when it's hard. They need to know you're a safe haven, reflecting God's unwavering love. And what about keeping ourselves "unstained from the world"? Friends, we risk losing our influence if we succumb to discouragement, anger, or even apathy. Let your religion be the kind that turns hearts back home.

Dear Father, thank you for the power of pure, unadulterated love and integrity in this war. In Jesus' name. Amen.

The Cycle of Generational Curses

Ever felt like you're battling not just for your child but against a whole line of generational issues? Even if your family's previous generations had issues, you bear responsibility only for your own behavior, as 2 Chronicles 25:4 reveals.

> He did not put their children to death, but did as it is written in the law in the book of Moses, which the LORD commanded, saying, "Fathers shall not be put to death for sons, nor sons be put to death for fathers; but each shall be put to death for his own sin." (NASB)

King Amaziah understood something crucial: each individual is accountable for their actions. Yes, the legacy of dysfunction or sin can follow a family, but God's law clarifies that each person stands or falls on their own choices.

Here's the good news: you and your child are not handcuffed to past mistakes, whether yours or your ancestors'. You can both make new, life-affirming choices rooted in God's grace. The generational chain can be broken, and you're just the parent to start that change with God's help. Hold on to this truth. Pray it over your wayward child and over yourself. The past does not have to dictate your family's future. So let's get to breaking some chains.

Dear Father, thank you for breaking generational curses for my family. In Jesus' name. Amen.

november

Trust God in Your Struggles

Are you feeling beaten down by the constant struggles with your wayward child? It's draining, both emotionally and spiritually. But let's pause and consider Psalm 146:5 to learn where our help and hope come from. "Blessed is he whose help is the God of Jacob, whose hope is in the LORD his God" (ESV). Our help is not from worldly sources such as books or one-step formulas. Our unfailing help and everlasting hope are in the Lord our God.

God is in it for the long haul. He's not a fleeting solution or a temporary fix. He's the God of Jacob, the God of generations, deeply invested in you and your family's well-being. Trusting him doesn't mean you won't have battles, but it means you'll never fight them alone.

If you're at your wit's end, take a moment to lean into God. You'll find an anchor for your soul and a wellspring of hope to refresh your weary spirit in him. You'll also discover the divine strategy you need to help bring your child back from the far country of rebellion. You are blessed when your hope and help are in God.

Dear Father, thank you that I can trust you deeply as I watch the atmosphere of my home transform. In Jesus' name. Amen.

One against a Thousand

Do you feel like the Enemy outnumbers you? Find powerful encouragement in Joshua 23:10: "One man of you puts to flight a thousand, since it is the LORD your God who fights for you, just as he promised you" (ESV). Here's a simple way to understand this: with God on our side, we can overcome anything. Think about it. One person, backed by God's power, can face a thousand challenges. This verse reminds us that in tough times, we're not alone. God is always there, fighting our battles with us.

As parents, we sometimes feel like we're up against a thousand problems with our children. But remember, God's love can bring incredible change even when things seem impossible. No matter what we're dealing with or how deep into sin our prodigals are, we become unstoppable when we team up with God. Even a child who has lost their way can find their path back with God's guidance. Let's keep our hope that we will always fight with the one true God, no matter how insurmountable the odds against us seem.

Dear Father, thank you that no matter how many challenges surround my family, we only need you. In Jesus' name. Amen.

Guidance in the Journey

Are you at a crossroads, unsure of the right path? A compass awaits you in Proverbs 3:5–6: "Trust in the LORD with all your heart, and do not lean on your own understanding. In all your ways acknowledge him, and he will make straight your paths" (ESV). Here Scripture guides us toward a profound trust in God's wisdom over our limited understanding. It's an encouragement to rely not on our instincts but on God's omniscient guidance.

Trusting "with all your heart" means surrendering the illusion of control, a challenging but liberating act, especially for parents. We acknowledge that we don't have all the answers despite our best efforts. God's Word invites us to lean into a deeper wisdom to recognize that God's perspective on our children's lives is far more expansive than ours.

Submitting "in all your ways" involves praying to God for every worry, decision, and hope. It's a daily, even minute-to-minute, practice of handing over our parenting fears and aspirations, believing that he will guide us and our children. This Scripture passage reassures us that God's hands will make the path straight. It might not be free of obstacles, but it will lead to the right outcomes.

Dear Father, thank you for the promise that you guide me when I am lost. In Jesus' name. Amen.

Turning Away from Idols

It's heartbreaking to see our kids searching for satisfaction and happiness in all the wrong places—harmful relationships, substance abuse, or even achievements that lead them away from God. We can't find happiness outside of God, as we see in Hosea 14:8, where the Lord cried, "What have I to do with idols? It is I who answer and look after you. I am like an evergreen cypress; from me comes your fruit" (ESV).

This verse is a wake-up call. God says, *Why mess with fake gods when the real deal is right here?* God is the provider of all good things, the giver of life, love, and every perfect gift. So if you're discouraged, remember that the same God who provides for you wants to provide for your kid too. Don't forget to turn to him for wisdom, peace, and the strength to intercede for your child when they chase idols.

As idols leave your child dissatisfied, stand firm in your faith. They may see in you the contentment that comes from God alone. Keep praying, keep loving, and, most importantly, keep turning to the one who has the real answers. Let's put our trust where it belongs. God is our everything.

Dear Father, thank you for giving me all I have.
In Jesus' name. Amen.

God's Mercy

If you're losing sleep worrying about your wayward child, let's stay here for a moment and consider this powerful thought from Ezekiel 18:23: "'Do I take any pleasure in the death of the wicked,' declares the Lord GoD, 'rather than that he would turn from his ways and live?'" (NASB). Can you grasp the magnitude of that? God longs for those who are lost in their sins to turn to him and find salvation. He wants to show mercy to your struggling child and forget their offenses (v. 22). Maybe your child needs to hear today that their repentance will lead to an abundant and everlasting life.

Even though your child may be far from righteous right now, God sees them for what they can become and how he desires them to live. And don't forget that he also sees you, the parent striving for righteousness and doing the hard work with mercy. So take heart. When the nights are long and the worries pile up, remember that God wants to see your child turn from their rebellion even more than you do. Your prayers and efforts are not in vain.

Dear Father, thank you for offering life to those who trust in you. In Jesus' name. Amen.

Turning Weakness into Strength

Have you ever felt weak, hanging by a thread while fighting for your wayward child? Read Hebrews 11:32–34.

> Gideon, Barak, Samson, Jephthah, of David and Samuel and the prophets…quenched the power of fire, escaped the edge of the sword, were made strong out of weakness, became mighty in war, put foreign armies to flight. (ESV)

These verses lay it bare—the heroes of faith were not made of steel from the get-go. They "were made strong out of weakness." There it is. Weakness turned into strength! This is a balm for your soul.

Maybe your prayers barely escape your lips, or you're emotionally drained from all the confrontations. But God specializes in turning our weakness into his strength. This is the arena where God shows up and shows off.

Your current situation is the battlefield where God's strength is made perfect in your weakness. All those nights spent in prayer, every tear-soaked pillow—they're not in vain. You're building spiritual muscle. You're becoming a warrior. Hold your ground. Your weakness is not your final chapter; it's just the setting where God turns you into a hero of faith. With God on your side, who can stand against you?

Dear Father, thank you for making me strong in the battle of my weakness. In Jesus' name. Amen.

Ultimate Healing in God's Hands

You've shed enough tears over your wayward child to fill oceans, right? Your pillow has been a silent witness to your midnight prayers, your eyes a reservoir for the tears you've held back in public. Many parents have been there. But imagine a future where God himself wipes those tears away. We can find this truth in Revelation 21:4, which states,

> He will wipe away every tear from their eyes, and death shall be no more, neither shall there be mourning, nor crying, nor pain anymore, for the former things have passed away. (ESV)

God understands your heartache and promises to bring it to an end. If you're nearly out of tears, hold on to this divine assurance. All the suffering, all the anxiety, all the prayers are not in vain.

Your child might be making choices that have you losing sleep, but God is in the business of turning things around. And those who turn to God will experience complete healing in heaven, where there will be no more tears, pain, or death. This transformative, eternal change will make the here and now look like a blink of an eye.

Dear Father, thank you for that promised future when every tear will be wiped away. In Jesus' name. Amen.

Unburdened Hearts

Do you carry guilt or shame because of your child's choices? Soak in Psalm 32:5.

> I acknowledged my sin to You,
> and I did not hide my guilt;
> I said, "I will confess my wrongdoings to the LORD";
> and You forgave the guilt of my sin. (NASB)

Sometimes it can be hard to face our own shame. But the reward is so worth it! The beauty of confession is that it's the gateway to freedom. We can carry the world on our shoulders, or we can lay it at the Lord's feet. We can bury our sins, or we can bring them into his marvelous light.

Your guilt or shame doesn't define you; God's forgiveness does. If you're blaming yourself for your child's path, it's time to unburden your heart. You're not God. You can guide your child, but you can't control their choices. Remember, you are at war with the Enemy, not with your child.

So go ahead and spill your secrets out to God. Keep the faith. He's ready to remove the guilt and flood your heart with grace. Living with transparency, unburdened before God, paves the way for transformation. This is the freedom your soul has been craving.

Dear Father, thank you for forgiving me of all my sins. In Jesus' name. Amen.

Words of Life

Maybe you're up late again, scrolling through your phone to see if your child has finally texted you back. Your heart is heavy. In John 6:63, Jesus told his disciples, "It is the Spirit who gives life; the flesh provides no benefit; the words that I have spoken to you are spirit, and are life" (NASB).

Feeling powerless is an awful experience, but remember: Jesus' words are not just words; they're also spirit and life. They contain the power to break every chain holding your child captive. Imagine these life-giving words infiltrating your home, flooding your child's thoughts, and reviving their spirit. That's the kind of power we're talking about here. Your tears, prayers, and sleepless nights are not in vain. God's words don't return void.

Let the life-giving words of Jesus be your source of hope and strength. Don't underestimate the power of speaking life-giving words, rooted in the promises of God, over your child. The world's words are empty, but Christ's are full of life and spirit. Hold tight to this truth, take your worries to God, and let the Word do its work. Your child may struggle today, but God's words have the final say.

Dear Father, thank you. Your words are life and can change everything for good. In Jesus' name. Amen.

Unclean Spirits Be Gone

Do you feel like your child is under the grip of something you can't even see? Does it seem like a destructive force guides their actions, and you're helpless to do anything about it? You're not alone, and you're definitely not powerless. Acts 8:7 says,

> In the case of many who had unclean spirits, they were coming out of them shouting with a loud voice; and many who had been paralyzed or limped on crutches were healed. (NASB)

Here we see the apostle Philip was dealing with the same kind of spiritual heaviness. But through prayer and the authority given to him, unclean spirits were ousted, and lives were transformed. Just like Philip, you have access to that same power through prayer.

Don't underestimate the power of intercession. Sometimes our kids are trapped in ways that defy logic and understanding. This isn't just a matter of willpower or good parenting; it's spiritual warfare. When you're up against our world's dark, evil forces, God has a track record of breaking chains and healing brokenness. Your prayers have the power to rebuke unclean spirits and to heal the emotional and spiritual paralysis gripping your child. Trust God to shout into the chaos and bring peace and deliverance to your prodigal.

Dear Father, thank you for your healing power, which can deliver my child. In Jesus' name. Amen.

Unconditional Love

Sometimes it's so hard not to judge some of our children's bad choices. For me, Romans 14:1 was an eye-opener. "Accept the one who is weak in faith, but not to have quarrels over opinions" (NASB).

When your child begins to follow Jesus but makes decisions you don't agree with because of their weak faith, your fear and anger can be overwhelming. You might think, *How can they make such choices?* Or you may face each day expecting your child will argue again, be disrespectful, and disobey you. But let's shift focus. Instead of laying out a courtroom in our minds, why don't we lay out a welcome mat in our hearts?

Your child may be weak in faith right now, and that's okay. Don't allow that weakness to be the basis for your judgment. God is in the business of strengthening the feeble. Just as he strengthens us, he'll strengthen our children. Think about this: What if your unconditional love and acceptance are the strongest bridge and most solid path for your child to mature their faith? We can't control their actions, but we can control our reactions. Keep that welcome mat out and your arms open.

Dear Father, thank you that I can keep the welcome mat out for my child through your love. In Jesus' name. Amen.

Understanding Spiritual Battles

Do you ever feel blindsided by your child's self-destructive choices and wonder, *How could this happen? How could they choose the same wrong path again?* Luke 22:3 explains why. "Satan entered Judas, the one called Iscariot, who belonged to the number of the twelve" (NASB).

Let's not kid ourselves. The struggle for your prodigal isn't just physical or emotional; it's also spiritual. Judas, one of Jesus' own disciples, was susceptible to satanic influence, which led him to betray the Lord. Think about it: if Satan can enter one of Jesus' Twelve, no one is off-limits, including our kids.

But here's the hope. Just as evil seeks to infiltrate, the Spirit of God is far more powerful and desires to fill, guide, and redeem our wayward ones. Keep praying and warring in the Spirit for your child. While the Enemy is real, so is God's redemptive power. Never underestimate the lengths to which God will go to rescue your child from the Enemy's grip. God is so generous and has already given us his only Son. So you're not fighting this battle alone. Remember that God is greater than the forces your child is following.

Dear Father, thank you for the power I have over the Enemy influencing my prodigal and that you can deliver. In Jesus' name. Amen.

A Night on the Mountain

Do you feel like you're spending a whole lot of nights agonizing over your wayward child? Luke 6:12 says, "It was at this time that He went off to the mountain to pray, and He spent the whole night in prayer with God" (NASB). Notice that Jesus didn't just pop off a quick prayer and call it a day. He spent the whole night in conversation with God. That's intense. Sometimes the issues we face as parents are so heavy that they require deep, extended prayer times.

Look, I know how it feels. Your child might be away, but they're never off your heart or mind. Maybe it's time to pull a Jesus—spend an entire night laying it all down in prayer. And don't just ask for change but dialogue with God about your heart, fears, and hopes. You're not alone on this mountain. Like Jesus, we sometimes need a whole night or even a season of concentrated prayer to see breakthroughs. So don't rush it; God has all night. And trust me, it will be time well spent.

Dear Father, thank you for helping me pray and find more time for you so that breakthroughs will come soon. Thank you for allowing me to go right to you in prayer. In Jesus' name. Amen.

Equal in Love

Parenting is a balancing act, especially in families with more than one child. Let's examine James 2:1: "My brothers and sisters, do not hold your faith in our glorious Lord Jesus Christ with an attitude of personal favoritism" (NASB). Here we are reminded of a critical principle that extends into our homes: God calls us to love all equally, without favoritism. This isn't always easy, especially when our children have different personalities, challenges, and needs. However, showing preference can create divisions and hinder the loving atmosphere we strive to nurture.

James urged us to reflect Jesus' impartial love in our parenting. Each child is uniquely crafted by God and deserves unconditional love and equal attention. Favoritism affects not only sibling relationships but also how children perceive their value and worth.

Let's embrace this divine wisdom in our daily interactions. Treating our children with equal love and fairness mirrors God's impartiality and fosters a family environment where every child feels valued and loved. In doing so, we cultivate a home that reflects the inclusive and unconditional love of Christ.

Dear Father, thank you for helping me be an impartial parent. In Jesus' name. Amen.

Unchanging through Every Challenge

In the ebb and flow of parenting, amidst the trials and triumphs, one constant remains: Jesus Christ. We find this truth highlighted in Hebrews 13:8: "Jesus Christ is the same yesterday and today, and forever" (NASB). The fact that he is unchanging can bring profound comfort. In every challenge, from the sleepless nights of our children's infancy to the tumultuous teenage years to every moment of worry for our prodigal children, Jesus remains steadfast.

Hebrews reassures us that the God who has guided countless generations through their struggles is with us too. His wisdom, strength, and love are as available to us now as they were to those who walked before us. In moments of uncertainty or despair, this unchanging nature is our hope.

Let this promise fortify your faith. God's character—his goodness, mercy, and love—doesn't waver based on our circumstances. As you navigate the complexities of parenting, lean into the unchanging nature of Jesus.

Dear Father, thank you for being the same God who fights for me despite my different challenges. In Jesus' name. Amen.

Unleashing Miracles

Are your prayers bouncing back unanswered? Do you wonder why you're not seeing miracles? Reflect on Mark 6:5: "He could not do any miracle there except that He laid His hands on a few sick people and healed them" (NASB). That's right—Jesus, the miracle worker himself, faced limitations where there was unbelief. Now let's flip that around. What would happen if we crank up our faith? What if we dared to believe God could perform a miracle in our children's life?

Let's get this straight: miracles aren't limited by God's power but by our belief. It is hard to believe in a miracle when our children are far off the path we hoped for. Can you ramp up your faith? Your child's breakthrough might be a prayer away. Dig deep. God isn't holding back, so why should we?

Don't settle for just a few small wins when God wants to unleash a full-blown miracle. Faith is the currency of the kingdom, and you have an endless account. Ready to make a withdrawal? Believe big. Stand in faith, expecting that God can move soon.

Dear Father, thank you for stretching my faith to believe more deeply in the miracles you can perform in my broken child's life. In Jesus' name. Amen.

Unlock Freedom

Often the weight of the world seems to be on your shoulders as you fight for your wayward child. But let me share something life-changing with you. In John 8:32, Jesus said, "You will know the truth, and the truth will set you free" (NASB).

Freedom sounds impossible, right? But it's not, not with God. The truth isn't just a concept; it's a person, and his name is Jesus. The fact that he offers us the truth is life-giving. It breaks chains and topples lies. The Enemy wants to feed you despair, bring you feelings of guilt, and make you believe the lie that things will never change. But God's truth says otherwise.

So here's the strategy: be relentless in seeking God's truth. Let it fill your mind, guide your decisions, and fuel your prayers. Apply it like spiritual armor against every lie the Enemy throws at you and your child. And then stand back and watch what God will do. Yes, it's that simple and that powerful. This battle for your child's soul might feel like you're always going uphill, but don't underestimate the leveling power of God's truth. Let it free you from crippling fear and uncertainty. The truth sets captives free and equips warriors.

Dear Father, thank you for the truth and the freedom it promises. In Jesus' name. Amen.

God Knows How to Rescue

Listen up; great news comes from 2 Peter 2:9: "The Lord knows how to rescue the godly from a trial, and to keep the unrighteous under punishment for the day of judgment" (NASB). I know it can be excruciating to feel like you're surrounded by evil when your child stumbles down a path toward sinful influences you never wanted for them. But anchor yourself today in the truth that God knows how to rescue the godly from trials. Maybe you're up to your eyeballs in a trial, but God specializes in rescues. He can create an escape route for you.

It's not a question of if God can rescue you from evil; it's a question of when he will. And while only he knows the timing, your job is to stand firm in faith and prayer. No matter how far your child has wandered down an unrighteous path, if they repent, God can also rescue them. The day of judgment hasn't come yet. Keep fighting the good fight of faith even when it seems like the prodigal child in your life is a million miles away from a turnaround.

Dear Father, thank you for knowing exactly how to rescue the godly from trials. In Jesus' name. Amen.

Faith through Jesus

You're on your knees daily, calling out your child's name in prayer, but don't forget the most powerful name—Jesus. The name of Jesus has unmatched power to heal, deliver, and set captives free. We see this powerful truth in Acts 3:16. After healing a man who was lame from birth, Peter preached,

> On the basis of faith in His name, it is the name of Jesus which has strengthened this man whom you see and know; and the faith which comes through Him has given him this perfect health in the presence of you all. (NASB)

You know the hurt and ache from watching your child stray. But don't let your child's current state cloud the promise of God's transformative power. Through Peter, Jesus didn't just heal that lame man; he gave him "perfect health." If he can do that, imagine what he can do for your wayward child.

Even in the darkest moments, remember Acts 3:16. It's not just about having faith but specifically about having faith "through Him," through Jesus. That's the faith that transforms lives. Yours. Mine. And our prodigal kids'. Jesus is the best partner in this struggle. Let the name of Jesus infuse your prayers.

Dear Father, thank you that I can find healing and miracles in the name of Jesus. In Jesus' name. Amen.

The Alpha and Omega

Do you know that God truly is the beginning and the end? We find this in Revelation 1:8, which says, "'I am the Alpha and the Omega,' says the Lord God, 'who is and who was and who is to come, the Almighty'" (NASB). This verse changes everything, especially when your home feels more like a battlefield than a sanctuary.

Think about it. God isn't just the starting block or the finish line. He's the entire race. That includes every twist, turn, and obstacle you're facing right now with your wayward child. When looking into the eyes of a straying child, it's easy to forget that God saw this moment before you did, and guess what? He's already there and in the moments that come after.

So when your heart is breaking, remember this: the Almighty holds yesterday's regrets, today's challenges, and tomorrow's victories in his hands. Whether you see it or not, he's already at work in your child's life. Trust him, warfare parent. God is not just the author but the finisher of our faith, including the chapter on your family. Hold the line because the Almighty is with you every step of the way.

Dear Father, thank you for always being the author of my family's lives. In Jesus' name. Amen.

When God Steps In

If you're on the front lines, battling for your child's soul, I want you to zero in on Acts 13:11.

> "Behold, the hand of the Lord is upon you, and you will be blind and not see the sun for a time." And immediately a mist and a darkness fell upon him, and he went about seeking those who would lead him by the hand. (NASB)

This isn't just a story from ancient history. It's also a lesson in God's power to change lives even when things seem far gone. In the account, Paul and Barnabas encountered Elymas, a sorcerer actively opposing the gospel. Paul, filled with the Holy Spirit, delivered a chilling message: Elymas would be blind for a time. This divine intervention led to Elymas seeking guidance, literally groping in the dark.

How does this relate to your wayward child? Sometimes our children are blinded by worldly temptations, bad influences, or harmful decisions. And it might take a spiritual shake-up—a moment when God intervenes in an undeniable way—to get their attention. Elymas went from hindering God's work to being humbled and led by the hand. Your child, too, can go from rebellion to redemption, from blindness to seeing the light.

Dear Father, thank you for supernaturally intervening to make blind people see. In Jesus' name. Amen.

Unlocking Wisdom for the Battle

Are you feeling a bit lost about how to handle your wayward child? Find some guidance in James 1:5, which says, "If any of you lacks wisdom, let him ask God, who gives generously to all without reproach, and it will be given him" (ESV). This verse isn't a suggestion; it's an open invitation from the Creator himself.

The fog of confusion can settle in quickly when you're in the heat of the battle for your child's soul. But guess what? You have a lifeline. When you don't know what to do, ask God for wisdom. Don't hold back or second-guess. Ask. God's wisdom isn't a limited resource that he reluctantly portions out. No, God gives it generously—without reproach.

And let's get real: Who is better to seek wisdom from than the one who knows your child even better than you do and who loves them even more than you do? God is invested in seeing your family healed and whole and walking in his purpose. So the next time you are stumped, are worried, or don't know where to turn, ask God for wisdom. Then brace yourself for insight, clarity, and divine strategies to flood your soul.

Dear Father, thank you for the wisdom you generously give to me when I ask. In Jesus' name. Amen.

Unmasking the Enemy

Do you feel like you're just spinning your wheels, making no progress with your wayward child? Many parents have been there. Here's some news you need to know from 2 Corinthians 2:10–11.

> What I have forgiven, if I have forgiven anything, has been for your sake in the presence of Christ, so that we would not be outwitted by Satan; for we are not ignorant of his designs. (ESV)

You're not just fighting flesh and blood here; you're up against spiritual forces. It's not about rules and curfews. It's a battle for your child's soul. And guess what? The Enemy has strategies, but so do you, and yours are divine! Don't let the Enemy outwit you. Remember, he is cunning and deceptive. Get in the game. Be alert. Understand that your fight is larger than you see in the natural world. Ask God for wisdom to recognize the Enemy's schemes and for the strength to combat them.

Warfare parents, equip yourselves with prayer, arm yourselves with God's Word, and stand your ground. You are not ignorant of the Enemy's designs, and he should never underestimate the power you wield through Christ. Remember, you are not at war with your prodigal child but with the forces of evil after them.

Dear Father, thank you for knowing the Enemy's tactics and having the strategies to win my prodigal back home. In Jesus' name. Amen.

Unshakable Confidence

Intimidation and fear can be constant companions if you're walking through the battlefield for your wayward child's soul. Let's turn our eyes to Philippians 1:28, where Paul told the people that he wanted them to be fighting for the faith "and not frightened in anything by your opponents. This is a clear sign to them of their destruction, but of your salvation, and that from God" (ESV). Can we pause and marinate in this? Intimidation can be a constant companion if you're walking through the battlefield for your wayward child's soul. The Enemy wants you frightened, second-guessing, and drained. But you know what? Your courage is a neon sign that reads, "God's got this!"

I know, it's easier said than done. The stakes are sky-high. But this isn't just about the battle for your child. It's a reminder of a much grander narrative. Your very response to these challenges can be a living testimony of God's promise, power, and grace. Even amid the storm, standing tall is a clear sign that the Almighty backs you.

If you feel those knees buckling today, lean into this verse. Your steadfastness isn't just for your benefit; it also sends a message to the Enemy. You are not alone. The creator of the universe fortifies you.

Dear Father, thank you that you will destroy the devil and erase my fears. In Jesus' name. Amen.

Mastering the Heart to Win

Is your heart full of worry? Find relief in Luke 16:13.

> No servant can serve two masters; for either he will hate the one and love the other, or he will be devoted to one and despise the other. You cannot serve God and wealth. (NASB)

This verse isn't just about money; it's about where our heart's loyalty lies. We can't serve both worry and faith. If we're all in with God, then we can't let fear or disappointment rule our lives, even when it comes to our wayward children. Who's the master of your heart today? Is it the anxiety churning over your prodigal, or is it the God of the impossible?

We could be channeling the energy we pour into fear into life-changing prayers, actionable love, and transformative faith. God is already fighting for our children's hearts, so why don't we align ourselves with the true Master and join the battle wholeheartedly? Let's put our trust in him today and starve worry away. When God is the Master, things change, hearts shift, and, yes, prodigals can come home. We can stand firm, for we're not fighting alone.

Dear Father, thank you for allowing me to come to you and for replacing my heart full of worry with a heart of faith. In Jesus' name. Amen.

Courage amid Chaos

Are you feeling defeated and overwhelmed? Ever wonder if you're making any progress at all? Let's look at Acts 23:11.

> The following night, the Lord stood near him and said, "Be courageous! For as you have testified to the truth about Me in Jerusalem, so you must testify in Rome also." (NASB)

We see here that Paul felt discouraged, probably the same way you do. Just when Paul needed it, the Lord showed up at his side and spoke courage into his life. And let me tell you that God wants to do the same for you.

This struggle with your wayward child is not the end of the road. It's just a chapter in a bigger story God is writing. Your witness to God's work in your life may be challenging now, but it prepares the stage for future victories—just like Paul's witness in Jerusalem led him to testify in Rome.

So take courage, dear parent. Hold your head up high. God's not finished with you or your child. You're about to enter a new chapter, and you won't walk it alone. The Lord is by your side, urging you on.

Dear Father, thank you for the confidence you give me today to believe that you will show up when I need courage. In Jesus' name. Amen.

Endurance Rewarded

Does the struggle with your wayward child feel like a marathon you didn't train for? Let's look at Matthew 24:13: "The one who endures to the end is the one who will be saved" (NASB). We're talking about endurance, that grind-it-out, keep-the-faith kind of staying power. It's not just about starting well; it's also about finishing strong. And guess what? There's a promise attached: the one with endurance "will be saved." In a world that demands quick fixes, the concept of enduring can be frustrating. But when it comes to your child's life, you're in it for the long haul, right? Let's not forget that salvation and restoration often come after a season—or even seasons—of enduring.

Don't let the hurdles, setbacks, or long stretches of silence deter you. Keep the faith. Enduring is more than just waiting; it's active, hopeful, prayerful waiting. Stay strong. The finish line holds a promise that makes every step worth it. In this marathon, you're not a bystander but a participant, strengthened by God's grace. You're making a difference every day even when it's hard to see. Endure with hope, for your steadfastness lays the foundation for a future filled with God's blessings.

Dear Father, thank you for helping me endure when I am so weary. In Jesus' name. Amen.

Unshakable Inheritance

Do you feel overwhelmed by the wickedness you see around you? Find peace in Psalm 37:28: "The LORD loves justice and does not abandon His godly ones; they are protected forever, but the descendants of the wicked will be eliminated" (NASB). That's a promise worth holding on to. Regardless of your child's current choices, you, as a godly one, are part of a lineage of faith that God promises to preserve. Hold on. God loves justice, which means he's into setting things right. God won't forsake those who lean into his justice.

Your child can also step into this inheritance if they "turn from evil and do good" (v. 27). They can walk away from the wickedness that currently ensnares them. God loves to bring close and protect those who accept him. Your wayward child isn't a lost cause; they may be on the brink of being God's next and best comeback story.

In God, you have a firm inheritance, the one that stands against time's test and triumphs over transgression. Keep this hope alive: you are secure in God's faithful hands. You're in this for the long haul, and so is God. Ready to claim that unshakable inheritance?

Dear Father, thank you for protecting the godly from the wickedness of the world. In Jesus' name. Amen.

Unstoppable Victory

Do you know the true power for victory over the world is inside you? Look at 1 John 4:4: "You are from God, little children, and have overcome them; because greater is He who is in you than he who is in the world" (NASB). If that doesn't light your fire, your wood is wet! This verse is a battle cry for every parent fighting for their wayward child. The Christian life is not just about overcoming worldly challenges; it's also about being equipped for spiritual warfare.

John was warning believers of false spirits that seek to mislead us. I get it: the tug-of-war for your child's soul feels endless. Society, peer pressure, and, yes, even evil are constantly pulling them away. But let's not forget that the power within us is far greater than any force that comes against us. And with Jesus, we can help guide our children toward the truth found in him.

You're not going into battle unarmed. You're armed with the strength of God, the same God who brought the universe into existence with a word. So when you're feeling helpless, remember you're not powerless. When God is for us, who can stand against us? Absolutely no one.

Dear Father, thank you for the power of Jesus that lives inside me, overcoming the world. In Jesus' name. Amen.

Unveiling God's Plan

Perhaps you've been wrestling with the mystery of your child's waywardness. The questions are constant: *Why is this happening? What's God's plan in all this?* You're waiting for something like a trumpet call to sound and shed light on this darkness you're feeling. It's found in Revelation 10:7: "In the days of the trumpet call to be sounded by the seventh angel, the mystery of God would be fulfilled, just as he announced to his servants the prophets" (ESV).

Let's be honest; life feels like a series of trumpet blasts at the moment, each one echoing uncertainty and despair. But listen up, warrior parent; God has a plan. Yes, even now, during your most challenging chapter, God's purpose is to march forward.

God has promised that someday his mystery will be fulfilled, so even when we don't understand what's happening, God does. He has set a time to unfold his perfect will. Your struggle, your fight, your child—none of these have caught God off guard. Know that the God who unravels mysteries and speaks through prophets cares about you and your family.

Dear Father, thank you for revealing the answers when the time is right and promising to fulfill your plan. In Jesus' name. Amen.

december

Unwavering Faith

Do you think that your dreams for your prodigal are dead? This story of Elijah in 1 Kings 17:21–22 shows us that resurrection is possible.

> He stretched himself out over the boy three times, and called to the LORD and said, "LORD, my God, please, let this boy's life return to him." And the LORD listened to the voice of Elijah, and the life of the boy returned to him and he revived. (NASB)

We see Elijah's lesson of persistence and faith. Here he was, in a room with a lifeless child. Instead of succumbing to despair, Elijah stretched himself over the child three times and prayed fervently. You might be emotionally stretching yourself over your wayward child, praying with tears and fervor, begging God for revival in their life.

Your prayers are not in vain! The Bible says the child's life "returned to him and he revived." Imagine that for your child—a divine turnaround, a coming back to life, a revival. The story reminds us of an invaluable lesson: be persistent in your prayers. Keep stretching, keep praying, keep believing. God hears you, just like he heard Elijah. Trust that a divine revival is possible for your child.

Dear Father, thank you for bringing dead things back to life. In Jesus' name. Amen.

Valley Walking

Are you stuck in a dark valley as you fight for your wayward child? Take heart from Psalm 23:4: "Even though I walk through the valley of the shadow of death, I fear no evil, for You are with me; Your rod and Your staff, they comfort me" (NASB). Valleys are challenging, scary places, but the great news is you're not walking them alone. When your child is so deep in the pit of sin, God is right there with you, rod and staff in hand. Those aren't just a shepherd's tools but also weapons and guidance systems for the journey.

Think of it this way: God's rod drives away the fears, doubts, and evil forces that try to derail you. His staff pulls you back when you wander off course. That's double protection and divine direction all rolled into one. This is also a picture of how you can guide your child toward God. What incredible comfort this gives.

So lift your head, square your shoulders, and keep going. The valley may be dark, but it's just a passage, not your final destination. In the struggle, you have divine company, and he knows the way out. Hold tight. You're walking through, not setting up camp.

Dear Father, thank you for being with me in the deepest valleys. In Jesus' name. Amen.

Victorious Parenting

Do you believe that God makes your battle his own? The truth is right here in 1 Chronicles 18:6: "David put garrisons among the Arameans of Damascus; and the Arameans became servants to David, bringing tribute. And the Lord helped David wherever he went" (NASB). God is your helper in every step of the war.

Are you feeling overwhelmed? Take heart. Just as God was with David in his battles, he's also with you in yours. David didn't win by his might. The Lord helped him wherever he went. Your battle for your wayward child isn't yours to fight alone. God is right there with you, strategizing, comforting, and, most importantly, fighting on your behalf.

You see, God can take your concerns and parental heartache and turn them into a triumph. The same God who helped David achieve victory over his enemies can do the same for you. He can transform your child's rebellious heart and make your home a peaceful kingdom once again. As he walks beside you, God makes sure you experience his presence. So suit up for battle, but remember who's leading the charge.

Dear Father, thank you for being by my side in the fight for my wayward child. In Jesus' name. Amen.

Deep Sorrow, Deeper Grace

When the heavy weight of sorrow over your wayward child distracts you from other parts of your life or even your relationship with God, lean into Matthew 26:38: "He said to them, 'My soul is deeply grieved, to the point of death; remain here and keep watch with Me'" (NASB). Jesus understands deep sorrow. In his darkest hour, he invited his closest friends to keep watch with him. There's a lesson here. Don't bear your grief alone. Ask God into it.

What you're going through is painful, and it's okay to acknowledge that pain. Jesus didn't put on a brave face. He spoke his sorrow. You can too. But don't stop there. Keep watch with him. Prayer isn't just asking for change. It's also inviting God to be present in your pain.

Pour out your soul to him. Lay down your hurt at his feet. Keep the faith, for even in the depths of sorrow, God is there. Remain vigilant, for divine comfort comes in the watches of the night. Always remember that God is keeping watch with you too.

Dear Father, thank you for Jesus' understanding of the depth of my sorrow. I am so grateful you are with me in the pain while I am waiting for my prodigal to return home. In Jesus' name. Amen.

Victory over Darkness

It can seem like you're wrestling against unseen forces for your child's heart, and you are. However, you can find great news in Luke 10:18, where Jesus told his followers, "I watched Satan fall from heaven like lightning" (NASB). Some days, it feels like evil is gaining ground. Maybe your child has relapsed, has been arrested again, or never came home, and you don't know where they are now. Or perhaps they are defying you or failing to comply with the rules of the house. But let this verse remind you that Satan has already taken a fall. Your child can still choose the path toward victory in Christ.

This isn't just poetic imagery. It's the reality of the spiritual realm. Every prayer you utter, every scriptural truth you instill, every loving act—you're participating in the kingdom work that topples the Enemy. Satan may be putting up a fight, but he's already defeated. He might have some influence, but he doesn't have ultimate power. That belongs to God.

When it feels like evil is winning, remember the spiritual scoreboard. The Enemy's loss is already recorded. The Enemy's defeat is the promise of eternal life for those who trust God.

Dear Father, thank you that Satan will never win in the end. In Jesus' name. Amen.

Walking among Wolves

Do you feel like wolves surround you as you share the gospel with your child? Let's unpack Luke 10:3, where Jesus said to his disciples, "Go; behold, I am sending you out like lambs in the midst of wolves" (NASB). You've likely felt this way, haven't you? But let me share a truth with you: the Shepherd is still watching over his lambs. It might feel like wolves surround you as you try to speak truth into your child's life, but don't forget who's leading the flock.

Experiencing wolves can deepen your worry over your child, who is interacting with the anything-but-gentle world, regardless of whether their faith is strong or nonexistent. The threat of bad influences, rebellious decisions, and the Enemy's schemes can make even the bravest parent feel anxious.

So when you worry about your child, remember that you're not sending them out alone; you're entrusting them to God's care. And in doing so, you're teaching them to walk in faith, not fear. Even amid wolves, a lamb under the Shepherd's care is the true picture of resilience and peace. Your "lamb" may wander, but the Shepherd knows how to guide them back home.

Dear Father, thank you for knowing how to protect people and keep them safe from the evil world that attacks like a wolf. In Jesus' name. Amen.

Remember Your Creator

I know the road you're on with your wayward child feels endlessly hopeless sometimes. You might even wonder where God is in all this mess. Let's look at Ecclesiastes 12:1 together.

> Remember also your Creator in the days of your youth, before the evil days come and the years draw near of which you will say, "I have no pleasure in them." (ESV)

When you're in battle, remember your Creator. Yes, you want your child to do the same—especially "in the days of [their] youth"—but don't forget that this applies to you too. Your Father knows your despair and hurt; he is your biggest ally in this fight. God knows how your heart aches and how scared you can get.

You may think it's too late for your child. But let me remind you that it's never too late with God. The days may be evil, but your child is not beyond redemption. Keep fighting the good fight. With God, you're armed with the strength to win this battle. And one day, you may look back and say, *Look what the Lord has done. My child has come home, and God has transformed the impossible into a miracle!*

Dear Father, thank you for knowing what the painful battle feels like and helping me get through it. In Jesus' name. Amen.

Divine Healing

Do you feel like the darkness is winning over your prodigal child? It's time to anchor ourselves in the miraculous. Acts 28:8 says,

> It happened that the father of Publius was lying in bed afflicted with a recurring fever and dysentery. Paul went in to see him, and after he prayed, he laid his hands on him and healed him. (NASB)

When we think we're defeated, remember that the apostle Paul faced impossible situations too. Yet he walked in divine authority and healing. This authority was not just for biblical times; this power is also available today. Your prayers and spiritual authority as a parent matter. Just like Paul, you can lay hands on your sick situation—whether it's addiction, rebellion, or anything dark ensnaring your child. There is power in prayer, and there's power in a parent's touch.

Stay in the fight. Keep praying and keep believing. Lay your hands on that lost child in prayer and claim healing in the name of Jesus. You're not in this fight alone. The same God who worked miracles through Paul wants to work miracles through you. Hold tight; deliverance is on the way.

Dear Father, thank you for the miraculous healing you give the sick. I pray that you heal my child. In Jesus' name. Amen.

Walking in the Spirit

Are you a parent whose child is falling prey to the evil lures of the world? Don't forget what Galatians 5:16 says, "Walk by the Spirit, and you will not carry out the desire of the flesh" (NASB). The world is loud, and it's pulling at your child. But here's the secret: the Holy Spirit is louder and stronger, especially when we let him lead. This isn't just good advice; it's an ultimate game plan. Walking by the Spirit is like having the best GPS that knows where you are and where you need to go.

When you're up against what seems like insurmountable odds, lean into the Holy Spirit. Let him guide your actions, your words, and, yes, even your discipline. You're not just fighting natural battles here. You're contending in the spiritual realm. And in that realm, the Spirit trumps the flesh every time.

Here's what you can know: you're not alone in this fight. The Holy Spirit is your ally, guide, and source of strength. Remember to walk by the Spirit when things get rough—and they will. That's how you outmaneuver the Enemy and show your child the power found in Jesus.

Dear Father, thank you for teaching me to trust in your divine guidance as I walk in your Spirit. In Jesus' name. Amen.

Weathering Life's Storms

Do you feel like your family is caught in a never-ending storm? I hear you. But hold on to this thought from Proverbs 10:25: "When the tempest passes, the wicked is no more, but the righteous is established forever" (ESV). In a world that feels shaky, you have a steadfast foundation. Storms may be brewing, but guess what? They pass, and what remains is what's built to last. You're like a tree with roots deep enough to last through any weather.

So what's the storm doing? It might be shaking things up, but maybe it's also clearing out the bad stuff. After all, we discover what we're really made of during the tough times. You're made of strong material.

And does your kid, the one out there in the storm right now, make you worry? Remember, nothing is too chaotic for God to calm, and no prodigal child is beyond his reach. Maybe they need a reminder that if they confess their sins and follow God, God will give them the strength to weather their storms too. Ready to find peace amid the whirlwind? Stay rooted in the one who stills storms.

Dear Father, thank you for helping me stand firm no matter what, knowing you outlast any storm. In Jesus' name. Amen.

Weighed Down by Worry

Are you carrying a heavy load of worry about your wayward child? Let me share a lifesaver from Psalm 55:22: "Cast your burden on the LORD, and he will sustain you; he will never permit the righteous to be moved" (ESV). It's easy to be weighed down by worry. But let's get real: the burden is too heavy for us to carry alone.

The good news? We don't have to. God says, *Give me that heavy load you're carrying.* God's not just willing but also eager to take it off our shoulders. Ready to lighten your load? Now I get that letting go is tough. We're parents; we want to fix everything. But some things are above our pay grade. That's where God steps in. Our role in our children's lives is to keep loving, guiding, setting boundaries, and trusting that God is working out the bigger plan. Let's trust that when we cast our cares on him, he's got us.

When he says he'll sustain you, he means he's there to keep you going even on your worst days. It's like having the best kind of support system there is. No matter what news you get about your child, you won't be shaken.

Dear Father, thank you for helping me overcome my worries and for sustaining me. In Jesus' name. Amen.

When God Reveals Himself

Do you need a word or touch from God today? You can get one just like Samuel did. Look at 1 Samuel 3:21: "The Lord appeared again at Shiloh, because the Lord revealed Himself to Samuel at Shiloh by the word of the Lord" (NASB). Samuel wasn't just hearing about God; he was experiencing God directly. The Lord revealed himself through his word. Let's not miss the message today in the battleground.

The key here is the phrase "the Lord revealed Himself." Our ultimate aim for our families in spiritual warfare is not just that they obey or follow a set of rules but that they experience God personally. What better way to turn around a prodigal than for them to have a direct encounter with the living God?

Let's make room for God to speak in the lives of you and your family. Set aside time to read his Word, pray, and listen. Then pray specifically for God to reveal himself to your child and change them forever. Remember, a personal encounter with God can melt the hardest heart and light up the darkest path. Your battles are not just yours to fight. God wants to reveal himself in your midst.

Dear Father, thank you for speaking to and touching me and my family today. In Jesus' name. Amen.

Unlocking Unlimited Authority

Today's your day for a boost of courage and empowerment. It's found in John 17:2: "Just as You gave Him authority over all mankind, so that to all whom You have given Him, He may give eternal life" (NASB). Can we pause and soak this in? Jesus was given "authority over all mankind," including your wayward child. Now what was the purpose of that authority? So that he could give eternal life to those whom the Father had given him. Your child has the choice to accept the gift of eternal life.

You might feel powerless, but the truth is that you have direct access to the one who has the ultimate authority. Jesus is in the business of life transformation. He wants to partner with you to bring your child to his arms. Remember, Jesus delegates his authority to you when you stand in faith. Your prayers, love, and unwavering stand for your child are backed by divine authority.

You're not a bystander in your child's life but a key player in their eternal destiny. Step into that authority. Pray bold prayers. Expect big changes. After all, you serve a big God, and nothing is impossible with him.

Dear Father, thank you that Jesus has authority over all, including my prodigal. In Jesus' name. Amen.

The Power of Sacrifice

Sometimes as parents, we mess up too. Let's delve into 1 Chronicles 21:26.

> David built an altar there to the LORD, and offered burnt offerings and peace offerings. And he called to the LORD, and He answered him with fire from heaven on the altar of burnt offering. (NASB)

David's mistake was taking a census instead of trusting in God, and this act unleashed turmoil. But his repentance and sacrifice led to a fiery divine answer.

Are you wrestling with guilt over your own missteps or your child's rebellious choices? It's heavy stuff. Yet remember that David's turnaround came through giving up his pride to seek divine intervention. That's our cue, isn't it? Our sacrifices—like relentless prayer, wrestling away despair, or swallowing pride to ask for help—echo a heavenly call for change. And believe me, God listens. His response might not be fire from above but rather a clear, powerful shift that steers your family's journey toward healing.

God is noticing every sacrifice you're pouring into your child's life now, every battle you're waging against the shadows. Your steadfast stand to bind your family together sends up a flare to the Almighty.

Dear Father, thank you for witnessing my battles. I lay my efforts and broken heart before you, trusting in your restorative touch. In Jesus' name. Amen.

When Heaven Breaks Through

Have you ever felt like you're locked in a seemingly hopeless situation? I have some good news to share. Chains can be broken, and freedom is possible, as we see in Acts 12:7.

> Behold, an angel of the Lord suddenly stood near Peter, and a light shone in the cell; and he struck Peter's side and woke him, saying, "Get up quickly." And his chains fell off his hands. (NASB)

Peter was chained and guarded in a cold, dark prison cell. Then suddenly, an angel appeared, light flooded the cell, and the chains fell off Peter's wrists. Just like that!

Let's apply this to our lives. Maybe you're in a hopeless season. Your child's rebellion feels like chains that won't break. But remember this: when God steps in, walls crumble, chains fall, and the impossible becomes possible.

That angel didn't wait for Peter to figure out an escape plan. No, heaven broke into that cell and brought freedom. And the same God who sent an angel to free Peter is the same God who can free your child from whatever is holding them captive. When heaven breaks through, nothing can stand against it.

Dear Father, thank you for breaking chains and giving me freedom from the bondage of sin. In Jesus' name. Amen.

God's Unbreakable Shield

Are you feeling exposed, vulnerable, and under attack as you watch your child stray? Here's a rock-solid promise from 2 Thessalonians 3:3: "The Lord is faithful. He will establish you and guard you against the evil one" (ESV). It's not that God might be faithful or that he could be, but he *is* faithful. The two life-transforming actions from God in this verse—establishing you and guarding you—are not passive. These are proactive moves from a God fully engaged in your circumstances. God's not just watching; he's also working. While you're up late praying for your child's safety, God is actively establishing and guarding. His protection isn't a mere shield. It's an unbreakable force field against evil.

This is God in action. With God by your side, you can remain faithful to him even when your child's choices discourage you. When you're scared and think that the Evil One is attacking you, remember this promise. God's faithfulness is your fortress. In your moments of doubt, when fear grips your heart, let this truth be your anchor. Trust in his unwavering commitment to guard and guide you through every storm.

Dear Father, thank you for being faithful and guarding me day and night. In Jesus' name. Amen.

Finding Hope

Do you feel like it's too late for your prodigal? The answer is clear in Ecclesiastes 12:5–6.

> Man is going to his eternal home…before the silver
> cord is snapped, or the golden bowl is broken, or
> the pitcher is shattered at the fountain, or the wheel
> broken at the cistern. (ESV)

Here it talks about the silver cord being snapped and the golden bowl being broken, but this flowery language is saying not to wait until it's too late. You might feel time slipping through your fingers as you battle for your wayward child's soul, and I get it. I've been there too. But let me encourage you today: now is the time to act. If your heart is heavy with what-ifs and could-have-beens, that's your signal to dive deep into prayer and action. God's still in control. No situation is too dire for him. Time may be of the essence, but God is the master of time.

Lean into him. Pray earnestly. And then act. Speak love into your child's life. Extend grace when it's the last thing you want to do. Show them God's love through your actions because sometimes actions speak louder than words. Remember that as long as there's breath, there's hope.

Dear Father, thank you for showing me it's never too late for
my child. In Jesus' name. Amen.

When Your Prodigal Is Sifted

Do you feel like your faith will fail? Hold on to Luke 22:31–32, where Jesus said,

> Simon, Simon, behold, Satan has demanded to sift you men like wheat; but I have prayed for you, that your faith will not fail; and you, when you have turned back, strengthen your brothers. (NASB)

Sifting wheat from chaff is difficult work as harvesters must separate what's useful from what's not. It feels a lot like parenting, doesn't it? The world throws our kids into the mix, trying to shake their faith and ours. But here's a comfort: Jesus is praying for us. If your child has ever given their life to Christ, Jesus is interceding for them just as he prayed for Simon Peter. You and your child might be getting shaken up now, but don't lose hope. Jesus' prayers are powerful; they protect and purify faith. And after the sifting, there's strength. Like Peter, your child will have a story to tell, lessons learned, a faith that's fire-tested and true when they return to Jesus.

Keep steady, pray, and be ready to walk alongside your child through their trials. The sifting isn't the end; it prepares you and them for a stronger testimony and a solid foundation.

Dear Father, thank you for Jesus, who is praying for my family. In Jesus' name. Amen.

Small Victories, Big Impact

As we see in 1 Samuel 14:14, small victories matter. "That first slaughter which Jonathan and his armor bearer inflicted was about twenty men within about half a furrow in an acre of land" (NASB). Jonathan and his armor-bearer faced an army, yet their impact was extraordinary! They took out twenty men in a tiny area of land. It wasn't a massive victory, but it made an enormous difference. You might think what you're doing for your wayward child seems small—maybe just a prayer here and there, a text, a meal, or even a new boundary. Yet just like Jonathan, these small acts can create ripple effects in the spiritual realm.

Jonathan didn't underestimate what two determined, God-trusting individuals could do. Neither should you. Your prayers, support, and even tough love hold more weight than you think. Just as God was with Jonathan, he's with you, strengthening you to have a meaningful effect on your child's life. The battlefield might look overwhelming, but don't underestimate the power of small victories. Each prayer is a stone slung at the Enemy. Each act of love penetrates the armor of rebellion. And with God on our side, those small victories can shift the tide of war.

Dear Father, thank you for helping me keep fighting those small battles. In Jesus' name. Amen.

Witnessing the Divine

Do you ever feel like you need some divine intervention? Dive into Deuteronomy 4:33–34, where Moses spoke to God's people.

> Has any people heard the voice of God speaking from the midst of the fire, as you have heard it, and survived? Or has a god ventured to go to take for himself a nation from within another nation by trials, by signs and wonders, by war, by a mighty hand, by an outstretched arm, and by great terrors, just as the Lord your God did for you in Egypt before your eyes? (NASB)

This isn't just ancient history. These verses remind us that God does the impossible to reclaim his people. If he could speak through fire and perform miracles to liberate a nation, think about what he can do for your child.

Yes, it's a battle, but we serve a God who specializes in miraculous rescues. The same God who spoke through the fire and performed wonders to save his people is the God you're calling upon to save your child. Stay hopeful and keep trusting, holding on to the promise that God can do mind-blowing things to bring your child back home.

Dear Father, thank you for being a God of signs and wonders. Thank you for your divine touch, which can rescue my child. In Jesus' name. Amen.

Word and Wonders

Do you feel like you're at a standstill with your wayward child? Check out Mark 7:29–30, where Jesus told the gentile woman, "'Because of this answer, go; the demon has gone out of your daughter.' And after going back to her home, she found the child lying on the bed, and the demon gone" (NASB).

All it took was a word from Jesus, and everything changed. That woman believed and acted on Jesus' word, and guess what? Her situation was turned around. The demon was cast out from her daughter. Even more astounding, the mother was nowhere near the daughter when God moved suddenly.

Maybe your child is struggling with addiction or anxiety. These are issues that God can deliver them from. Stand in faith that God can do this soon. Even if you don't know where your child is, God can act. Don't underestimate the power of God's Word in your life and your child's. Keep the faith. God's promises are your ammunition. Dare to believe that one word from God can change everything. Ready to return to your home, your situation, and find it transformed? Claim that word.

Dear Father, thank you for delivering people from the demons of this world. In Jesus' name. Amen.

Demonstrate Mercy

Are you feeling disappointed today that your child is still pursuing sinful and destructive habits? I get it. But listen, Romans 11:32 offers an uplifting message. "God has shut up all in disobedience, so that He may show mercy to all" (NASB). Here's the deal: everyone sins. Your child, you, everyone you encounter today—we have all sinned. But Jesus came to earth, died on the cross, and was raised again to save all who come to him. He offers salvation to your child, you, and everyone you meet.

So take heart, warrior parent. When you get frustrated over your child's sins, remember yours and remember the great mercy of God, who has forgiven your sins and remembers them no more. This does not excuse the real-world consequences of your child's choices, but even when your child faces punishment, you can have hope that God's mercy is still available to them. And maybe today God is calling you to show your child an act of mercy. This may be what your child needs to fully understand the overflowing mercy of God. Be an example of mercy today.

Dear Father, thank you for your mercy. In Jesus' name. Amen.

You Are Never Alone

Are you sick from worries over your child today? Hold on to this promise in Joshua 1:5.

> No man shall be able to stand before you all the days of your life. Just as I was with Moses, so I will be with you. I will not leave you or forsake you. (ESV)

This Scripture passage is a comforting reminder of God's constant presence in our lives. God promised his support to Joshua, telling Joshua that God would be with him as Joshua faced many uncertainties in a new leadership role.

Regardless of the struggles we face leading our children, God's promise to Joshua extends to us: he will never leave or forsake us. This assurance can transform how we approach our parenting journey, especially in difficult times. Instead of feeling overwhelmed, we can stand firm, knowing God is with us, providing strength and guidance.

This verse is an invitation to trust deeply in God's presence. In times of worry or doubt, we are encouraged to remember that we are never alone. God's steadfast presence is a source of courage and peace. God is there, an unfailing support and guide, just as he was with Joshua.

Dear Father, thank you for always being with me. In Jesus' name. Amen.

Heavenly Praise

Are you finding it hard to muster any praise for God? Maybe you are feeling isolated as you pray for your wayward child. Take in Luke 2:13–14: "Suddenly there appeared with the angel a multitude of the heavenly army of angels praising God and saying, 'Glory to God in the highest'" (NASB). See, you're not alone in this. There are angels all around you every day. They can praise God for you. This heavenly host, a divine support system, is ready to step in as God's plan unfolds. Just as they celebrated the miracle of Jesus' birth, they're also ready to celebrate the miracle in your child's life.

Praising in the storm is very difficult. But remember that God hears your unique noise when you praise him in the darkest hour while you are waiting for a miracle for your wayward child. Ready for some divine intervention? Expect a multitude of heavenly praise when the breakthrough comes. Hold on to hope because heaven is actively involved in your family's miracle. In these challenging moments, remember you're joined by a celestial choir, lifting your worries to the one who can turn them into wonders.

Dear Father, thank you that even these small praises are a sweet sound in your ear. Thank you for the angels who help support me, my child, and my family. In Jesus' name. Amen.

Trusting God's Plan

I know you may be confused about the way things are turning out with your child. But don't lose hope. Reflect on Joseph, whom God placed in the daunting role as Jesus' earthly father. Matthew 1:18 says,

> The birth of Jesus Christ took place in this way. When his mother Mary had been betrothed to Joseph, before they came together she was found to be with child from the Holy Spirit. (ESV)

Talk about a tough start. Joseph faced unimaginable challenges. Mary, his fiancée, was pregnant, and he knew the child wasn't his. Imagine the whispers, the side-eyes, the humiliation. But what did Joseph do? He trusted God. And God showed up in Joseph's confusion and uncontrollable challenges.

Just like Joseph, you may face an impossible situation, but you are not alone. Even in the confusion, God has a divine plan that the Enemy cannot steal. The Holy Spirit is at work even if you can't see the results right now. Pray as you've never prayed and love like you've never loved because God is in the business of turning messes into miracles. You and God make an unbeatable team. Believe that your prodigal isn't too far gone.

Dear Father, thank you for sending your Son to earth to offer us salvation in you. In Jesus' name. Amen.

Your Child Is Still a Gift

Battle-weary parent, I know how easy it is to forget that your wayward child is a gift from God, especially when they're rebelling against you and him. In these trying times, though, God speaks loudest. We see this in Psalm 127:3: "Behold, children are a gift of the LORD, the fruit of the womb is a reward" (NASB). Yes, even now, your child is a "gift of the LORD."

Here's the deal: God's gifts don't lose their value. And your prodigal child doesn't lose their worth just because they're lost right now. You see, God doesn't make mistakes. He gifted you your child not as a burden but as a blessing.

You might not see it now, but God is using this difficult season for something extraordinary. He's working on you and your child in ways you can't imagine. And just as he turned water into wine and raised Lazarus from the dead, he can turn your child's heart back to him. Stay rooted in prayer and never forget that your child is still a gift from God. Your wayward child, in all their complexity, is still a treasure. No rebellion can ever change that.

Dear Father, thank you for creating my wayward child, who is a gift from you. In Jesus' name. Amen.

Your Perpetual Advocate

When it seems like your wayward child is slipping through your fingers and all hope feels lost, remember who's fighting for you and them. As we see in Hebrews 7:25, Jesus is not sitting idle. "He is able to save to the uttermost those who draw near to God through him, since he always lives to make intercession for them" (ESV). Jesus is actively interceding for us. What a comforting thought—that our Savior always pleads our cause.

I know your battles are real, the sleepless nights are long, and the prayers seem unanswered. But let me encourage you that no one is beyond God's reach, not even your prodigal child. Jesus can "save to the uttermost." That means no situation is too dire and no child too lost for him to reach.

Christ is doing this work every single second. Are you worried at 2 a.m.? He's on it. Your tears during the drive home? He's aware. Your whispered prayers? He's amplifying them before the throne of God. You never have to win this battle on your own. It's not all on you. What a relief to know we have such a persistent and capable advocate!

Dear Father, thank you for Jesus, who intercedes for those who draw near to you. In Jesus' name. Amen.

Claiming God's Promises

Here's a life-changing truth from 2 Peter 1:4.

> Through these He has granted to us His precious
> and magnificent promises, so that by them you
> may become partakers of the divine nature, having
> escaped the corruption that is in the world on
> account of lust. (NASB)

Amazing, right? Listen, your struggle with your
wayward child is real. They're making choices that are
trapping them in the world's corruption. But here's where the
power lies: in God's "precious and magnificent promises."
They are your lifeline.

When you're wondering where your child is or what
they're doing, remember you can claim promises that go
beyond the current chaos because of Jesus' power and your
faith. And the beauty of these promises is that they give you
the power to partake in the divine nature—God's nature.
That means you're not relying on your strength to get
through this; you're tapping into God's.

You're fighting an unseen battle for your child, and the
weapons you have are not of this world. You have God's
Word, his promises, and his divine nature on your side.
Remember, you're not just escaping the world's corruption,
but you're also showing your child that escape route too.

*Dear Father, thank you for helping me stand on your
promises. In Jesus' name. Amen.*

Your Urgency in the Waiting

Time seems to stretch endlessly when you are waiting for your child to turn to God. Every tick of the clock can feel like a lifetime, each day a small eternity. But here's a wake-up call: time is short. Jesus is coming soon, as seen in Revelation 22:7: "Behold, I am coming soon. Blessed is the one who keeps the words of the prophecy of this book" (ESV).

Your prayers, sleepless nights, and endless love—don't think they're wasted for a second. They are your weapons in this spiritual warfare, and they matter now more than ever. Why? Because time isn't just ticking away; it's rushing toward an eternal deadline.

Revelation 22:7 contains a blessing for keeping "the words of the prophecy." In other words, don't just hear the promise; act on it. Keep praying, hoping, loving, and doing the hard work of parenting—even when it feels like you're getting nowhere. The Lord sees you and knows your struggle intimately. The Lord is coming soon, and you're shaping eternity in the here and now. Don't lose hope; the finish line is closer than you think. What you do today could shape your child's eternal destiny.

Dear Father, thank you for coming soon. In Jesus' name. Amen.

You're Not Fighting Alone

Do you question whether God is with your prodigal? Let's unpack 1 Corinthians 3:16: "Do you not know that you are a temple of God and that the Spirit of God dwells in you?" (NASB). This changes everything. When you're up at night worrying about your wayward child, remember this: if your child has ever accepted Christ, the Spirit of God resides in them. Yes, you read that right. This child is a walking, talking temple of the Holy Spirit.

What does this mean for you? It means you're not fighting this battle alone. Even when this child seems lost in the world's darkest corners, the Spirit of God is right there, nudging them back toward light and life. When the Enemy whispers lies, the Spirit whispers truth.

Believe that the Spirit is actively at work in your child's life even when you can't see it. Remember, God's Spirit doesn't vacate the building just because things get tough. He's steadfast and fighting for this child's heart from the inside out. Trust that God's Spirit is stirring profound changes. Even if your child has yet to accept Jesus, the Spirit dwells in you, giving you the words to witness to your child.

Dear Father, thank you for your Spirit, who lives within me and all those who believe. In Jesus' name. Amen.

The Party Heaven Throws

God throws a party for our repentant prodigals! We see this in Luke 15:7, which tells us, "There will be more joy in heaven over one sinner who repents than over ninety-nine righteous people who have no need of repentance" (NASB). Can we stop and breathe that in for a moment? Heaven throws a party when a lost one is found.

I know it's hard. Our hearts ache when we think about our wayward children. But here's the game changer: heaven is watching, and God orchestrates the most epic celebration for the day your prodigal returns home. Your tears, prayers, and endless love are not in vain. They're all seen by the one who can ignite a change in your child's heart. God isn't standing idly by. He's waiting for that grand moment of reunion, and so should you.

Let's hang on to this hope. When we're up at 3 a.m. worried sick, let's remember that heaven has the confetti ready. Your battle isn't in vain, and believe me, the party that awaits will be worth it all. Your prodigal is worth the heaven-sent celebration.

Dear Father, thank you for caring for the one over the ninety-nine and for throwing a party for sinners when they return. In Jesus' name. Amen.

Acknowledgments

To my extraordinary husband, Steve Craft. You have been my unwavering pillar of strength, my most fervent cheerleader, and my wise mentor for over four decades. You embody God's love and grace, and I am forever grateful for your presence by my side.

To my three children, Steven, Lawson, and Kaylee. You are the beat of my heart. Your triumphant victories over the devil declare the power of faith and God's miracles. And to my wonderful son-in-love and daughter-in-love, Keegan and Madison. You are a blessing to our family, and your love and support have been invaluable.

Above all, I offer my deepest praise to God. Your unconditional love has guided me through dark times. Thank you for entrusting me with this sacred mission to share your words of healing and hope with this world.

To BroadStreet Publishing and Jessica Pollard, my gifted editor. Thank you for believing in this message and working tirelessly to craft my words into a masterpiece.

To my family, friends, mentors, and fellow believers who have supported and encouraged me along this journey. I am forever grateful for your love, prayers, and unwavering belief in me.

To each of you who have bravely picked up this book as a lifeline in the fight for your precious child. You're not alone. I'm cheering you with my love and prayers.

About the Author

Laine Lawson Craft is an unstoppable force revolutionizing parenting. This best-selling, award-winning author, TV host, and podcast host from sunny Florida is a trailblazer of transformation, turning the impossible into awe-inspiring realities. Her groundbreaking book *The Parent's Battle Plan* clinched the 2023 Nonfiction Book of the Year Golden Scroll Award, and her *Warfare Parenting* podcast has skyrocketed to the top 10 percent globally.

Having faced the gut-wrenching challenges of raising prodigals, Laine knows warfare strategies that can help win the war for your child's future. Her infectious blend of humor, charisma, and raw authenticity has made her a global sensation, proving that victory in Christ is possible.

If you're struggling with wayward children, Laine is your ultimate ally. Connect with her at LaineLawsonCraft.com and unlock a treasure trove of free resources designed to empower you. From her popular online courses on forgiveness and reclaiming joy to her best-selling books and award-winning podcast, Laine is here to guide you.

Don't wait to start your transformation. Join Laine's army of triumphant parents and discover the power that can turn your family's story into a testament of hope. Connect with Laine today, follow her on social media, and start your journey to unshakable faith, unbreakable bonds, and unstoppable success.